THE CRYPTOZOOLOGICAL SOCIETY OF LONDON

A NATURAL HISTORY OF THE UNNATURAL WORLD

SELECTED FILES FROM THE ARCHIVES OF THE CRYPTOZOOLOGICAL SOCIETY OF LONDON

THOMAS DUNNE BOOKS

St. Martin's Press New York

This volume was collated and produced under the auspices of
THE CRYPTOZOOLOGICAL SOCIETY OF LONDON

by CARROLL AND BROWN LIMITED
20 Lonsdale Road
Queen's Park
London NW6 6RD

Writer JOEL LEVY
Editor DAVID GOULD
Copy Editor PETER HARRISON

Art Editor SIMON DALEY
Designer VIMIT PUNATER
Creative Consultant ROGER KOHN

Photography JULES SELMES, DAVID MURRAY
Picture research RICHARD PHILPOTT

Production WENDY ROGERS, CLAIR REYNOLDS

Index LAURA HICKS

Computer management JOHN CLIFFORD, PAUL STRADLING, ELISA MERINO

THOMAS DUNNE BOOKS
An imprint of St. Martin's Press

A Natural History of the Unnatural World

For information, address St. Martin's Press, 175 Fifth Avenue,
New York, N. Y. 10010.

Library of Congress Cataloging-in-Publication Data Available on Request.

ISBN: 0-312-20703-4

First U.S. Edition: January 1999

10 9 8 7 6 5 4 3 2 1

Reproduced by Colourscan, Singapore
Printed and bound in Singapore for Imago

100 PICCADILLY
LONDON W1

The President of the United States
The White House
1600 Pennsylvania Avenue
Washington DC

Dear Mr President,

What a great honour it was to meet you and the First Lady on your recent visit to the
United Kingdom. I will always treasure the memory of our dinner at Number 10 Downing
Street.

Mr President, I hope you recall as vividly as I our riveting conversation about the
North American Bigfoot, the Loch Ness Monster and the problems the Allies had with
gremlins during the last World War. It is rare to meet a layman who is so interested
and well-informed about the strange creatures who lurk in the dark and mysterious
corners of planet Earth, so we are truly blessed to have a world statesman who is also
an amateur cryptozoologist of some standing.

Over the coffee and petits fours, you sincerely asked me to send you more information
about the Cryptozoological Society of London, which it is my privilege to chair. It is
now my pleasure, sir, to enclose this dossier compiled specially to give you an
overview of the Society's activities. The documents in this binder offer a
representative cross-section of our archives and publications.

Mr President, cryptozoology has never been so popular. It is deeply ironic that the
Society's future as a learned institution is today under serious threat from government
cuts. As a man who spent six months in the Arizona desert hunting the Thunderbird, you
are in a unique position to remind our Prime Minister of the importance of our work. I
know how much you would treasure an honorary fellowship of the Society. We can only
make such awards if our future is secure.

The contents of this file, Mr President, are the cream of the Society's archives. I
hope that you enjoy reading them.

I remain, sir,

Your humble servant,

Henrietta Wensleydale

100 PICCADILLY
LONDON W1

A NATURAL HISTORY OF THE UNNATURAL WORLD

<u>Prepared for the President of the United States</u>

<u>From</u>: Joel Levy FCSL, Chief Archivist

Since its foundation in the golden age of Victorian exploration and discovery, the Cryptozoological Society of London has been at the forefront of learned research into the unusual — even mythical — creatures that populate the globe.

Cryptozoology remains an academic orphan, rejected by mainstream zoologists content to study more prosaic animals. However, the quality of research, rigorous standards of investigation and sheer wealth of anecdotal and material evidence in the Society's archives will convince even the most sceptical reader that cryptozoology is a genuine field of scientific endeavour.

In its 150 years of existence, the Society has conducted detailed investigations into all manner of unnatural phenomena and its dedicated experts have built up a valuable archive on practically every strange creature that has ever been identified. A team of press monitors keeps the clippings library up to date, and there is a picture library of more than 7000 images. The Society's researchers have delved into the world's libraries in search of elusive written material, frequently emerging with vital evidence in the form of a hitherto unnoticed dusty scroll or tattered scrap of paper. The Society has also commissioned expeditions to every corner of the globe, and its flagship magazine, the <u>CSL Review</u>, is among the foremost organs of cryptozoological scholarship.

This file represents a selection from the Society's vast collection of historical documents, expedition field reports, artefacts and biological samples. These are interspersed with offprints from the <u>CSL Review</u>, each giving a scholarly summary of the current state of cryptozoological learning on particular topics. Examples of the correspondence received from the Society's many friends and observers throughout the world are also included. Full-page reproductions of some of the paintings in the Society's collection, together with specially-commissioned maps, help to explain how the world's legendary heroes and heroines have been instrumental in understanding cryptozoological phenomena such as the giant, the roc and the kraken.

Perhaps the best way to gain an initial appreciation of the Society's history and its work is to read the short publication immediately following. It forms part of the information pack issued to new members, accredited researchers and other interested parties.

Welcome to the Cryptozoological Society of London

IN 1848, VICTORIAN BRITAIN WAS entering a golden age of exploration and discovery. Britons around the world were pushing deep into unknown lands and extending the boundaries of knowledge. Just twelve years earlier, Darwin had returned from the journey on board HMS *Beagle* which would contribute so much to the publication in 1858 of *Origin of the Species*. In the following decades, Burton and Speke's expedition to the source of the Nile and Livingstone's epic treks would start to unlock the 'Dark Heart' of Africa. The many strange and wonderful animals which they discovered gave fresh impetus to scientific endeavour in biology, zoology and geology.

Against this backdrop, a number of scholars nurtured a passion for the marvellous and fantastical. Excited by the possibility of finding and bringing back exotic creatures like the unicorn they pored over dusty tomes, trawled through news reports and planned expeditions in search of clues. Their aim was to study, using the latest scientific principles, all the animals that their conventional zoologist colleagues did not. They termed their science 'cryptozoology' (from the ancient Greek for 'hidden' and 'animal'), and called themselves cryptozoologists.

Many of these gentlemen knew each other by reputation or association, and it did not take long for the idea of a Society that would further their interests to gain currency among them. Inspired by their shared passion to pursue the unknown, 51 distinguished scholars, explorers, antiquarians, doctors and scientists gathered in London's Piccadilly to found the new Cryptozoological Society of London. On April 1st, 1848, they signed the charter of the Society. Nearly £2000 was raised by subscription, and the Society leased the premises at 100 Piccadilly that have remained its headquarters to this day.

Shunned by the establishment

The Fellows of the Society immediately sought a Royal Charter that would place them on the same

☞ *FROM A BOOK OF CARTOONS OF THE EARLY DAYS OF THE CSL COMES THIS DEPICTION OF A TYPICAL CLUB HOUSE ARGUMENT. SIR ARCHIBALD BLANTYRE (CENTRE) OFFENDS VISCOUNT TITTERTON BY CASTING ASPERSIONS ON THE MORALS OF MERMAIDS.*

footing as prestigious institutions such as their great rival, the Royal Geographical Society (founded in 1830). Setting a pattern typical of the low esteem in which cryptozoology continues to be held, however, the Society ran into official disapproval, and was refused such a Charter. To this day it remains simply the Cryptozoological Society of London, or CSL for short. In 1934 members voted unanimously to abandon their charter bid.

In 1848 cryptozoology was a science in its infancy, beset with poor standards of evidence in the form of unsubstantiated travellers' tales, fairground fakes and blatant forgeries. The founders of the CSL were determined to raise the standards of their science to the same levels of rigorous method and meticulous research and proof which applied in all other fields of scientific endeavour.

Field studies, past and present

The writers of the past, from Pliny to the authors of the medieval bestiaries and beyond, were often unreliable sources, making little distinction between fact and fantasy. The Society needed hard evidence and proper field research in place of wild conjecture. In September 1848 they dispatched Douglas George Pendleton, a noted antiquarian and founder-member of the CSL, to darkest Rumania on the Society's first field study. Pendleton's successful expedition initiated a practice that has become an important part of the CSL's *modus operandi*.

Today's field workers are carefully trained in at least three languages, foreign etiquette and

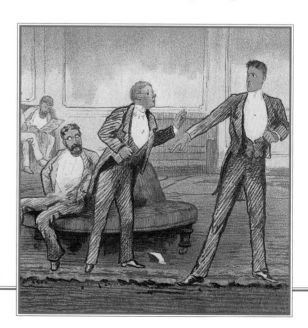

☞ *LIBRARIAN CHARLES LLOYD ASSESSES THE COLLECTION OF CRYPTOZOOLOGICAL DOCUMENTS AND BOOKS BEQUEATHED IN 1958 BY THE AMERICAN STEEL MAGNATE OSCAR MELLONHEAD II, AN IMPORTANT PART OF THE TOTAL 25,000 VOLUMES IN THE CSL LIBRARY.*

THE CSL REVIEW

THE ORIGINAL RESEARCH CONDUCTED BY THE CSL'S FIELD WORKERS IS USED, TOGETHER WITH MANY OTHER SOURCES, IN THE PREPARATION OF PAPERS FOR INCLUSION IN THE SOCIETY'S MONTHLY PUBLICATION, THE CSL REVIEW. THIS PUBLICATION HAS GROWN FROM BEING AN UNILLUSTRATED ACADEMIC JOURNAL INTO A FULL-COLOUR MAGAZINE WITH A DUAL MISSION. ON THE ONE HAND, THE CSL REVIEW REMAINS THE SOCIETY'S JOURNAL OF RECORD, PUBLISHING NEWS, ACADEMIC ESSAYS, LEARNED DEBATE AND A REGULARLY-UPDATED GAZETTE OF CRYPTOZOOLOGICAL SIGHTINGS; ON THE OTHER HAND, IT SEEKS TO RAISE PUBLIC AWARENESS OF THE SUBJECT. ITS REGULAR CREATURE PROFILES, AND THE OCCASIONAL SERIES INSIDE CRYPTOZOOLOGY, HAVE HELPED TO CREATE INTEREST AMONG LAY READERS BY INCORPORATING ACCURATE INFORMATION IN A LIVELY AND ACCESSIBLE FORMAT.

CSL review

VOL 138 No10

THIS ISSUE: GIANTS AT LARGE

customs, tracking skills, advanced zoology and ethology, navigation and survival and the use of firearms, dart guns and tranquillisers. Training aside, the most important skill of the field worker is, and always has been, observation.

Before setting off, every researcher will make a detailed reading of all the available sources to learn as much as possible about the habits and history of the animal under investigation. In 1848 the Fellows relied very much on their own resources, as well as talking to colleagues and visiting the great libraries of the day, such as the Bodleian Library in Oxford and the Bibliotheque Nationale in Paris. Nowadays they also can call on the extensive library and voluminous files of the Society itself, housed in almost a mile of corridors and cellars beneath 100 Piccadilly. In the future, much of this material will be digitised and made available in database form.

Field workers then draw the necessary clothing and equipment from the Society's outfitters. The Society can also help to organise travel to the remote and dangerous parts of the world that are home to some of our most mysterious creatures.

Once on location, the researcher's priority must be to respect the subject's natural rights. This means minimising disturbance caused to the

Physical evidence is hard to come by. Cryptozoological creatures have been systematically marginalised by millennia of human antagonism. They have been pushed into the farthest, wildest corners of the Earth, reduced to perilously small population sizes and have learned to be elusive and shy of human contact. They are forced to skulk in the shadows of the human world, becoming monsters of the imagination as much as monsters of reality. The CSL is committed to changing this. Members believe that cryptozoological creatures are not only fascinating in their own right, but offer potentially exciting new insights in a wide range of fields, from evolutionary biology to quantum physics.

creature and its habitat. Recovery of material evidence, such as photographs, samples or even a specimen that has died of natural causes is a secondary objective. Killing or taking live specimens is forbidden.

After the expedition is completed, the field worker may follow it up with supplementary research. All relevant material is then appended in a field report kept in the Society's files.

Common problems in cryptozoology

Cryptozoology is bedevilled by certain critical issues that prevent it from gaining recognition as a legitimate science. The most obvious is the lack of hard evidence with which to convince sceptics. There are few specimens available for study and most photographs, videos and samples are regarded with suspicion. The bulk of information about cryptozoological species comes from eyewitness reports – insufficient evidence to satisfy the conventional scientific establishment.

The CSL's facilities

The main burden of work at the CSL lies in maintaining the academic resources for which it is renowned. The magnificent library on the first floor of the headquarters also houses a small display of the many artefacts collected by the Society over the years. Archive material is stored in basement stacks, and can be consulted in the library or the reading room. The Society also offers dining facilities, a well-stocked bar, and a small number of bedrooms for visitors from out of town. The world-famous collection of paintings of strange beasts provides a fitting backdrop for all the activities of the Society.

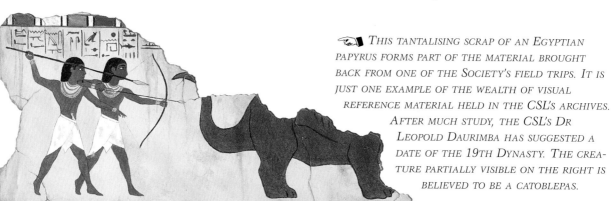

APPLICATION FOR MEMBERSHIP

APPLICATION NO.

All applicants must be nominated and seconded by existing members of the CSL.
Applications will be considered by the Membership Committee as soon as possible after receipt.

To: The Membership Secretary
Cryptozoological Society of London
100 Piccadilly
London W1

I wish to nominate the following for membership of the
Cryptozoological Society of London.

Mr/Mrs/Ms/other (please specify) _____

Name _____

Address _____

_____

_____

Telephone _____

Relevant qualifications and experience _____

_____

Nominated by _____

Seconded by _____

Nominee's signature _____ Date _____

Joining fee: £450
Annual membership: £650
Life membership: £15000
Overseas membership (annual only): £350
Special rates for students available on application.

i

CSL R E V I E W

INSIDE CRYPTOZOOLOGY

Basic principles of cryptozoology explained in simple terms for schools, colleges and new readers. Created by the Education Department of the Cryptozoological Society of London.

Taxonomy Guide

The spirit of human inquiry expresses itself as a constant quest to bring order to a chaotic world. For the philosophers of classical Greece and Rome and the Arab sages who succeeded them, the classification of the natural world was the first step towards solving the mysteries of the universe.

Taxonomy – the classification of organisms by structural or other categories – starts, as do so many things, with Aristotle (384–322 BCE), the most famous of the Greek natural historians. His work over 2000 years ago laid the foundations of modern taxonomy (from the Greek for 'arrangement of names') . Aristotle classified over 500 species according to a *Scala Natura* – an ascending order of complexity based on the animal's 'spirit' – a system still in use as late as the 18th century.

St Augustine (354–430 AD), the key early Christian philosopher, proposed three basic divisions of living things: harmful to humans, useful to humans and 'superfluous' (neither harmful nor useful).

Two names for everything

The first logical system of classification was devised by the Swedish botanist Carolus Linnaeus (1707–78). He introduced what we now call the binomial system of nomenclature, which gives every living thing a Latin name consisting of two or more words. The first

word describes the genus, which is a group of closely related animals; the second word reveals the species. All dogs, for example, are of the genus *Canidae*: the coyote is *Canis latrans*, the domestic dog *Canis familiaris* and the wolf *Canis lupus*. The dingo, which evolved from a common ancestor by crossbreeding with domestic dogs, has an extra name: *Canis familiaris dingo*. Despite protests from the zoological and biological establishment, the Cryptozoological Society of London has adopted the Linnaean system. As this method of classification was devised for use in conventional science, cryptozoologists have had to make certain adaptations for the unlikely creatures they study. The paucity of sightings, the rarity of evidence and the lack of specimens combine to make the classification of many of these creatures difficult, but by no means impossible.

Different approaches

Some animals are simply outsized or peculiar examples of existing genera (e.g., the goblin – *Homo kobalis*). Others are clearly a genus of their own (e.g., the sphinx, with its Egyptian and Middle Eastern species of *Sphinx aegyptus* and *Sphinx orientalis*). Hybrid creatures have genus names that reflect their mixed genetic heritage (e.g., the minotaur, of the genus *Buhomo*, from the Latin words for ox and man).

The reader should be aware that although ordinary taxonomy is often contentious, cryptotaxonomy (the classification of strange animals) can be doubly so (see Fig 2).

FIG 1 CAROLUS LINNAEUS

Linnaeus was a Swedish naturalist who trained as a doctor. In his early work, he classified plants by the characteristics of their flowers. In 1749, he introduced a more developed system based on giving all species – plant and animals – two Latin names. It forms the basis of all biological classification today.

FIG 2 THE UNICORN'S PLACE IN THE TAXONOMIC HIERARCHY

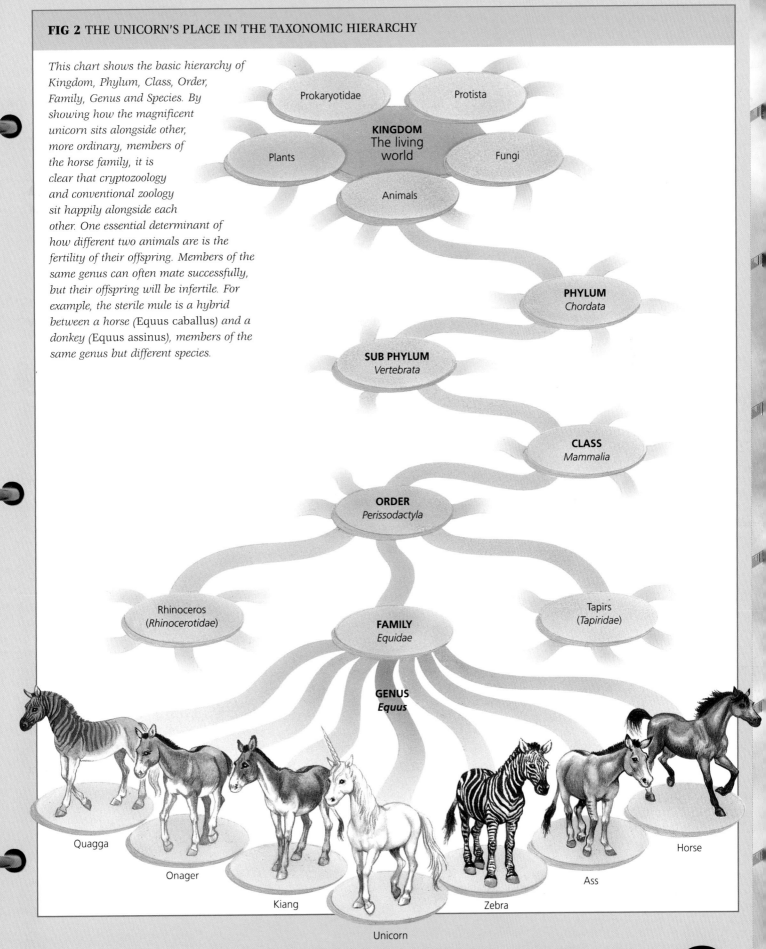

This chart shows the basic hierarchy of Kingdom, Phylum, Class, Order, Family, Genus and Species. By showing how the magnificent unicorn sits alongside other, more ordinary, members of the horse family, it is clear that cryptozoology and conventional zoology sit happily alongside each other. One essential determinant of how different two animals are is the fertility of their offspring. Members of the same genus can often mate successfully, but their offspring will be infertile. For example, the sterile mule is a hybrid between a horse (Equus caballus) and a donkey (Equus assinus), members of the same genus but different species.

Prokaryotidae

Protista

Plants

KINGDOM
The living world

Fungi

Animals

PHYLUM
Chordata

SUB PHYLUM
Vertebrata

CLASS
Mammalia

ORDER
Perissodactyla

Rhinoceros
(*Rhinocerotidae*)

FAMILY
Equidae

Tapirs
(*Tapiridae*)

GENUS
Equus

Quagga

Onager

Kiang

Unicorn

Zebra

Ass

Horse

From: Joel Levy,
Chief Archivist

**100 PICCADILLY
LONDON W1**

Presidential file summary

Here is a brief outline of the contents of the file. The material is drawn from a number
of sources: principally back issues of the <u>CSL Review</u>, archive field reports and correspondence. It is arranged in seven sections: Insects, molluscs and amphibians; Reptiles; Birds;
Mammals; Hybrids; Manimals; and Hominids.
   Each section starts with a divider and an offprint from the <u>CSL Review's</u> <u>Inside</u>
<u>Cryptozoology</u> series that briefly outlines the state of current scientific knowledge about
the creature in question.

There is a full index at the end of the file.

CONTENTS

*Please turn the pages with care and be careful with the documents and objects in this binder. Many are fragile and old,
AND SOME ARE IRREPLACEABLE. They will be DAMAGED unless they are handled CAREFULLY!*

Section 1

INSECTS, MOLLUSCS & AMPHIBIANS

Insects are the most numerous and varied of the
Earth's animals, but to humans their biology and
lifestyle are almost incomprehensibly alien.
Freakish giant insects have the power to
terrorise entire communities.
We marvel not only at the strangeness of some
of the creatures living in the sea, but also at
their ability to live in an environment we find so
threatening and mysterious.

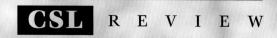

Basic principles of cryptozoology explained in simple terms for schools, colleges and new readers. Created by the Education Department of the Cryptozoological Society of London.

Insects, Molluscs & Amphibians

It would be considered strange in normal zoology to group insects, molluscs and amphibians together. For the cryptozoologist, however, the three present fascinating examples of unusual habits or immense size.

The many reports of giant squid, spiders and strange amphibians such as the giant salamander present a challenging opportunity for the crypto-zoologist. These animals may be very different from each other, but they exhibit intriguing parallels when considering size and habits.

Definitions

Members of the phylum *Arthropoda* (principally, arachnids, crustaceans and insects) are the most numerous of all animals. There are over 2 million known insect species, for example, far outnumbering the total of animal and plant species.

Molluscs (phylum *Mollusca*), with some 50,000 species, are characterised by their soft bodies and tough outer skeletons. Scallops, cuttlefish, clams, snails, squid and octopuses are all molluscs.

Scientists are familiar with about 4000 species of amphibians (phylum *Chordata*), ranging from the familiar frog to the worm-like, legless caecilians that can reach lengths of 5 ft (1.5 m). Most amphibians spend at least part of their life cycle in the water, and undergo a process of metamorphosis to become adults.

A matter of size

Insects, molluscs and amphibians are familiar to everyone and zoologists have closely studied spiders, octopuses and salamanders. However, salamanders that flourish in fire, spiders as big as horses, and octopuses the size of ships belong firmly to the world of cryptozoology: Their habitats, diets or dimensions put them beyond the bounds of conventional science.

Among insects, molluscs and amphibians, unusual size is

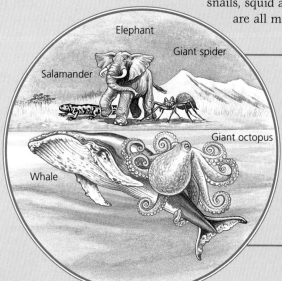

FIG 1 COMPARATIVE SIZES

This scale drawing shows the largest animals known to conventional zoology, together with oversized salamander, spider and octopus. The latter are shown at a size estimated from eyewitness reports. The feasibility of such giant animals surviving in the wild depends on many factors. These include the absence of parasites and predators; the availability of food and air and the ability of the creatures' skeletons to bear their massive bulk.

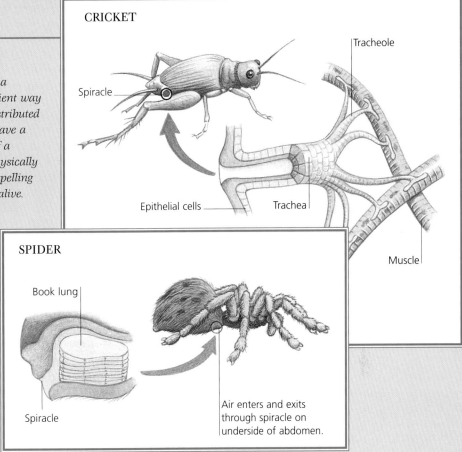

FIG 2 INSECT BREATHING APPARATUS

Fully-developed lungs or gills, combined with a system of circulating blood, are the most efficient way to absorb and deliver oxygen to the widely-distributed organs of a large animal. Most insects only have a rudimentary respiratory system, consisting of a network of tracheal tubes. These tubes are physically incapable of supplying enough oxygen and expelling enough carbon dioxide to keep a giant insect alive. The book lung of the spider is slightly more advanced, and may have been adapted by other giant insects.

CRICKET

Spiracle

Tracheole

Epithelial cells

Trachea

Muscle

SPIDER

Book lung

Spiracle

Air enters and exits through spiracle on underside of abdomen.

overwhelmingly the attribute that most interests the working cryptozoologist. The mysterious Scottish kelpie, for example, may well be the largest known amphibian, while (if mariners' reports are to be believed) the terrifying sea creature known as the kraken must be among the largest creatures that ever lived (see Fig 1).

The phenomenon of oversized creatures raises several important questions. Why have these creatures become so much bigger than their conventional relatives? One explanation was that they have mutated because of exposure to radiation, but this has now been rejected by cryptozoologists. It is a generally accepted wisdom that for many of these creatures, being big is actually an evolutionary advantage.

Supported by the sea

Many sea animals have evolved to great size – the whales, the great sharks and the elephant seal to name but a few. Large creatures have a lower ratio of surface area to volume, which helps them to retain heat in the cold sea.

The salt water in which they spend their lives provides support for a bulk that on land might collapse under its own weight. The vastness of the ocean also provides the nutritional resources for huge creatures – vast amounts of plankton, krill and fish.

Giant insects avoid some of the problems that face giant land mammals. Their exoskeletons, made of a cartilaginous material called chitin, afford

greater structural strength than the bony internal skeleton of a vertebrate. Insects' simple internal organs weigh less than the bulky liver, heart and kidneys of the mammal, and do not require as much fluid to function.

Air supply problems

Another major problem in cryptozoology is how these giant creatures overcame the physiological constraints that restrict their lesser relatives. The size of conventional sea creatures is in part limited by the availability of food, and the amount of energy they have to expend in order to find it.

In insects, however, the primary problem is gas exchange. Oxygen is distributed in higher animals via a system of circulating fluid (blood) that carries it from the lungs or gills around the body. Insects, however, only have a network of tubes (tracheae) that lead from air holes (spiracles) on the skin to a network of tracheoles, fluid-filled structures that transfer oxygen directly to every internal organ (see Fig 2).

Oxygen can only pass along these narrow passages at a limited rate.

Although larger and more active insects, such as wasps and grasshoppers, can move their bodies or flex their tubes to increase ventilation, there is an inverse relationship between the volume of usable gas and the length of the tube. The amount of fresh air that can reach the tracheole grows less as the trachea gets longer. Careful analysis has shown that even if an ant were to reach a length of 1 ft (30 cm), its tracheae could not deliver enough oxygen to keep the creature alive.

Alternative lungs

Scientists are at a loss to explain how the Earth's many reported gigantic insects surmount this problem. However, the arachnids (spiders) and some molluscs have primitive 'book lungs'. These consist of parallel thin plates filled with blood and separated by air spaces. Air enters the lungs by a spiracle, and oxygen diffuses into the blood through the plates. Giant spiders must have a highly developed form of book lung, and it is possible that other giant insects and molluscs have a similar type of breathing apparatus.

The insect world is so varied that new species are being discovered all the time. There are over 2 million different species of these uniquely adaptable creatures, and many have bizarre life cycles and strange feeding habits. A few species have reached a remarkable size.

INSECTS, MOLLUSCS & AMPHIBIANS

Giant Insects

LATIN NAMES
*Giant mantis:
Mantis
giganticus; giant
spider: Araneida
giganticus; giant
ant: Formicidus
giganticus*

HABITAT
*Forest,
rain forest and
deep jungle*

LIFESPAN
*Mantis:
15–20 years;
spider: 15–20
years; ant: 2–3
years*

SIZE
*Mantis: c. 7 ft
(2 m); spider: up
to 10 ft (3 m)
across; ant:
c. 5 ft (1.5 m)*

**INFORMATION
SOURCE**
CSL Review

DISTRIBUTION
*Giant mantis
and ant:
S. America;
giant spider:
Africa, Europe,
SE Asia*

CREEPY CRAWLIES

VERY LITTLE IS KNOWN ABOUT THE several species of insect that have grown to an unnatural size. The size and strength of these creatures has created such disbelief and fear in humans that few effective observations have been made, and no scientist has been able to put forward a credible explanation of how and why the Gigantica, as they are known, have evolved to such unusual dimensions.

ANTY MATTER

Giant ants are said to construct enormous colonies using whole tree trunks instead of the plant stems and leaves favoured by ordinary ants. The extraordinary strength of the common ant is shared by its giant cousin: a giant soldier ant can crush rocks to powder using its mandibles. Finally, giant ants spread terror and mayhem when they migrate *en masse* to a new site, destroying everything and everyone in their path.

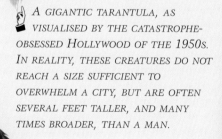
A GIGANTIC TARANTULA, AS VISUALISED BY THE CATASTROPHE-OBSESSED HOLLYWOOD OF THE 1950S. IN REALITY, THESE CREATURES DO NOT REACH A SIZE SUFFICIENT TO OVERWHELM A CITY, BUT ARE OFTEN SEVERAL FEET TALLER, AND MANY TIMES BROADER, THAN A MAN.

Giant ants are known for their extraordinary strength, but perhaps more noteworthy is the way in which the queen ant controls and coordinates the activities of the entire colony, so that it functions as if it were a single, intelligent creature.

BLINDINGLY POISONOUS

The giant mantis, by contrast, is habitually a lone hunter, and often uses varicoloured camouflage to disguise itself in the thick, humid rain forest that forms its habitat. It closely resembles a scaled up version of its normal-sized relative the praying mantis (*Mantis religiosa*), from which it probably evolved in the isolated conditions of the deepest rain forest basins.

The mantis is famed both as a deadly predator and a creature of supernatural powers. It excretes into its saliva a highly potent toxin that can kill animals as large as a horse, but seems only to affect the optic nerves of humans, causing blindness and disorientation. The mantis feeds mostly on medium sized herbivores such as the tapir, but it has reportedly attacked more fearsome predators like leopards or jaguars – proof of its unnatural strength and size. The name mantis derives from the Greek word for 'diviner', and it seems that the creature is gifted with powers of prophecy – although how it could communicate these insights to humans is unclear.

WEBBED TO DEATH

Enormous spiders are the best known of the giant insects, and are the only species to have spread beyond the deep jungle, occurring as far afield as Northern Europe and Mexico. They share their smaller cousins' patience, and have adapted well to a variety of niches, including some aquatic forms. They are, however, most commonly found lurking at the fringes of a huge web hidden in the dark recesses of a forest or cavern. From here they either pounce on unwary victims, injecting deadly poison with their fangs, or wait for their prey to become ensnared in the strong and sticky web, whereupon they descend and envelop the creature in a silken death shroud.

EXAMPLES OF THE WORLD'S BIGGEST COCKROACH SPECIES LOOM OVER A RATHER MORE CONVENTIONAL SPECIMEN. NATIVE TO QUEENSLAND, AUSTRALIA, THESE HUGE INSECTS ARE SUFFICIENTLY FRIENDLY TO BE KEPT AS PETS BY SCHOOLCHILDREN AND HAVE BEEN KNOWN TO RESPOND TO CRIES OF 'HERE, COCKY!'

Giant ants, spiders and mantises have been rumoured to exist since the Classical era, but only in the 19th century, when Victorian explorers began to penetrate the depths of the 'Dark Continent' and chart the vast equatorial rain forests of Central Africa and the Congo, did the first credible reports emerge. Other unnaturally large insects, including enormous wasps and beetles and man-sized moths, are rumoured to exist, but scientists have in general dismissed these as fables.

STRANGE ENCOUNTERS

While carrying out a series of geological surveys of equatorial Africa for the British Colonial Office between 1883 and 1889, the Very Rev. Arthur Symes, a Fellow of the CSL, gathered dozens of folk tales about giant spiders. He dismissed these as mere fables until three of his porters were caught in an enormous web close to the shores of Lake Kyoga, in what is now Uganda. Before he could rescue them, a colossal arachnid shot out from behind a tree and killed them all with its poisonous fangs

Major-General Grover J Blunkett, a prominent CSL member of the interwar years, claimed to have shot a mantis while journeying in the upper reaches of the Zambesi. Since the colonial era, however, deforestation and exploitation have dramatically shrunk the potential range of the Gigantica, and it is doubtful whether any still survive in Africa. More probably these species persist in the vast wilderness of the Amazon basin, much of which remains uncharted even now.

INSECTS, MOLLUSCS & AMPHIBIANS

Giant Octopus & Squid

LATIN NAME
Octopus:
Octopus
giganteus; squid:
Architeuthis
princeps

HABITAT
Octopus: wrecks
and reefs in
warm waters;
squid: deep
ocean

LIFESPAN
Unknown

SIZE
Octopus: up to
60 ft (18 m);
squid: up to
75 ft (23 m)

INFORMATION
SOURCE
Field Report

DISTRIBUTION
Worldwide

A 26 FT (8 M) SQUID CAUGHT IN THE PACIFIC OCEAN, SOME 310 MILES (500 KM) OFF NEW ZEALAND'S SOUTH ISLAND.

BACKGROUND NOTES

The giant octopus and the giant squid, both types of mollusc called cephalopods, are the largest invertebrate animals in the world. Many stories of these creatures are dismissed as sailor's tall tales, but there is plenty of evidence to support the existence of octopods and squid up to 75 ft (23 m) long. In 1887, for instance, a giant squid carcass some 48 ft (14.7 m) long was found in New Zealand, and in 1873 two men in a rowing boat off Newfoundland were attacked by a giant squid, only escaping after hacking off one of its tentacles. Until recently, the Smithsonian Institute in Washington held a specimen of a giant octopus washed ashore in Florida in 1896.

For this field expedition, one of the first to be commissioned by the CSL, naturalist and oceanographer Dr Charles Varney, FCSL chartered the barque <u>Dawn Rose</u> at Kingston, Jamaica. Under the captaincy of John Percy May, he set out into the Atlantic in search of unusual marine life. The relevant parts of his field report follow.

THE *DAWN ROSE* MAKES HEADWAY IN CHOPPY MID-ATLANTIC WATERS.

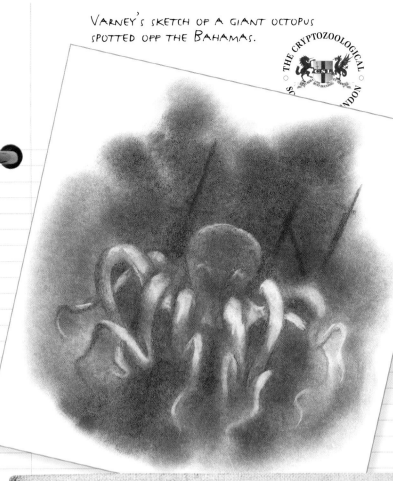

THE CRYPTOZOOLOGICAL SOCIETY OF LONDON

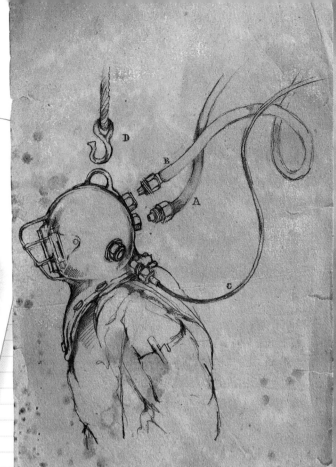

Diagram of air supply and other features of the 'Acme Imperial' diving suit worn on this field trip.

22 November, Great Inagua, Bahamas; E 72° 52', N 21° 2'
   We hove to in shallow water and sent out a boat with glass-bottomed viewers, in order to examine the undersea grottoes. The water here is wonderfully clear, and there is an abundance of fish and coral. Alas, no sightings of the giant octopus (Octopus giganteus) although I am convinced that conditions are ideal. Giant octopuses prefer warmer climes and shallower waters, and they are most likely to be found lurking in an undersea cavern or shipwreck. They may, however, be extremely hard to spot, since they have a remarkable chameleon-like ability to control the pigmentation of their skin, They use this ability to great advantage to blend in with their surroundings.

24 November, Long Island, Bahamas; E 75° 10', N 23° 12'
   Today we put the diving apparatus through its paces. Diving to the wreck of an old Spanish slave ship, I got a good view of a huge octopus. It had a hard, bony beak in the centre of its body, where the tentacles joined, and must have been at least 40 ft (12 m) in total diameter. I beat a hasty retreat, but must have scared the beast anyway, for it released a cloud of thick, inky dye, which soon obscured the entire wreck. Mine was a lucky escape, since giant octopuses are known to ensnare divers, or even, with the truly huge specimens, entire boats.

3 December, Sargasso Sea; E 59° 22', N 25° 46'
   We have skirted the most dangerous currents, but Captain May is disquieted all the same. He tells me tales of sea serpents and strange voices. I have attempted to set his mind at ease by explaining my theory that many sightings of sea serpents result from a misidentification of the giant squid - Architeuthis princeps. Two of its ten tentacles are far longer than the rest, with enlarged pads at their tips. This arrangement, if lifted out of the water while the rest of the body barely breaks the surface, might give the

Dr Varney starts his descent to the wreck.

impression of being a serpentine neck bearing a head, forward of a massive body. Since the giant squid is found only in the cold, polar seas, and probably eats only fish and shellfish, we should be quite safe here.

12   December; North Atlantic; E 56° 30', N 43° 44'
   Yesterday we sighted a sperm whale which was marked with terrible scars. The crew were aghast to imagine what could have caused them, and nature soon provided us with an answer. Around noon we spotted an enormous disturbance in the ocean ahead. We soon beheld that its cause was a struggle between two titans of the ocean. Thrashing the water into a boiling storm was a great sperm whale. Wrapped around its girth were several mighty tentacles, some of which must have been nearly 60 ft (18 m) in length. Occasionally we caught sight of a gigantic squid's body, with a vicious looking beak. Suddenly the squid broke free and shot off into the deep at an astonishingly high speed, pursued by the hungry whale. Smaller squid propel themselves by forcing water through a funnel-like tube, and the gigantic Architeuthis princeps must be able to generate tremendous force in this fashion.
   I count myself lucky to have made this sighting, but have resigned myself to the scepticism of my conventional colleagues in London. Why they should find the idea of giant squid so impossible I do not understand. Members of the phylum Mollusca have been remarkably successful in colonising almost every habitat on the globe, and the cephalopods are no exception. In the vast and inhospitable reaches of the ocean abyss big is probably better, and the giant squid has doubtless taken advantage of the riches of the polar seas to attain its extraordinary dimensions, driven also by the need to defend itself against the predations of the giant toothed whales.

WOODCUT BY CAPTAIN MAY OF THE DAWN ROSE BERTHED IN THE BAHAMAS.

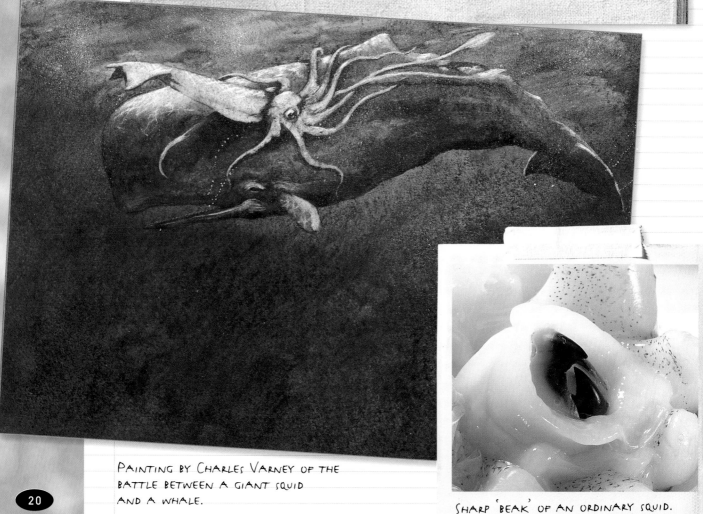

PAINTING BY CHARLES VARNEY OF THE BATTLE BETWEEN A GIANT SQUID AND A WHALE.

SHARP 'BEAK' OF AN ORDINARY SQUID.

Kraken

The kraken may well be dead, poisoned by marine pollution. Those who have studied its history claim that it lives yet, but in a state of hibernation, sleeping, in the words of Tennyson, 'far, far beneath the abysmal sea'.

HE KRAKEN WAS DESCRIBED BY THE renowned naturalist Erik Pontoppidan, Bishop of Bergen, as 'the largest and most surprising of all the animal creation'. This was no exaggeration, for this immense beast was, or is, the largest animal of all time. Whether there is more than one kraken, what is its gender, how long it lives and many other important questions remain unanswered, for the creature has not been sighted for more than a century.

LATIN NAME
Kraken kraken

HABITAT
Deep ocean

LIFESPAN
Unknown

SIZE
Vast – up to 1 mile (1.6 km) in circumference

DISTRIBUTION
North Sea, North Atlantic and beyond

GIANT OF THE DEEP

Descriptions are sketchy, perhaps because the creature is too vast to make a proper observation (except from the air), or because sailors who

SO LONG SUCKER

As well as devouring ships whole, the kraken can be stealthy and cunning. Some say that the Marie Celeste, found intact but abandoned in mid-ocean, was attacked by the beast.

encounter it are badly traumatised. Although some accounts describe it as an enormous whale- or turtle-like creature, the general consensus is that the kraken is a tentacled, slimy monster up to 1 mile (1.6 km) in circumference. On the rare occasions that the kraken surfaces from the ocean depths, it is easily mistaken for an island. Sailors of old would weigh anchor, 'go ashore' and light fires, waking the slumbering titan which would promptly submerge, creating an enormous whirlpool which sucked ship and crew down with it. Occasionally the kraken would drag down entire ships with its tentacles.

TRENCH TOWN

On the whole the kraken restricts its range to northern waters, its favourite haunt being those off Scandinavia. It probably lurks in the Norwegian Deep, the trench that cuts into the continental shelf off the coast of Norway, but it has occasionally been sighted further afield. Sailors in the waters off Scandinavia are used to monsters. They regularly see sea serpents, but the kraken is the most fantastic, and the most feared.

Numerous ships lost without a trace have been credited to its predations, although much les so in recent times. The North Sea is one of the most heavily polluted stretches of water in the world, and it is possible that radioactive and toxic waste have driven the kraken deep into open ocean or even killed it. If it is still alive, it may simply be dormant – a state of affairs that will not last forever. Some fear that continued oil and gas extraction in the North Sea might attract the kraken's wrath, and that retribution will follow.

LITERARY MONSTER

In myth and folklore the kraken has been linked with the biblical Leviathan, and the Norse 'world-serpent' Jormungandr.; but it is perhaps best remembered in the English-speaking world by Tennyson's epic poem *The Kraken* and John Wyndham's science-fiction novel *The Kraken Wakes*.

SINDBAD AND THE KRAKEN

by Nicholas Harris, MCSL

THE JOURNEY OF SINDBAD THE SAILOR

 The tales of Sindbad the Sailor have come down to us from the famous collection Alf Laylah Wa Laylah *(known in the West as* A Thousand and One Nights *or* The Arabian Nights)*. *In the story of the Seven Voyages of Sindbad the Sailor, we learn about the adventures that befell this pioneering merchant (and singularly unlucky seafarer) from Baghdad.*

Nicholas Harris' magnificent painting of Sindbad (reproduced on the two preceding pages) is one of many that hang in the Dining Room of the Cryptozoological Society of London at 100 Piccadilly. It was commissioned in 1990 to mark the 60th anniversary of the presentation of a set of valuable cutlery to the Society by the Shah of Iran, in gratitude for the CSL's help in the Alburz incident, when his son and heir nearly lost his life to a rogue lamassu on a hunting expedition

Sindbad's story preserves a remarkable record of a life spent in repeated encounters with cryptozoological phenomena. The ancient map shown here, part of the Dixon Codex bequeathed to the CSL in 1984, provides a key to his progress around the early medieval world.

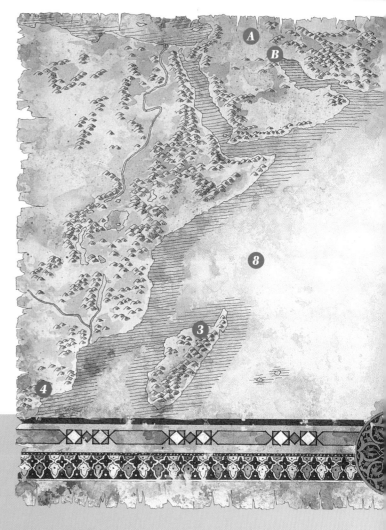

FROM BAGHDAD TO BASRA

A TO **B** Sindbad lived in Baghdad, Iraq, in the 8th century AD, during the reign of the greatest of the city's caliphs, Haroun al-Rashid. It was then one of the greatest cities in the world.

Despite being several hundred miles upriver from the Arabian Gulf, Baghdad was the centre of a trading empire. Spices and silk came there overland from the Central Asian deserts and China and fleets of ships went out from Basra that reached every corner of the Indian Ocean. At the start of the first of his epic journeys, Sindbad followed the route used by all Baghdad merchants before him. He went down the River Tigris to Basra, where he clubbed together with a group of other merchants wishing to charter a ship.

FIRST VOYAGE

1 Sindbad did very nicely until his ship moored at what the captain thought was a small island. Passengers and crew decided to stretch their legs, at which point the island submerged, leaving Sindbad and sundry others paddling desperately in mid-ocean. Sad to say, the 'island' had been a kraken all along that had decided to roll over and return to the depths from which it had come. Sindbad survived by clinging to a handy piece of timber.

2 After being washed up on a strange shore (probably Sri Lanka), Sindbad describes witnessing the mating of the King of Mahrajan's mares with some sea horses – presumably hippocampi.

SECOND VOYAGE

3 It was on this journey that, marooned ashore in Madagascar, Sindbad managed to escape by tying himself to the feet of a giant roc which had fortuitously landed nearby. At this time rocs still hunted on mainland Africa, and so the giant bird carried him across the Mozambique Channel and dropped him in the 'Diamond Mountains' (probably the modern Drakensberg range).

4 Making his way to the coast he saw many strange beasts including what he called a karkadan. Descriptions of this creature, its single horn and its perpetual battle with the elephant, led many medieval writers to believe it was a unicorn, but it is far more likely that it was a rhinoceros.

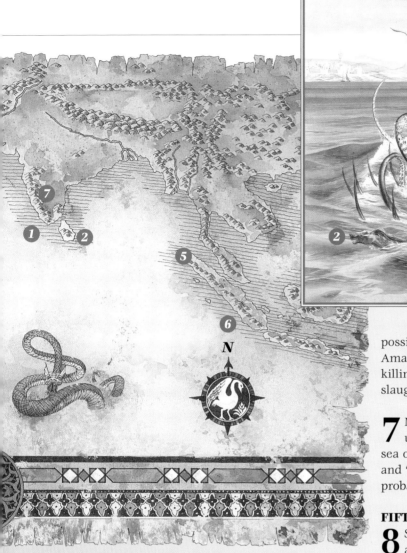

possibility. More impressive reports come from the Amazon, where Lt-Col. Percy Fawcett reported killing a 62 ft (19 m) anaconda in 1907, and soldiers slaughtered a 115 ft (35 m) snake in 1948.

7 Making his way back to Baghdad, Sindbad sailed up the west coast of India and saw many strange sea creatures, including one which 'resembled a cow' and 'one with the head of a donkey' (they were most probably dugongs).

FIFTH VOYAGE

8 Sindbad's second meeting with the roc went awry after his crew mates broke open a roc's egg and ate the contents. A vengeful flock pursued them, dropping boulders to smash the ship (displaying an interesting ability to generalise their feeding tactics to offensive ends, a cognitive leap usually thought to be beyond birds). This is the violent incident depicted in Nicholas Harris's superb painting in the CSL Dining Room.

SEVENTH VOYAGE

In his last voyage Sindbad ventured further afield then ever, ending up in Indochina. There he encountered a race of winged humans. They may have been harpies, although more civilised than other reports describe them. They were, however, only one among the amazing number of cryptozoological sightings granted to this legendary mariner.

THIRD VOYAGE

5 Sindbad's third journey was as eventful as the first two. He and his crew mates were blown far off course, crossed the Indian Ocean and drew close to Sumatra. Here they met an unpleasant band of furry dwarves, a description strikingly reminiscent of the *orang pendek*, or 'little man' of Sumatra – a possible *Homo erectus* relic and the subject of much modern day cryptozoological interest.

6 Having escaped various torments and perils, Sindbad's remaining companions were swallowed by an enormous snake. This was probably a very large python, and, while it must have been a frightening specimen, a snake large enough to swallow a human is well within the bounds of

Kelpie

LATIN NAME
*Hippopotamus
uisge*

HABITAT
*Lochs, pools and
upland rivers*

LIFESPAN
Unknown

SIZE
*Equivalent to a
large horse*

**INFORMATION
SOURCE**
*Colleague's
Field Report*

DISTRIBUTION
*Scotland, parts
of Ireland*

FIELD REPORT

THE CRYPTOZOOLOGICAL SOCIETY OF LONDON

THIS UNUSUAL FIELD REPORT WAS FILED BY A US AIRMAN STATIONED IN SCOTLAND DURING THE SECOND WORLD WAR.

I write this report on leave from Camp Mead, the US Air Force training school near Loch Awe, in Scotland. As a long-time associate of the CSL, I figured I'd be doing it a favor by checking out local reports of the kelpie. This critter is known throughout the Scottish Highlands and Islands, the Lowlands and even parts of Ireland, and it seems to have a dozen different names. The most common alternative is 'water-horse', but it's also called each uisge (the Gaelic term) and hippotam (which is where its Latin name comes from).

A FANCIFUL VICTORIAN PICTURE OF A KELPIE. UNLESS THE CREATURE IS CAPABLE OF ASSUMING DIFFERENT FORMS, THIS CANNOT BE AN ACCURATE IMAGE — IT BEARS NO RESEMBLANCE TO LENTON'S SKETCH.

AUGUST 1. CAMP MEAD, KILCHRENAN, LOCH AWE
My furlough comes through tomorrow, so I thought I'd kick the dust of this crummy camp off my boots and do a little research. The locals are real mines of information, and I've heard a dozen conflicting descriptions of the kelpie - apparently it can look like a horse, a bull, a cow-shaped creature, a hairy man or a beautiful fairy maiden. Usually the kelpie is black, but occasionally it's yellow, and although it's at home on land for short periods of time it seems to have to stay near to water at all times, living around lochs and mountain tarns. My best guess is that it's some sort of amphibian. The description of a hairy man or a beautiful woman is probably the result of confusion with water-dwelling creatures like nixies or nereids.

AUGUST 2. FORD, LOCH AWE
Spent the day traipsing along the shore, but didn't see anything except ducks. My research in the local bar was more effective. I bought this ancient old guy a 'wee dram', as they say (a large Scotch where I come from). He said it was a bad omen to see a kelpie, and told me how the kelpie hangs around looking like a horse and waiting for someone to climb aboard, and then jumps into the nearest loch, drowning the person before eating him or her. I bought the old guy another 'wee dram' and he started to tell me about Kitchener and Khartoum. Crazy story, and I just loved his accent.

Maybe the kelpie has evolved to look like a horse, so that people will come within striking range - like the angler fish's lure, or the manticore's human face. The old guy told me it was a pub, not a bar.

AUGUST 3. MCALLISTER'S FARM, LOCH AWE
I'm staying with Alasdair McTavish, who's running this farm while Kelvin McAllister's fighting Jerry down in Sicily. McTavish insists that there's a 'right big bogger' of a kelpie in the Loch, and goes around with a shotgun loaded with silver sixpences for self-defence! He even says you can catch a kelpie. Apparently Cuchulainn, the great Irish folk hero, used a water-horse as a mount, and St Cummein employed the each uisge of Loch Ness to till the land around his church at Fort Augustus. Whenever one of his mares comes into season, McTavish ties

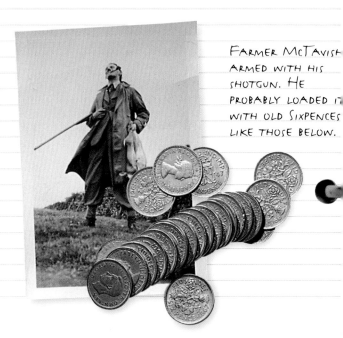

FARMER McTAVISH ARMED WITH HIS SHOTGUN. HE PROBABLY LOADED IT WITH OLD SIXPENCES LIKE THOSE BELOW.

THE CRYPTOZOOLOGICAL SOCIETY OF LONDON

KELPIE.

As described by Alasdair McTavish.
He says this is a good likeness.

Horse-like head and ears
help to explain the kelpie's
nickname of 'waterhorse.'

I've drawn webbed feet, but
some accounts give the kelpie
hooves.

The kelpie's long dorsal
fin is probably hard to
see until it emerges
from the water.

her up near the shore, hoping that the kelpie will come out of the water and impregnate her. The offspring have long ears and shiny black hooves, and are worth a fortune. I'd have to say this sounded kinda far-fetched, especially if the kelpie is an amphibian.

In the evening McTavish showed me where he'd seen the monster come out of the water a few times, but nothing unusual happened. I drew a sketch from his description. Then I went out to a dance with some of McTavish's cute land girls. Golly, what a night! Did they teach me how to reel!

AUGUST 4. INVERARAY, LOCH FYNE

Spent the afternoon in the library here doing a bit of research. It seems Farmer McTavish was right about catching the critters – Sir Walter Scott tells a story of how a guy called Clanronald attempted to

catch a water-cow that lived in a small lake. In his diary of November 23, 1827, he says Clanronald and his kin tried to hook the kelpie using anchors baited with dead dogs, but 'to their confusion, the baits were found untouched.'

As I said before, there are lots of different names used for kelpies: in Gaelic – each uisge (pronounced ech ooshkya), tarbh uisge (meaning water-bull) and beiste. Related creatures include the Scottish nuckelavee and the Irish water-horse, the aughisky (pronounced agh-iski) – Hippopotamus goidelis. There's also a notorious Australian monster called the bunyip, which is a lot like the kelpie – it's probably a local variety, so a good name would be Hippopotamus australiensis.

Tomorrow I'm due back at camp. I guess I'm still not convinced that the kelpie really exists, but these Scottish lochs sure hold some secrets.

INSECTS,
MOLLUSCS &
AMPHIBIANS

Salamander

LATIN NAME
*Salamandra
pyra*

HABITAT
*Fire – furnaces,
active volcanoes,
fireplaces*

LIFESPAN
5–10 years

SIZE
*Up to 4 ft
(1.2 m) long*

**INFORMATION
SOURCE**
CSL Review

DISTRIBUTION
*Southern and
Central Europe*

*The salamander
was revered as a
symbol of purity,
permanence and
fire. It also filled a
gap for medieval
natural historians,
who insisted that
there must be a
beast of fire to
complement those
living in the air, in
water and on earth.*

TOO HOT TO HANDLE

THE STAR-SHAPED MARKINGS SPANGLING the dog-sized salamander's golden skin are umistakable. It is from these star markings that it exudes a milky fluid that is one of the most potent toxins known to man. Human skin burns and shrivels on contact, and the victim's flesh withers instantly on the bone. The hair drops out and only a blackened, shrunken corpse is left to bury.

PORKY PROBLEM

The salamander's vicious excretion can poison fruit trees on contact, and make the water in rivers and wells undrinkable. It is said that 2000 of Alexander the Great's horses and 4000 of his men died in India after drinking from a salamander-poisoned stream. The only animal able to tolerate this venom is the pig, which gobbles salamanders with impunity, but stores the toxins in fat deposits under the skin, making it toxic in turn. This is one reason why travellers often regard spicy pork sausages with suspicion.

Apart from its evil toxin, which it can spit or inject by biting, the salamander has extraordinary heat-resistant properties. Indeed, it can only thrive amidst heat and flames, and the intense conditions of a furnace or even lava flow provide an ideal habitat. However, it is also able to extinguish flames at will, projecting a wave of intense cold which can douse the fiercest blaze.

A SIZZLING LITTLE NUMBER

Regarded, for obvious reasons, with some trepidation by early chroniclers like Aristotle and Pliny the Elder, the salamander was a popular inclusion in medieval bestiaries where it was used as a moral and Christian allegory for indestructibility and the triumph over desires of the flesh. Alchemists used it as the symbol for the element of fire; King Francis I of France (1494–1547) adopted it as his emblem, with the motto, 'I nourish and extinguish'.

It was also in the time of Francis I that weavers learned how to make the salamander's cocoon into a textile. Clothes made of salamander, as the material was known, could be cleaned simply by throwing them onto the fire.

Salamandra pyra is closely related to other members of the genus *Urodeles*, especially the Common Salamander and the Black Salamander.

Section 2

REPTILES

Reptilian monsters are familiar to many people, but only as dinosaurs, the long-dead masters of a vanished world. Most dinosaurs died out 65 million years ago, probably as the result of a meteorite strike that caused such rapid change to the Earth's climate that they could not adapt. Those that survived are now thought to have evolved into birds. What if some of these creatures bypassed the evolutionary process, however, hidden away in the world's most remote places? The abyssal depths of the oceans, the uncharted expanses of virgin rainforest, the gloomy waters of lakes and the desert wastes may harbour many such fugitives, far away from most human eyes.

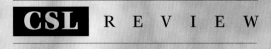

2

Basic principles of cryptozoology explained in simple terms for schools, colleges and new readers. Created by the Education Department of the Cryptozoological Society of London.

Reptiles

Reptiles once ruled the Earth and, as if to prove the point, survived a global disaster to remain significant players in the game of Life. Despite currently weighing in with a meagre 600 species, the class Reptilia still has the capacity to spring a few cryptozoological surprises.

Reptilian monsters are familiar to many people, but only in the form of dinosaurs, the extinct dominant species of the Mesozoic era. Despite the pyrotechnics of science fiction – epitomised in the film *Jurassic Park*, where dinosaurs were resurrected from fragments of DNA left in fossilised amber – everyone knows that the dinosaurs died out 65 million years ago, probably as the result of a meteorite strike that wiped out their entire habitats.

What if some of these creatures had survived and succeeded in hiding themselves away in the world's most remote places? If so, the very deep trenches of the ocean floors, the still uncharted areas of rain forest and the very still, cold waters of mysterious lochs, far from human eyes, might all provide secure habitats for creatures living far out of their times. This theory offers a plausible explanation for the presence of lake monsters and dragons in the contemporary world.

Prehistoric survivors

This hypothesis is reinforced by several examples of creatures which have survived from prehistoric times to the present. The horseshoe or king crab has remained unchanged for 150 million years, and the ancient tuatara lizard of New Zealand is the relic of a 200 million-year-old group.

More dramatic are the discoveries of species which were thought long

FIG 1 KOMODO DRAGON

A species of monitor lizard native to the Indonesian islands of Flores, Pintja, Padar and Komodo, this reptile is the world's largest lizard. Its main prey is pigs and deer, but it is capable of attacking and killing a human being. The Komodo dragon is an example of a living dinosaur, proving that large reptiles do not need to hide in lakes or caves in order to prosper.

extinct. The most famous example is the coelacanth, a primitive type of fish which was thought to have become extinct about 70 million years ago – roughly the same time as the dinosaurs. The capture of a specimen in 1939, off the coast of South Africa, astonished the scientific community (not least because the ancient coelacanths were believed to have lived in freshwater), and proved that, given the right combination of biological and ecological circumstances, ancient creatures can survive to the present day.

On the trail of the lonesome pine

Just as remarkable is the tale of the Wollemi pine, a fern-like conifer that belongs to a 300 million-year-old group, thought to have been extinct for at least 2 million years. In 1994 a stand of living specimens was discovered by Park Ranger David Noble, deep within Australia's Wollemi National Park, and just 90 miles (150 km) from Sydney, Australia's largest city. The pine only grows in two places, and genetic testing has revealed that all the plants are clones of each other. This means that, in genetic terms, a single individual has survived for 2 million years longer than anyone thought possible.

The case of the Wollemi pine has encouraged cryptozoologists to embrace the prehistoric survivor hypothesis for lake monsters, sea serpents and the like. In the case of the pine, a very small population (of one) lived for millions of years. Lakes like Loch Ness, with their great depths and stable ecology, provide the kind of cover needed for a complex organism to survive despite long-term human scrutiny

Further evidence to support this theory emerged in 1998, when Australian scientists discovered a species of beetle with a combination of scales and spines that proves it has remained unchanged since the Jurassic period, some 200 million years ago. The beetle, say entomologists, evaded detection (and possibly survived without needing to evolve) simply because it spends most of its life underground.

Body of evidence

A familiar problem for those who argue that giant reptiles do exist is the absence of material evidence – there are no specimens. This is the essential difference between known prehistoric survivors like the coelacanth and putative ones like the *mokele mbembe*: the scientific community has accepted the existence of the former because of the presence of actual specimens. Plesiosaurs, zeuglodonts and giant sea snakes persistently fail to wash up on beaches or get caught in fishermen's nets, or at least fail to make it into the hands of scientists when they do.

Scientists at odds

Some cryptozoologists believe that the mass of sightings represents a sufficient weight of evidence, but conventional scientists riposte that extraordinary claims require extraordinary proof. Even the much-studied dragon is the object of suspicion among conventional biologists, although centres of dracology, such as the Götlingen Institute for Cryptozoology in Germany, carry on their work regardless of the prevailing scientific opinions. Their general attitude is that important research should not be hampered by the lack of a scientific consensus over the actual existence of the subjects.

Ignoring the presence of huge and extremely dangerous reptiles just because they refuse to pose for the world's media, will not stop them from killing people. The more we know about them, the more we can avoid the conflict between them and humans which damages both sides.

REPTILES

Dragons

LATIN NAME
Draco

HABITAT
*Varied:
mountains and
caverns, or
underwater*

LIFESPAN
*more than
400 years*

SIZE
*Varies, but
generally
similar
dimensions to
African
elephant or
small roc.*

**INFORMATION
SOURCE**
CSL Review

DISTRIBUTION
*Europe, Middle
East, Asia
Minor, India
and South-east
Asia*

CREATURE PROFILE

A GENUS OF EXTREMELY LARGE, LONG-lived, winged lizards, the species *Draco* should not be confused with any of their lesser cousins, including the false dragon, or wyvern (*Pseudodraconis*) and the drake (*Ophidio draconis*), or their distant relatives, the winged serpents. True dragons constitute the most advanced race of lizards known, far surpassing other orders in size, intelligence, and lifespan. Habitat, appearance and lifecycle vary widely between the five major species of dragon, which are divided along geographical lines. The five species have therefore been named the European, Near and Middle Eastern, Indian and Oriental.

EVERY CRYPTOZOOLOGIST KNOWS THE ERROR IN UCCELLO'S DEPICTION OF ST GEORGE: THE 'DRAGON' HAS ONLY TWO LEGS AND IS THEREFORE A WYVERN.

THE

Prehistoric leftover or just a lizard that got too big for its boots? Whatever it is, the dragon is the most feared and esteemed of beasts.

LIZARD
KINGS

32

FOUR-LEGGED FIENDS

There are many terms used to refer to dragons, and incorrect terminology is often applied. Wyvern, hydra and firedrake, in fact completely different species, have all been mistakenly used. Common names include: orms, worms, wyrms, serpents, flying serpents and winged snakes. Specific types of dragon include *peluda* (a furred dragon that spits water), *tarasque*, *guivre* and *gargouille* (another water-spouting dragon, one of which nearly destroyed Rouen in 520 AD), which are all from France; and lindorms or lyndwyrms in England. Other cultures have thrown up various names, such as the Persian *musshussu* and the Irish *peist*.

We in the West are, of course, familiar with the classical form of the common European dragon (*Draco magnificens*), a four-legged creature with a tough, scaly hide, an eagle's talons, a long, sinuous tail, and a reptilian snout crowned with a pair of horns. It has bat-like wings which spring from extended rib bones just behind the front legs.

Dragons of the Near Eastern and European variety tend to adopt a terrestrial lifestyle, living high in remote mountainous areas, although there are exceptions: Irish dragons (*Draco magnificens goidelis*), for example, have an exclusively aquatic habitat. Caverns adopted by dragons as lairs are marked with a number of telltale signs: the cavern itself will be spacious, often enormous, with a sizeable passage connecting it to the outside world. The mouth of the passage, though probably well hidden,

es bestes que elles apœrent
let gens alixᵉ en ocillrent mlt.

cuer sou oft cuiſt eſte deſconfite.
Coument Alixᵉ entry enla chite de

will be scorched and blasted, and bear the imprints of the creature's passing. Scales shed by the dragon, and the bones and carcasses of its prey will litter the floor, but the real give-away will be the dragon's hoard of treasure and gems, glittering in a well-guarded corner.

GRANDMA WAS A VELOCIRAPTOR

The evolutionary origins of the dragon are shrouded in mystery. Scholars have traditionally assumed a line of descent from lizards such as the monitor lizard, pointing to the Indonesian Komodo dragon as the modern descendant of a putative dragon/lizard common ancestor. However, another school of thought has been gaining followers in recent years, arguing for a draconian lineage stemming directly from carnivorous dinosaurs such as the velociraptor. The fossil evidence is scant, and in the absence of any successful capture of a dragon

MEDIEVAL BARDS LOVED TO RECOUNT THE EXPLOITS OF ALEXANDER THE GREAT. DRAGONS WERE AMONG HIS MANY FEARSOME OPPONENTS AS HE RAMPAGED ACROSS EUROPE AND ASIA MINOR.

SOME SPECIES OF DRAGON CAN GROW UP TO 45 FT (14 M) LONG. THE BAT-LIKE WINGS IDENTIFY THIS SPECIMEN AS A COMMON EUROPEAN DRAGON.

Dragons

since medieval times, a definitive resolution of the debate seems unlikely in the immediate future.

However, there is a growing weight of evidence in favour of the new theory, particularly the recent hypothesis that dinosaurs such as the velociraptor were warm-blooded. If this is true of dragons, as many cryptozoologists have speculated, it could help explain their ability to survive in colder climes (such as Scandinavia and Iceland) and how they can produce the sort of sustained metabolic output necessary for flight.

Flight provides another clue linking *Draco* to velociraptor: they both have similar bird-like hip and breast bones. These are present in the dragon to provide the broad base necessary for attachment of the massive pectoral muscles that power the wings. Evidence like this has led cryptopalaeozoologist and CSL member Dr Basil Iske to propose that dragons evolved from bird-like dinosaurs, much as birds themselves are thought to have done. He has predicted that there should be a draconian equivalent of the proto-avian *Archaeopteryx*, and indeed one exists: the recently unearthed *Kuehnosaurus*, a winged lizard from the Cretaceous era, which many palaeontologists believe may prove to be the vital missing link in draconian evolution.

CARELESS FATHERS

Dragons of the most common European species (*Draco magnificens*) are dormant for much of the year, and even when awake are rarely active, preferring to concentrate on guarding their hoard of gold and precious items.

These dangerous creatures are solitary in their habits, coming together only at very infrequent intervals to mate – a spectacularly violent event. Gestation lasts for approximately one month, after which the female lays a clutch of 3–12 large, leathery eggs (similar in size to those of an ostrich) for which she has the sole responsibility. These must be kept at temperatures of around 50°C, and incubation can last up to one year, during which the father plays no role in feeding or caring for the broody mother.

☞ *FRIEDRICH BERTUCH SPOTTED THIS UNUSUAL SPECIMEN IN GERMANY IN 1792. THE 'EYES' ON THE WINGS, AS IN SOME BUTTERFLIES, ARE THE EFFECT OF SCALE PATTERN AND DESIGNED TO INTIMIDATE.*

Large numbers of cattle and sheep form the dragon's basic source of sustenance, but they are fond of human flesh, particularly the most tender examples – namely children and young maidens. Western dragons are notorious for using comely maidens as bait for foolhardy heroes, whom they enjoy eating as a tasty variant on their otherwise monotonous diet of raw beef and mutton.

THEY STOOP TO CONQUER

First-hand reports of hunting dragons reveal that they employ similar methods to birds of prey like the hawk and the falcon. Typically the dragon will use thermals and air currents to rise high into the sky until it spots a likely meal. Having closed in on its target, the dragon draws back its wings and goes into a 'stoop', gaining speed for its attack run. As it approaches the ground the wings are unfurled and the hind legs brought sharply forward to meet the forelimbs, with the unfortunate prey in the middle. The enormous claws on each talon slice deeply into the animal, bringing instant death. The dragon will then either settle with its kill, or remove it to a less disturbed spot, where it uses its claws and razor sharp teeth to rend and tear the flesh.

Reports of dragon physiology are generally unreliable, since all date from the Middle Ages or earlier. It seems likely they possess two or more stomachs, with one potentially involved in flame production. Like many other carnivorous reptiles – especially snakes like the python – dragons can make one meal last a long time, and may take up to a month to fully digest a single carcass, not needing to feed again for two or three months.

Western dragons' bodies are adapted to flight in ways

IN A FAMOUS 18TH-CENTURY EXPERIMENT, A FLYING DRAGON WAS USED TO TEST THE ABILITY OF THE HUMAN EYE TO TRACK A FAST-MOVING OBJECT.

exploited by the Nordic hero Siegfried, who lay in a pit waiting for the dragon Fafnir to pass overhead, and successfully skewered it from below.

HUMANS VERSUS DRAGONS

The earliest known artefacts depicting dragons come from a Neolithic site in Liaoning province in Northern China. Dating from the fourth millennium BCE, they include burial pieces complete with scaly tails, and ornaments representing pig-snouted dragons. Stone cylinder seals decorated with serpentine dragons, found at Bannu in north-western Pakistan, date from *c.*2000 BCE.

Dragons often appear as protectors and guardians in the earliest recorded Middle and Near Eastern myths and legends, where they are frequently captured and pressed into service by kings and gods. This tale features in the Babylonian Epic of Creation; in Egyptian mythology (like the 15th century BCE *Am-Duat*, or *Book of What is in the Underworld*), where serpent-dragons guarded the various gateways of the underworld; and in Greek myth: one of the twelve labours of Hercules was to defeat a fearsome dragon.

By the Middle Ages dragons had spread to all parts of Europe. Their carved simulacra adorned the prows of Norse longships, and lavish descriptions and drawings appear in medieval bestiaries. It was at this time that dragon killing became a favourite sport. One of its most famous practitioners was the Syrian Saint George, who was later adopted as the patron saint of England and Portugal. In the face of such sustained human aggression, European dragons became truculent and pettish, devouring babies and small children at will. Naturally this quickened the tempo of dragon hunting and the dragon population declined sharply.

Most scholars agree that dragons are nearly extinct in Europe and western parts of Asia, and there have been very few sightings since before Victorian times. Whatever the size of the remaining population, one thing is certain: steps must be taken to safeguard the future of one of nature's grandest designs.

SEE ALSO WYVERNS AND DRAKES P38–39.

similar to birds': hollow bones combining strength and lightness; broad breast bones with a deep keel, necessary to provide an attachment base for the powerful wing muscles; and a long, sinuous body, with smooth aerodynamic scales to reduce drag. But there are also flaws in their wing structure that (in theory, at least) make flight impossible.

Firstly, their wings are essentially extended ribs with membranous flaps between them (*Kuehnosaurus* was more primitive, but essentially similar), and neither the bones or the membrane are, theoretically, strong enough to withstand the massive pressures that each downstroke would produce. Secondly, the area of each wing is typically only 15 m², which – even with a theoretical maximum possible pressure of 120 kg/m² produced by each down-stroke – should only generate enough lift to raise a rhinoceros, or perhaps a large hippopotamus, off the ground.

SOFT UNDERBELLY

Over the ages the hosts of dragon-slayers and would be dragon-slayers have amassed a plethora of hints and tips for hopefuls to follow, most of which lack any real credibility – for example, dragons are said to be repulsed by the 'sweet' smell given off by panthers, and in some instances by male nudity. A better documented weak point in the dragon's armoury is its soft underbelly, which contrasts with its hard and almost invulnerable upper hide (composed of tough, heat resistant scales). This 'Achilles' Heel' was

A 16TH-CENTURY ENGLISH CHURCH CARVING DEPICTS THE DRAMATIC SLAYING OF A TWO-HEADED, TREE-DWELLING DRAGON.

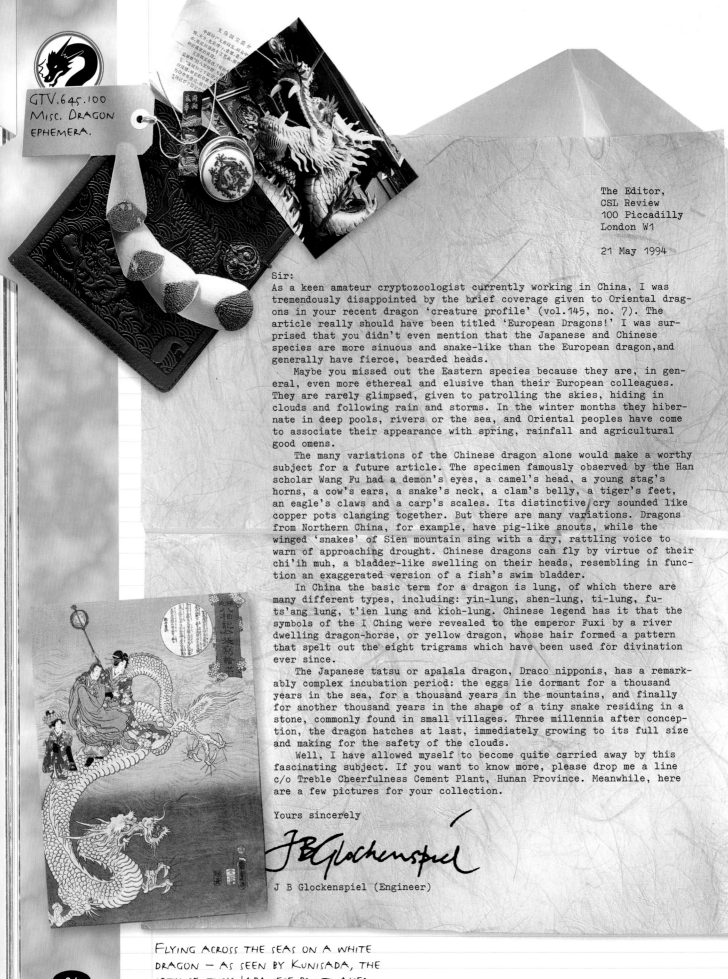

The Editor,
CSL Review
100 Piccadilly
London W1

21 May 1994

Sir:

As a keen amateur cryptozoologist currently working in China, I was tremendously disappointed by the brief coverage given to Oriental dragons in your recent dragon 'creature profile' (vol.145, no. 7). The article really should have been titled 'European Dragons!' I was surprised that you didn't even mention that the Japanese and Chinese species are more sinuous and snake-like than the European dragon, and generally have fierce, bearded heads.

Maybe you missed out the Eastern species because they are, in general, even more ethereal and elusive than their European colleagues. They are rarely glimpsed, given to patrolling the skies, hiding in clouds and following rain and storms. In the winter months they hibernate in deep pools, rivers or the sea, and Oriental peoples have come to associate their appearance with spring, rainfall and agricultural good omens.

The many variations of the Chinese dragon alone would make a worthy subject for a future article. The specimen famously observed by the Han scholar Wang Fu had a demon's eyes, a camel's head, a young stag's horns, a cow's ears, a snake's neck, a clam's belly, a tiger's feet, an eagle's claws and a carp's scales. Its distinctive cry sounded like copper pots clanging together. But there are many variations. Dragons from Northern China, for example, have pig-like snouts, while the winged 'snakes' of Sien mountain sing with a dry, rattling voice to warn of approaching drought. Chinese dragons can fly by virtue of their chi'ih muh, a bladder-like swelling on their heads, resembling in function an exaggerated version of a fish's swim bladder.

In China the basic term for a dragon is lung, of which there are many different types, including: yin-lung, shen-lung, ti-lung, fu-ts'ang lung, t'ien lung and kioh-lung. Chinese legend has it that the symbols of the I Ching were revealed to the emperor Fuxi by a river dwelling dragon-horse, or yellow dragon, whose hair formed a pattern that spelt out the eight trigrams which have been used for divination ever since.

The Japanese tatsu or apalala dragon, Draco nipponis, has a remarkably complex incubation period: the eggs lie dormant for a thousand years in the sea, for a thousand years in the mountains, and finally for another thousand years in the shape of a tiny snake residing in a stone, commonly found in small villages. Three millennia after conception, the dragon hatches at last, immediately growing to its full size and making for the safety of the clouds.

Well, I have allowed myself to become quite carried away by this fascinating subject. If you want to know more, please drop me a line c/o Treble Cheerfulness Cement Plant, Hunan Province. Meanwhile, here are a few pictures for your collection.

Yours sincerely

J B Glockenspiel (Engineer)

FLYING ACROSS THE SEAS ON A WHITE
DRAGON — AS SEEN BY KUNISADA, THE
19TH-CENTURY JAPANESE PRINTMAKER.

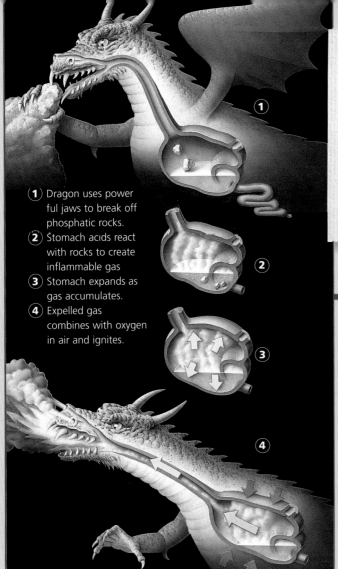

These excellent diagrams were first printed in the catalogue for an exhibition at the Kansas City Museum of Unnatural History. They are the clearest and most up-to-date illustrations I have seen on two important areas: how European dragons make fire and the development of the Chinese dragon.

1 Dragon uses powerful jaws to break off phosphatic rocks.

2 Stomach acids react with rocks to create inflammable gas

3 Stomach expands as gas accumulates.

4 Expelled gas combines with oxygen in air and ignites.

CAT NO. 354

FIRE-BREATHING

The dragon's mysterious ability to produce bursts of flame is one of the most potent weapons in its arsenal. Dragon observers claim to have recorded emissions up to 200 m long, attaining temperatures of over 1000°C, and many people have sought to explain how this remarkable feat is achieved.

Professor Heinz Diebtrich, of the Götlingen Institute for Cryptozoology in Germany, has proposed that dragons ingest phosphor-laden rocks which break down in the acidic conditions of the digestive system, possibly in a special stomach (termed the phosphorocatabolic stomach by Professor Diebtrich), to release a volatile gas, which is flammable on contact with the air. Attempts to investigate the phenomenon – and to reproduce it in the laboratory – have proved difficult, and frequently fatal.

CAT NO. 373

DEVELOPMENTAL STAGES OF THE CHINESE DRAGON
DRACO SINENSIS

Centuries of study by Chinese scholars have allowed us to build up a fairly complete picture of the 4000-year birth cycle of the Chinese dragon. After 1000 years of gestation as a gemlike egg (**1**), the young dragon spends 500 years as a water snake (**2**), slowly developing the head of a carp, at which stage it is known as a *kiao* (**3**). Over the next millennium the dragon acquires scales, four limbs tipped with claws and an elongated, bearded face; it is now known as a *lung* (**4**), meaning 'deaf', for the dragon cannot yet hear anything. It takes another five centuries to grow horns, through which it can hear, and becomes a *kioh-lung* (**5**) – the classical form of oriental dragon. The final stage of growth (**6**) takes another millennium, during which the dragon sprouts a set of wings and becomes a fully mature *ying-lung* (of which there are several varieties).

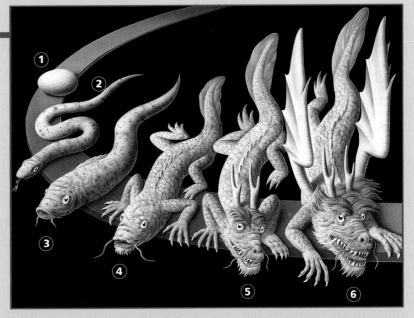

Wyverns & Drakes

LATIN NAME
Wyverns:
Pseudodraconis
sp.; Drakes:
Ophidio
draconis

HABITAT
Forests, caverns,
mountains

LIFESPAN
Up to 30 years

SIZE
Wyverns:
6–18 ft
(1.8–5.4 m)
long; Drakes:
3–5 ft
(1–1.5 m) long

INFORMATION
SOURCE
Letter

DISTRIBUTION
Europe, esp.
northern parts

TDY.102.136
TRADITIONAL FRENCH
WYVERN'S CLAW-PATTERN
DOOR KNOCKER.

Hans Dietmar MSc PhD
Draconian Studies Dept.
Gotlingen Institute for
Cryptozoology
Vienna, Austria

6 Feb 1998

Dear Sirs

Professor Diebtrich has passed to me your letter of 23 January,
asking for information on wyverns and drakes. I am pleased to reply
with the following brief details.

I must point out that you have made an error in classing the wyvern
with the drake. They are both close relatives of the dragon, but they
do not belong to the same order. I understand that in England you
call them 'dragonets' because they are like little dragons, but it is
quite inaccurate to put them together.

They have fundamentally different body plans. The drake's wings, like
those of the dragon, have developed from extended ribs with
membranous flaps between them. The wings of the wyvern, on the other
hand, are true wings (derived from the forelimbs) like those of bats
or birds. As a result the drake looks like a miniature dragon, but
the wyvern has a distinctive two-legged stance.

Both types live in caverns or similar protected lairs, which can be
identified by the debris of bones and valuables. These they gather
because, like dragons, they are attracted to shiny objects and
baubles. 'Dragonets' are far less discerning and their 'hoards' will
contain as much rubbish as gold.

Drakes are more timid than the wyvern, and live in remote mountain
areas. They have highly toxic blood which is saturated with a
volatile sulphur salt. This makes it extremely corrosive on contact
with almost any surface other than the drake's own skin or veins, and
it is actually flammable on contact with air. Drakes do not possess
fire-breathing capabilities, but because of their blood they are
sometimes known as firedrakes. They are reclusive, and sightings and
interactions with humans are rare. One example is the medieval story
of an encounter between a knight and a drake at Mount Pilatus in
Switzerland. The knight killed the drake, but was killed in turn by
its poisonous blood.

Wyverns, or <u>Pseudodraconae</u>, live in forests and woods. They have
eagle-like talons, and deadly barbed stings at the tip of their
tails. They are aggressive by nature, and attack on sight anything

DRAKE'S
SULPHUROUS
BLOOD.

that might provide a meal. Broody females should never be approached when they are with young.

Wyverns are far less timid than drakes and were once well known in Europe, especially in England, before weapons technology and the growth of human populations depleted their numbers. Leonardo da Vinci recorded an encounter between a wyvern and a lion, although it seems unlikely that he observed it first hand. In the bestiaries of the Middle Ages, the wyvern was used as an allegory of Satan, and was associated with war, pestilence and sin. It was especially said to spread plague, a heinous charge in a medieval Europe reeling from the horrors of the Black Death.

The wyvern was given other meanings too. The medieval alchemists dressed their knowledge in esoteric codes and allegories, and the wyvern was used to represent matter in its 'base', or untransmuted, state. The alchemist himself was depicted as the worthy knight overcoming the beast – that is, transforming it into gold.

The wyvern survives today mainly as a heraldic emblem, and both it and the drake must be considered practically extinct. The relatively undisturbed mountains and forests of Eastern Europe and Russia might, however, conceal a few surviving specimens.

If you wish to have more information or amplification of the above points, you are welcome to write again. I will be pleased to fill the evident gaps in your knowledge and correct any more of your glaring mistakes.

Yours faithfully

H V Krump

H. Dietmar

A SWISS KNIGHT PREPARES TO SLAUGHTER A DRAKE HE HAS CORNERED IN ITS LAIR.

HERCULES AND THE HYDRA

by Nicholas Harris, MCSL

THE LABOURS OF HERCULES

Reproduced on the preceding pages is Nicholas Harris' Hercules and the Hydra, commissioned to commemorate the Society's 125th Annual General Meeting. It now hangs in the Upper Reading Room at 100 Piccadilly. Hercules and other heroes of the past– the Argonauts, Sindbad the Sailor, Odysseus – represent the earliest examples of cryptozoological research in practice, a long and proud tradition which the Cryptozoological Society of London continues today. During his lifetime Hercules met (and killed) a host of strange and marvellous creatures. His story provides a remarkable account of the sheer diversity of ancient Mediterranean cryptozoological life.

THE TWELVE LABOURS

Hercules' cryptozoological travels are usually placed within the narrative framework of his legendary Twelve Tasks or Labours. In reality he was probably a Bronze Age princeling from Southern Greece, but by the 6th century BCE a story cycle had grown up around him.

1 THE NEMEAN LION

Hercules' first task was to subdue an enormous lion that was terrorising the area of Nemea (near Corinth). Its hide was invulnerable, so he strangled it with his bare hands and skinned it with its own claws. This beast was possibly a cave lion, not extinct on mainland Europe until the Roman era or later or, possibly, a rare surviving Megantereon – a prehistoric sabre-tooth cat.

2 THE LERNEAN HYDRA

Hydra are related to dragons. They are wingless, however, do not breathe fire and have several heads. According to legend Hercules cut off the Hydra's heads, whereupon it grew two for every one cut off. The creature was only defeated when Hercules' companion Iolaos cauterised the stumps.

3 THE HIND OF KERYNEIA

In the legend this animal, although female, had golden horns. Hercules had to track it for a year before he finally caught it. Stories of supernatural deer, such as this, may have sprung from accounts of another prehistoric survivor – *Megaceros*, the giant Irish Elk, which could grow antlers up to 13 ft (4 m) in span.

4 THE BOAR OF MOUNT ERYMANTHUS

For his fourth task Hercules had to capture alive a huge boar which was ravaging the countryside around Mount Erymanthus.

5 AUGEAN STABLES

Augeas, King of Elis, kept vast herds of cattle in an enormous stable which he could not keep clean. Charged with the role of sanitary engineer, Hercules diverted the courses of two rivers to flow through the stable.

6 THE STYMPHALIAN BIRDS

These appear elsewhere in legend as the foes of Atalanta, one of the Argonauts (see page 64). They haunted the lake of Stymphalos, in Arcadia, until Hercules drove them off with his bow.

9 THE BELT OF HIPPOLYTE

Hippolyte was the queen of the Amazons, a nation of warrior women who lived on the shores of the Black Sea. Hercules captured her belt – in most versions after killing Hippolyte.

10 THE CATTLE OF GERYON

Geryon, an ogre with three bodies attached to one pair of legs, may have been a mythologised reference to an ancient Siamese triplet. Hercules stole his cattle from Tartessus, on the Iberian peninsula, with the aid of a flying bowl borrowed from Helios the sun god.

11 THE GOLDEN APPLES OF THE HESPERIDES

In order to obtain the golden apples from the garden of the Hesperides, in the Atlas Mountains in North Africa, Hercules needed the help of Atlas – the Titan who carried the world on his shoulders. He was required also to fight a dragon, which the ancients seem to have viewed as a mere distraction, suggesting that North African dragons were not particularly impressive.

7 THE FIRE-BREATHING CRETAN BULL

This beast was menacing the island of Crete until Hercules wrestled it into submission. The creature's fiery breath was probably a fanciful embellishment, but the legend almost certainly refers to a real animal – the aurochs (*Bos primigenius*), a giant ox which was the ancestor of modern cattle, and did not become extinct until 1627, when the last individual was killed in Poland.

8 THE MAN-EATING MARES OF THRACE

King Diomedes of Thrace kept a herd of fierce horses who ate human flesh. This is unusual behaviour for horses, although under modern farming practices many livestock have animal protein added to their feed. Hercules subdued the mares by feeding them their master's body.

12 BRINGING BACK CERBERUS FROM HADES

Hercules' final task was to bring Cerberus, the three-headed hound that guarded the entrance to the Underworld, into the world of the living. Denied the use of any weapons by Hades, the ruler of the Underworld, Hercules used brute strength to haul the dog into the daylight, so completing his twelve labours.

REPTILES

Sea serpents

LATIN NAME
*Hydrophiidae
giganteus*

HABITAT
*Ocean, both
deep and
coastal waters*

LIFESPAN
Unknown

SIZE
*Up to 200 ft
(61 m) long,
20 ft (6 m) thick*

**INFORMATION
SOURCE**
CSL Review

DISTRIBUTION
Worldwide

HE WORLD'S OCEANS COVER TWO-thirds of the Earth's surface, and reach a depth of 11 miles (17.7 km). It has often been said that scientists know less about they do about come as little sur-tures like the sea evaded the grasp While the size and markings of this awesome animal obviously vary with maturity, most sightings confirm that fully grown adults are 200 ft long, and have a body some 20 ft thick, with dark brown or black skin, often with a white or yellow underside. Some reports describe a seaweed-like 'mane' (which may be a secondary sexual characteristic, designed to help attract a mate) and almost all describe fiercely glowing, mesmeric eyes that stare up through the water.

the ocean depths than outer space. It should prise, then, that crea-serpent have largely of conventional zoology.

EGGS-EMPT

In addition, sea serpents share a number of adaptive features with their smaller brethren the sea snake, ideally suiting them for a life in the ocean. On the top of their heads they have nostrils that can be sealed with a special valve, and their tails are deep but laterally compressed in order to act more effectively as paddles. The structure of their scales prevents them from moving on land, restricting them to a marine environment. This presents difficulties in reproduction. Most reptiles, even amphibious ones such as sea turtles, need to come ashore in order to lay eggs –

☞ *PHOTOGRAPHER ROBERT LE SERREC
SNAPPED THIS GIANT TADPOLE-LIKE
CREATURE IN AUSTRALIA'S BARRIER REEF.*

a perilous exercise that leaves the reptile vulnerable to predators. The *Hydrophiidae*, the group to which most cryptotaxonomists consider sea serpents to belong, bear live young (are viviparous) – completing their adaptation to the aquatic world.

Sea serpents have been sighted in both coastal waters and the deep ocean, and are probably at home in either habitat, freely adapting their diet to

include fish, sharks, dolphins, squid and even humans, if the opportunity presents itself. There have been several attacks on boats and even large ships, and one report relates a titanic tussle between a particularly large sea serpent and a sperm whale.

FANGS VERY MUCH

Classical writers often claimed that the sea serpent had a venomous bite. Other, smaller sea snakes are very poisonous, so there is good reason to suspect that the classical authorities are accurate. The sight of these fearsomely fanged monsters would be enough to strike fear into the heart of even the saltiest of salty dogs. Huge sea serpents were also a common fea-ture of many of the world's great mythologies: Jormungandr, the serpent that encircled Midgard (Earth) in Norse mythology, was a perennial foe of Thor's. Aristotle, writing in the 4th century BCE, provides one of the earliest accounts of real sea serpents. In his *Historia Animalium*, he describes them as 'very large,' and relates how mariners off the coast of Libya saw the bones of oxen eaten by sea serpents before coming under attack themselves. One of their triremes was capsized by the combined efforts of several angry serpents.

Documented reports exist spanning the classical era and the Middle Ages. One well-known sighting was by Olaus Magnus, Archbishop of Uppsala, who tells in his *History of the Northern People* (1555) of an enormous sea creature that haunted fishermen around the coastal waters of Norway. His description is detailed: 'He hath commonly hair hanging from his neck a cubit long, and sharp scales and is black, and he hath flaming shining eyes.' One of the most influential reports was that of the renowned Norwegian Bishop Hans Egede. En route to Greenland in 1734, the clergyman encountered a serpent that raised itself out of the water so that its head was higher than the main mast. When it fell back into the sea, its tail was observed to be much longer than the ship itself.

The general climate of opinion remained biased against the existence of sea serpents until the famous 1848 sighting by the crew of HMS *Daedalus*, a British Navy ship, between the Cape of Good Hope and St Helena. Captain Peter McQuhoe made a careful record of the sighting, and was brave enough to report the matter to his superiors on returning to London. His description of a 60-ft long, brown-skinned, white-throated creature with 'something like the mane of a horse ... washed about its back' sparked off a flood of similar stories from other mariners around the world. It seemed that there were many sailors whose fear of being ridicules had

THE CREW MARVEL AS THE GIANT SEA SERPENT PASSES BEHIND THE STERN OF HMS Daedalus. *THE CREW'S PROFESSIONAL STATUS LENT VERACITY TO THEIR STATEMENTS, AND SPARKED A FLOOD OF REPORTS.*

have fallen through a combination of general pollution and a great increase in naval traffic. There remains a persistent tendency to dismiss sightings of the sea serpent as mere giant squid or whales, or even as a school of porpoises – which might give the impression of being a single, long creature as they leap through the air in procession.

Most cryptozoologists believe that sea serpents are in fact plesiosaurs or pliosaurs – like their cousins the lake monsters, living fossils from the age of the dinosaurs. The current scarcity of sea serpents, and the extreme difficulty of catching a specimen for study, means that this may well be the last word on this giant of the seas.

A WOODCUT FROM KONRAD VON GESNER'S BOOK OF FISH SHOWS HOW A SEA SERPENT CAN EASILY OVERWHELM A SMALL SAILING VESSEL.

deterred them from telling their tales.

TRAFFIC CASUALTY

Most observers now accept that such serpents exist. However, although sightings continued into this century – a creature known as Cadborosaurus was seen off the Canadian coast as recently as September 1994 – they fell dramatically in frequency. The serpent's geographical distribution has also changed: in classical times, the creatures were common in the Mediterranean, but since the Industrial Revolution, sightings became increasingly confined to very remote parts of the oceans. The most likely explanation is that their numbers

UP FROM THE DEEP

Far from being dismissed as fables inflated by seafarers' love of tall stories, the quantity and consistency of reports has convinced many members of the scientific community that gigantic sea serpents really do exist.

A SEA SERPENT PICTURED IN THE 1840s – THE GREAT AGE OF SEA SNAKE SIGHTINGS. NOTE THE THICK FOLDS OF HEAVY SKIN.

REPTILES

Lake monsters

LATIN NAME
Unknown

HABITAT
Remote, isolated, deep lakes

LIFESPAN
Uncertain

SIZE
Up to 40 ft (12 m) long

INFORMATION SOURCE
Field Report

DISTRIBUTION
Worldwide

46

BACKGROUND INFORMATION

More than 250 of the world's lakes and rivers are reported to have some sort of monster; 24 of these are in Scotland alone. Despite a wealth of testimony, with over 3000 reported sightings at Loch Ness, cryptozoologists have been unable to make a clear identification of any of the world's lake monsters. Consistent features of the sightings and habitats in question suggest that one genus, or at least one family, of creature is responsible, but scientists are still debating what class that might be.

Much of the evidence about lake monsters is drawn from studies of the Loch Ness Monster, by far the most famous and investigated of the world's lake monsters. The first recorded reference to the Loch Ness Monster comes from St Columba, the Irish abbot who brought Christianity to Scotland in the 6th century AD. Sporadic encounters occurred over the following years, but there was often confusion between Scotland's many lake monsters and the equally widespread water-horse, or kelpie.

The story of the Loch Ness Monster really took off in 1933, the year a new road was opened along the side of the

TOP: A PLAYFUL MODEL OF OGOPOGO, WHO LIVES IN LAKE OKANAGAN IN BRITISH COLUMBIA. BOTTOM: A SKETCH BY THE SIBERIAN BIOLOGIST N F GLADKIKH OF THE MONSTER OF LAKE KHAIR, WHICH HE OBSERVED IN 1964

Loch. Shortly after the road was completed, a Scottish couple named McKay saw a 30 ft (9 m) long animal with a serpentine neck and head. A rash of sightings followed, culminating in Lt-Colonel Dr Robert Wilson's famous photo purporting to show the monster's head in 1934. The scientific community, however, dismissed the whole affair, and interest in the 'Nessie' died down.

Interest was renewed in the early 1960s, when post-war developments in technology brought valuable new evidence about the Loch and its mysterious inhabitant. In April 1960 an English engineer, Tim Dinsdale, captured on 16mm film a hump object moving across the loch at a speed of about 7 mph (11 km/h). Military experts, skilled at analysing aerial reconnaissance film, agreed that it

---

Missionary Gazette, 13 October 1924

Warriors of Christ

IN TIMES PAST, as today, the way of the missionary was beset on all sides by the torments of the Devil. Where today the earnest prose-lytiser, engaged in God's holy work, must contend with the evil influences of the secular world, in times gone by our forebears had to face dangers of a more tangible kind. In 565 AD the Irish missionary Columba was travelling through Scotland to spread Christianity, when he came across the funeral of a man savaged by the creature of Loch Ness. Taking heart from his Faith, Columba resolved to face and defeat this wicked serpent. Summoning his courage, he bade one of his companions swim out to retrieve the man's boat. When the monster appeared, Columba made the sign of the Cross, forcing the beast to retreat far into the depths of the Loch.

SEE ALSO
KELPIE,
PAGE 26.

THE TIMES, 30 April 1934

'CREATURE IN LOCH' CAUGHT ON FILM

SCIENTISTS SCEPTICAL OF SNAPSHOTS

THE FRENZIED MONSTER-hunting of the last few months appeared to have finally borne fruit last night, with the publication of sensational photographic evidence. The pictures, taken by army surgeon Lt.- Col. Dr Robert Wilson, clearly show the long neck and small, snake-like head reported by so many witnesses. Professor Gordon Willoughby, President of the distinguished Cryptozoological Society of London, commented yesterday that as far as he was concerned, "these pictures provide definitive proof that there is a prehistoric survivor in the Loch. In my opinion the general public should be advised that bathing could be hazardous."

But government scientists were quick to dismiss the claims as "misguided". "This so-called monster is most likely a grey seal, specimens of which frequently find their way into the Loch," said a Home Office spokesman, adding that there was no cause for alarm.

was a living, aquatic creature. In the same year, an echo-sounding expedition found a large unidentified trace off Urquhart Castle, where most of the sightings have been made. Intensive observation projects rendered very little worthwhile evidence, while several forays with submarines proved unsuccessful.

The next breakthrough came in 1972, when an American team, led by Dr Robert Rines, used a special underwater camera to obtain a startling picture of what looked exactly like a plesiosaur's flipper. Rines followed this in 1975 with a controversial photograph purporting to be the creature's head and neck. Investigations since have centred on the use of sonar; definitive proof has still not emerged.

In June 1996 I undertook to review the activities of the CSL's Loch Ness Observation Station (LNOS), near Urquhart Castle on the Loch. The station is manned by a dedicated team of researchers, whose complete logbooks, going back to 1984, are held in the Society's archives.

APRIL 7, 1976

THE TELEGRAPH

NESSIE 'IS REAL'

Astonishing photo seems to show entire monster

Veteran monster hunter Robert Rines today issued a blurry picture he took last year and vowed to to return to Loch Ness until he has definitive proof of the monster's existence. Dr Rines, President of the New Hampshire based Academy of Applied Science, says that the picture shows a bulbous body with flipper-like appendages, a thin neck and a tiny head.

The New York Times has offered to pay $25,000 towards the cost of the Academy's planned expedition this year. Today's murky picture, taken under water with an advanced stroboscopic camera and enhanced by NASA computers, has been examined by a team from the Cryptozoological Society of London. Officials said that the photographic evidence appeared to confirm the theory that the monster is a type of plesiosaur (an aquatic dinosaur), but warned that further research would be needed.

Three years ago, Dr Rines issued two pictures of what appears to be a rhomboidal flipper passing a sonar-activated camera in the Loch.

REPTILES

Lake monsters

FIELD REPORT

FIELD NOTES
13 June

Today was a rare sunny day, providing ideal conditions for observations. All too often the weather here is overcast and gloomy, just one of the problems that hamper investigations. The loch is huge - 24 miles long and 1 mile wide (38 x 1.6 km), and we can only see a small part of it, but the LNOS is sited at Urquhart Castle, where many of the best sightings have occurred.

Mist frequently covers the water, which is dark and murky from particles of peat washed down from the surrounding hills. As a result, visibility underwater is close to nil. Attempts at echo-sounding (sonar), the most useful way to spot underwater movements, are hindered by the depth of the loch (up to 975 ft/297 m) and the canyons of its deeply ridged floor.

Together with the overhangs of the loch's steep sides, these create 'sonar-shadows' where sonar beams cannot reach.

We scanned the waves for four hours, our video and still cameras bristling with zoom lenses and ready for action. I was excited by a strong V-shaped wake until Hannah, one of the student volunteers, pointed out the duck that was making it. She'd seen floating logs, fish breaking the surface and even a seal, but no monsters. She said that most sightings describe the same elements: a large submarine mass moving through the water creating a wake, often seeming humped (like an 'upturned boat') or undulating; a long, swan-like neck topped with a small head, often described as horse-like; dark, slimy skin; and flippers or paddles. Hannah told me that the total length is said to be about 30 ft (9 m).

SLIME-COVERED VEGETATION FROM THE LOCH SHORE.

MEMBERS OF THE LOCH NESS OBSERVATION STATION USE POWERFUL TELEPHOTO EQUIPMENT AND BINOCULARS TO SCAN THE WATER'S SURFACE IN 1968. TODAY'S INVESTIGATORS USE A BATTERY OF COMPUTERS AND SPECIALIST INSTRUMENTS.

STUDENT UNAL KOZAK TOOK VIDEO FOOTAGE OF A PART-SUBMERGED CREATURE ON LAKE VAN.

14th June

Broken cloud today. When the water is in shadow, it is surprisingly difficult to see under the surface, and you realise how hard it is to judge distance and size – yet more complications for would-be Nessie-hunters. At lunchtime it began to rain, and we retreated to a pub. I bought Hannah a few whiskies, and we got quite comfy in a corner of the snug. Then her boyfriend Alasdair, the local caber-tossing champ, came in and I decided to take a look at the saloon bar, where I was buttonholed by a couple of middle-aged Americans who urged me to explain 'this Nessie thing'.

I explained that the most widely favoured candidates for the role of lake monster are plesiosaurs, a family of aquatic dinosaurs believed to have become extinct some 65 million years ago. Fossil remains show that plesiosaurs had many of the same features as lake monsters, including the long swan-like neck, the small head, the large, oval body and the paddle-like flippers. A similar candidate is the pliosaur.

My new American friends had read that the Loch Ness Monster is especially hard to spot because it spends a great deal of time away from the loch, migrating to the open sea via underwater tunnels linking the loch to the sea. Although this would tie in with the high frequency of sea-serpent sightings in the North Sea, it could not apply to many of the world's other lake monsters, which are often found in lakes well away from open water. For instance, a lake monster exciting much recent interest is the monster of Lake

Van, in Eastern Turkey. Lake Van is high in the mountains and more than 185 miles (297 km) from the nearest large body of water, the Black Sea.

15th June

After lunch I persuaded Hannah to stroll with me along the loch shore. The fringes of the loch are thickly wooded, with almost impenetrable undergrowth right down to the waterside, but we did come across something unusual: an area where the undergrowth was flattened in a broad swathe, as if something heavy had dragged itself out of the water. The vegetation seemed slimy, and there was a rank smell.

It occurred to me that the Loch Ness Monster is often seen on land – crossing a lochside road, or plunging into the woods. On at least one occasion it was reported to be carrying a sheep in its mouth, and it has been linked with the occasional slaughtered sheep. The creature might also be dangerous to humans. The first record of the Loch Ness Monster

49

The London Mercury. November 14th, 1897.

SWEDISH VILLAGERS LAUNCH HUNT FOR LAKE CREATURE.

If the reports of two young girls are to be believed, Lake Storsjo in Sweden harbours an unsavoury creature. Responding to the girls' claim that they were molested by a large, slimy monster, the locals have set out to trap and kill the monster. Brandishing a fearsome collection of harpoons, hooks and irons, they gather by the lake shore or put to in small boats. This reporter can only speculate that something in the Scandinavian temperament is given to flights of fancy. Let us be thankful that the British, for the time being at least, are immune to such nonsense.

The Telegraph June 9, 1971

· Your Letters

Dear Sir,

In my thirty-two years as Head of Palaeontology at the National Museum of Prehistory I have often been asked to comment on the likely existence of a prehistoric survivor in Loch Ness, and have therefore thought long and hard about the matter. In light of the flurry of media interest that has surrounded the announcement of plans for a submarine exploration of the loch, I would like to put a number of questions to the expedition's leader.

If the creature in the loch is indeed a plesiosaur, as is usually suggested, it has survived the extinction of its fellows by some 65 million years. How large a breeding colony would be needed for the beast to survive this long? How could such a population evade detection or fail to leave any evidence? If a prehistoric cold-blooded resident of tropical seas is assumed to be behind the mysterious sightings, how does it survive in the cold temperatures of the higher latitudes? (Lake monsters have been reported in Ireland, Norway, Sweden, Canada and Chile, among others.) How is it that lake monsters are equally at home in freshwater or marine environments, in and out of the water ('Nessie' has often been spotted on land), and in warm and cold waters? Lastly, there is the question of breathing. If lake monsters are reptiles then they can't breathe underwater, but need to come to the surface. Why aren't more monsters spotted? Can they last all day without air, only coming up at night?

I would advise potential 'monster hunters' to think twice before committing huge sums of money to such an ill-conceived project.

Professor Zoltan Kuczynskcyz,
National Museum of Prehistory,
Hartlepool.

reports an attack on a man, and in 1897 a Swedish monster in Lake Storsj chased two girls along the lake shore.

Later that night, as the light was fading, I was standing by the loch and noticed a disturbance in the water. The surface seemed to be churning, and there were flashes of silver. The monster! I thought to myself - but then realised that I was seeing a shoal of fish, a mixture of trout, salmon and others, all swimming frantically towards shallower water. It was an extraordinary sight, but then I noticed a strange V-shaped wake moving up the loch. I could clearly see that there was nothing on the surface causing it, and I did get the distinct impression of very large, dark mass or hump just below the surface in the water. It was moving very quickly, and soon passed out of sight, but at one point I distinctly saw something break the surface at least 20 ft behind the front of the wake. I went to bed a happy man - not least because I bumped into Hannah on the way back from the Loch.

PERHAPS SOME PLESIOSAURS SURVIVED THE CATASTROPHE THAT WIPED OUT THE DINOSAURS SOME 65-70 MILLION YEARS AGO AND LIVE IN THE DEEP, FRESH WATER OF BIG LAKES SUCH AS LOCH NESS.

I made a few sketches of the fish and the monster.

Leaping fish (top) announced the imminent arrival of the monster. A shiver ran up my spine as I watched it glide silently past.

REPTILES

Lake monsters

DRAWING OF THE CONGOLESE MOKELE MBEMBE,
BASED ON EYEWITNESS DESCRIPTIONS.

SUPPLEMENTARY NOTES

At the time of writing, interest in the Loch Ness Monster seems to have subsided for a while. Other lake monsters have created interest elsewhere in the world. Recently the Migo of Lake Dakatua in New Britain was supposedly filmed by a Japanese film crew - although experts claim the footage shows, variously, a large crocodile, two crocodiles swimming together or a dugout canoe with a man standing on it. On the whole, though, sightings excite interest from the media rather than officialdom, with serious study left to a few dedicated crypto-zoologists. Until more definite proof emerges, lake monsters will have to carry on being speculative creatures, without being properly named or identified, remaining officially non-existent.

There have been so many lake monsters reported from around the world that it is impossible to list them all. Notable examples include: Manipogo (Lake Manitoba, Canada); the White Lake monster (Chile); the Hvaler Serpent (Norway); Slimey Slim (USA); Waitoreke (Australia), the Lake Bala monster (North Wales); Ogopogo (British Columbia), Ponik (Lake Pohenegamook, Quebec) and Champ, the Lake Champlain monster (USA/Canada). Cynics claim that these beasts are creatures of the imagination, invented to drum up tourist business. Explanations offered for these creatures range from giant sturgeon, rogue elephant seals and enormous otters to zeuglodonts - a long, slender aquatic dinosaur that propelled itself by vertical undulations of its body. This motion would produce the 'rolling arches' effect reported by so many observers.

In folklore and fiction, lake monsters are often confused with other water-based monsters, including the sea serpent and even the dragon. Most likely this is the case for some sightings of these creatures, particularly sea-serpents, but most of their true relatives would have died some 65 million years ago in the great extinction that ended the age of the dinosaurs.

An intriguing exception is the creature known to the pygmies of the Congo as mokele mbembe, almost certainly a surviving sauropod related to the gigantic brontosaurus of ancient times - in other words, a 70 million-year-old living fossil. For cryptozoologists specialising on lake life, the mokele mbembe shares many characteristics with lake monsters. Its favourite haunts are lakes, it has a long neck and tail, a small head and massive body, and has proved as elusive as its aquatic cousins. Perhaps lake monsters are a form of mokele mbembe, adapted to suit a water-based lifestyle.

The Inverness Star, September 14 1933

Strange monster sighted on new road

A couple driving on the new lochside road at Loch Ness were yesterday startled by the appearance of a strange creature.

Mr McKay reported that his wife was "terrified" and "really quite upset" by the 30 foot long apparition which confronted them as they rounded a bend. "It was a horrible monster," said Mrs Mackay, "with a head and neck like a big snake. It took me three cups of sweet tea before I could stop shaking!"

The couple claimed that the monster appeared out of the long grass on one side of the road and plunged into the undergrowth by the loch shore. The news has created a sensation across the country, although the government has yet to comment on the reports.

Section 3

BIRDS

The popularity of bird-watching today reflects the powerful presence that birds have in our collective subconscious. It is no surprise, therefore, to find that legendary birds have intrigued and terrorised humans over the ages. The titanic thunderbird and roc, the wise simurgh, the therapeutic caladrius and the legendary phoenix have all touched the human soul in complex ways that reflect this privileged position. Sadly, all of the species discussed in this section are either extinct or severely endangered, emphasizing how fragile is the balance between the human and the marvellous and how important the cryptozoologist is in maintaining that balance.

3

CSL R E V I E W

INSIDE CRYPTOZOOLOGY

Basic principles of cryptozoology explained in simple terms for schools, colleges and new readers. Created by the Education Department of the Cryptozoological Society of London.

Birds

Birds soaring in the air have fascinated humans over the ages, perhaps because they symbolise the spirit of freedom and peace. Some birds, like the titanic thunderbird and the gigantic roc, have struck fear into human hearts. Others, like the therapeutic caladrius, the wise simurgh and the phoenix, have inspired love or awe.

Millions of keen enthusiasts and bird-watchers around the world have helped to ensure that birds are among the most closely studied of all fauna. Sadly, they are also among the most endangered: theft of eggs, erosion of habitat and shooting for sport pose a serious threat to their survival. All the species studied by cryptozoologists are either extinct or in peril.

The flightless dodo, the last specimen of which was killed in about 1761, has become the very emblem of extinction. Other famous lost avians are the dodo-like solitaire, the great auk and the passenger pigeon. To their ranks cryptozoologists can add the phoenix and the caladrius. All these birds suffered a fatal blow – either directly or indirectly – from humans.

Sink or swim

Species are constantly being extinguished through natural causes, as part of the continuing evolution of life on planet Earth. Accepting and understanding this mechanism will help us to gain a deeper appreciation of the many

FIG 1 THE MOA

Like Madagascar and Australia, New Zealand has a unique, protected ecosystem, lacking many of the predators and competing species found in Europe and the Americas. As a result, flightless birds were able to evolve and flourish. The arrival of humans from Europe changed all that. Marauding rabbits and cattle proved stiff competition for food, while domestic cats and dogs wreaked havoc with native species who had not evolved to deal with such predation. The moa, which reached heights of 10 ft (3 m) was a slow-moving forest dweller native to New Zealand. Like the American passenger pigeon, human hunters could not resist such easy pickings. By the mid 19th century the moa was extinct.

problems facing cryptozoological populations today.

Populations wax and wane in response to several different factors. Climatic change, an increase in the numbers of predators or prey,or a sudden natural disaster can all devastate creatures who depend on a particular environment. A flexible, adaptable animal (in evolutionary terms, a genetically 'fit' species) will come through such hard times, enabling them to take advantage of better conditions when they come.

Upsetting the balance

Species become especially vulnerable when they lose the ability to adapt to change (see Fig 1). This can happen when they become too specialised or too closely tied to a particular niche. The dodo could not adapt because it depended on the specific, fragile, ecosystems of the islands of Madagascar, Mauritius and Reunion. Human immigrants from Europe, accompanied by dogs, rats, goats and pigs, quickly upset that equilibrium.

The long-tailed North American passenger pigeon, on the other hand, was simply hunted to extinction. Millions of birds used to migrate in flocks along the eastern seaboard every spring and autumn. These vast clouds of birds were, it seems, too tempting for 19th-century huntsmen to ignore. As rifles grew cheaper, more accurate and more powerful, the death toll steadily grew: man as predator had fatally upset the balance. The last passenger pigeon died in Cincinnati Zoo in 1914.

Cryptozoological species face similar pressures. The chimaera was hunted to extinction by the Ancient Greeks, but change or damage to habitats is more often to blame. The bizarre lifecycle of the phoenix, for example, was interrupted by human exploitation of the spice groves in which it gathered its own funeral pyre. The caladrius was over-dependent on the generosity of human benefactors for its food supply, in stark contrast to its adaptable (and successful) cousins, the crow family.

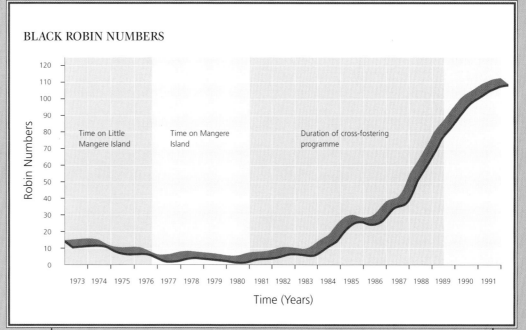

BLACK ROBIN NUMBERS

FIG 2 CONSERVATION IN ACTION – THE BLACK ROBIN

In the late 1970s, the tiny black robin (Petroica traversi) of New Zealand's Chatham Island group was in danger of extinction. By 1980 human settlement and the predations of cats had reduced its numbers to just five specimens. The New Zealand Wildlife Service launched an emergency cross-fostering programme, based on the birds' habit of laying a second clutch of eggs if it loses the first. Wardens transferred the birds to a predator-free island and carefully removed the first clutch from the nest and placed the eggs with local tomtit foster-parents. Numbers gradually recovered. In 1989, when the population reached 100, it was decided that the fostering programme could be halted.

Critical mass

One of the greatest obstacles to adaptability is low population size. Any species that reaches a critical level of population becomes vulnerable to misfortune: a single natural disaster or outbreak of disease could wipe out all remaining individuals (see Fig 2).

A related problem affects the cheetah. At some point in the last few million years, the cheetahs of Africa passed through a catastrophic event that left only a few individuals to found the current population. All the cheetahs alive today are therefore very closely related. As a consequence, they suffer from low sperm counts, infertility and susceptibility to disease and the species is gravely endangered.

The challenge of survival

Cryptozoological species like pegasi and rocs are thought to suffer similar problems. Unsurprisingly, human encroachment and environmental changes have restricted their numbers. It has always been a feature of the cryptozoological corpus that its members require absolute solitude to breed and multiply. Human tampering with the Earth's air and water have simply added to problems created by geometrically increasing populations. The result has been small breeding populations and dangerously low levels of genetic diversity.

The problems highlighted by such extinctions are shared by many species today. If creatures as rare and marvellous as thunderbirds, *lamassu* and lake monsters are to survive, international action is needed now and on a wide scale. Conservationists working with the cheetah have shown what can be done. Is cryptozoology ready for the same challenge?

BIRDS

Phoenix

LATIN NAME
Phoenos immortalis

HABITAT
Light woodland

LIFESPAN
500–1000 years

SIZE
*Wingspan:
c. 8–12 ft
(2.5–3.5 m)*

INFORMATION SOURCE
CSL Review

DISTRIBUTION
India, with migration route to Egypt via Middle East

The phoenix is a symbol of rebirth, but also has a lifecycle defying biology. Truth really can be stranger than fiction.

C'MON BABY, LIGHT MY
PYRE

ANY CREATURE THAT SETS ITSELF ON FIRE in order to guarantee its survival is bound to compel attention. The phoenix has been for centuries a very powerful human symbol of the desire for spiritual rebirth and has, inevitably, become a multi-faceted emblem. It embodied the purifying power of fire; the Chinese female principle, or yin; imperial grace and elegance; immortality and rebirth; purity and piety. Now extinct, its end, like its beginning, is shrouded in a smokescreen of mystery. But such was man's regard for this bird that even now, some 500 years after it is believed to have vanished, there is a roaring trade in purported phoenix relics.

UP IN SMOKE

Making its home in a beautiful wooded glade in central India, the phoenix presented a magnificent sight. Resembling a very large eagle, with red and golden feathers, rainbow-hued wings and scarlet feet, it lived for at least 500 years – in some incarnations, as long as 1000. Ancient zoologists believed that it subsisted on air and dew, for it was never seen to feed. Modern knowledge of bacteria and other microscopic life forms, however, suggests that the phoenix was probably a filter feeder, using some sophisticated form of extraction mechanism like a plankton-eating sea creature.

As the phoenix approached the end of its allotted span, it would begin the long migration west. Flying to the Arabian peninsula, it would gather leaves and branches of cinnamon, myrrh and many other spices, before travelling on to Phoenicia (modern Lebanon). Here it would construct a pyre out of the materials it had gathered, strike its beak against a piece of flint, set the pyre and itself ablaze, and become completely consumed by the flames. By the next day a tiny worm-like creature could be seen amongst the embers, growing quickly into a bird exactly like its parent. After three days, the

GIVING THE PHOENIX A HALO SUGGESTS THE BIRD'S POWERFUL SPIRITUAL SYMBOLISM.

鳳凰

☞ DORÉ BASED THIS RENDITION ON AN IMAGE IN A CHINESE TEMPLE.

new phoenix was said to gather up its predecessor's ashes and take them to Heliopolis in Egypt, location of the Sun-God's temple, before flying back east to India.

CLONE RANGER

This apparently courageous act of self-immolation by the phoenix impressed human observers beyond measure. In reality the practice was probably not the altruism it seemed. Because there was only ever one phoenix, it must have reproduced by parthenogenesis (developing an egg without being fertilised), a phenomenon common among chickens. The resulting offspring was thus an identical clone of its mother, and the incineration was probably a mechanism to encourage an internally-produced egg to hatch. The phoenix's self-destruction was in fact only the means to a state of which people have dreamed for millenia: genetic immortality.

The song and scent of the phoenix were said to be so beautiful that all the birds of the Earth would follow it, and when its plumage caught the sun it would appear to flare and shimmer in the sky. In the Far East its appearance was an auspicious omen, heralding the birth of a great emperor, or the dawn of a new age.

Although its western name is Greek (meaning 'Phoenician'), the Chinese were probably the first to record the phoenix, calling it the *feng huang*. For them it was a symbol of the empress and the female principle, *yin* to the emperor's dragon *yang*. Classical scholars learned of the bird through the Egyptians, and Hesiod and Herodotus both wrote about it. Later, the Christians were impressed with many of its features, seeing an allegory for Christ's resurrection in the three days it took for the young phoenix to develop, and arguing that it was free of corruption and sin because it never ate flesh.

SPICE INVADERS

However high their regard for it, the medieval Europeans were to prove the phoenix's undoing. Their rapacious demand for spices lead to the over-exploitation of the Arabian spice groves on which it depended. With a population of one, the species could neither adapt nor evolve. By the end of the 16th century, the phoenix's fragile lifecycle had been fatally interrupted, and one of nature's most extraordinary creations had been lost forever.

THE PHOENIX WAS PROBABLY RELATED TO THE PERSIAN SIMURGH (SEE PAGE 62).

AMY'S BAR
CREEK ALLEY.
BEER AND LIQUOR.
PRIVATE ROOMS.

Hangman's Gulch Hera

ISSUE 437.   26TH APRIL 1890.   SIX PAGES.

WINGED MONSTER IN HUACHUCA

RANCH HANDS TELL OF
PRODIGY OF NATURE.

Sheriff's Men Seek Remains.

*By Our Reporter J. C. Rees.
Hangman's Gulch, Weds.*

THE SHERIFF RODE OUT THIS morning to collect the remains of an enormous bird shot down in the Huachuca desert yesterday. Last night William Hancock, 34, and James Cody Bradshaw, 26, hands at the Big T Ranch in Green Valley, breathlessly rode in to Hangman's Gulch and hurried into Billy's Saloon. A bottle of whiskey later they had calmed down enough to tell of their extraordinary encounter.

NERVOUS HORSES
Travelling between the Whetstone and Huachuca Mountains, the ranch hands saw a large bird circling overhead. Their mounts suddenly became nervous, and it was only when the bird settled to the ground nearby that the men understood why.
Hancock explained: 'This was like no other bird I ever saw. It musta been the size of a horse. I looked at Jimmy and he was real spooked.'
At this point Bradshaw intervened, claiming that it was Hancock who had been shaking with fear. The men briefly left the saloon 'to sort things out'. Ten minutes later, Hancock resumed the tale.

BIG BIRD
'I guess we were all pretty frightened,' he said, spitting out fragments of broken tooth. 'The bird looked real tired, like it had been flying a long time and could hardly go any further.'
The ranch hands followed it, and eventually drew close enough to open fire with their Winchester rifles.

The giant bird attacked Jimmy Bradshaw, who fired ba

Bradshaw hit it in the wing and it fell from the sky. The angry bird ran after the men and started to attack them. Bradshaw fired three rounds straight into its brain, and it fell down dead. "It had eyes as big as saucers, two legs the size of horse's and a wing span of at least 36 feet," said Hancock, "and I ain't exaggerating."

SHERIFF DESPATCHED
The two men decided that they could not bring the monster to town alone and resolved to get help. After hearing the tale, Sheriff Hooper and a team of prominent local men, including Jebediah Lewis, the McIlroy brothers and Dr Baker, left this morning for the desert to collect evidence which will surely be sent East to be examined by the finest scientists.

Continues on page 2.

Pastor's Dog has Fleas.
And the Rest of the Local News: Page 3.

d

ESERT.

n self-defense.

IAN'S

MEDY.

INE EMETIC,
D ASTRINGENT.
URES DROPSY,
, INFLUENZA,
UINSY, FEVER,
OCKJAW, POX AND
GUE. RELIEVES
AND AIDS CHILD-
VE OVER FIVE
MONIALS ON FILE,
EM GENUINE.

IN THE EXCESSIVE USE OF DR
ILITY OF THE MANUFACTURER,
ENSES OR ANY OTHER DISORDER

WINGED MONSTER
IN DESERT.

Continued from page 1.

Continued from page 1.

This encounter is not the first one to meet this reporter's attention. Indeed, outside of civilized society some of the local Indians are quite familiar with such a creature. Amongst the Indians of the wild Northwest it is known as the *Thunderbird*, because it arrives with the summer storms. The Cherokee call it the *Tlanuwa* and the Indians of New England name it the *Pilhannaw* or *Mechquan*.

FIRING RANGE

Travellers on the Missouri River, in the state of Illinois, are apt to see a ghastly sight on the bluffs at Alton, where the Indians of ancient times have carved a petroglyph (stone image) of a giant bird. This apparition is known to the local Illini as the *Piasa*, and they scarcely go by without firing their rifles at it. It seems probable that the *Piasa* and the *Thunderbird* are one and the same.

CSL ARCHIVE NOTE: Unfortunately this intriguing story has no conclusion. Nothing further was ever reported about the strange animal in the Huachuca desert, although persistent rumours have circulated about a photograph of it, or one like it. Palaeontological research has uncovered a candidate for the identity of the mysterious beast, in the shape of the Magnificent Argentine Bird (Argentavis magnificens), a type of bird called a teratorn, and probably the largest bird that ever lived (with the exception of the roc). Although teratorns were thought to have died out between 5 and 8 million years ago, many cultures have stories of giant birds. To the Maori they were known as pou-kai and to the Persians as the imgig. Lapps in Northern Norway reported a vuokho carrying off several reindeer as recently as 1991.

SAN BERNARDO OPERA ON TOUR.

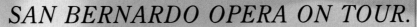

SPECIAL TRAIN TAKES VERDI AND WAGNER ACROSS THE ROCKIES.

– From Our Arts Correspondent.

The San Bernardo Opera Company will be performing Verdi's *Aida* in Cooper's Field next Thursday. Last year, opera-loving wheat magnate Milton B. Hammerhead II, who believes that only opera has the power to tame the Wild West, gave the company $4 million to take full-scale productions of *Aida* and Wagner's *Ring Cycle* across America. Tomorrow's Herald will reprint some recent, and it must be said, rather mixed, reviews of the production.

Our picture shows members of the chorus with the train chartered to take the company, the orchestra and the 1500-seater portable theatre from Atlanta to Sacramento.

Roc

LATIN NAME
Argentavis maximus

HABITAT
High mountains

LIFESPAN
30–40 years

SIZE
Wingspan up to 60 ft (18 m)

INFORMATION SOURCE
Field Report

DISTRIBUTION
Madagascar

A COMMON ALTERNATIVE SPELLING FOR ROC IS 'RUKH'.

SCALE DRAWING SHOWING RELATIVE SIZE OF ROC AND HUMAN.

BACKGROUND INFORMATION

Rocs are probably the biggest non-marine animals in existence. Chinese and Arabian merchants who traded across the Indian Ocean were familiar with this fearsome bird, and they are mainly known today through the 14th-century Arabic classic, the <u>Thousand and One Nights</u>. The roc is now on the endangered list, with the population restricted to a very few breeding pairs living in Madagascar's loftiest and most northerly mountain range, the Massif du Tsaratanana.

There have not been any attested sightings since the 14th century, when Marco Polo reports that Kublai Khan was presented with a roc's wing feather about twelve paces long.

FIELD NOTES

12 November, Antsiranana

From here, the northernmost town of Madagascar, the mountains of the Massif du Tsaratanana are within easy reach. I started my field trip on the coast, in search of the roc's hatcheries. The female lays a single vast egg on the beach and leaves it to be incubated by the sun and hot sand, freeing her to spend more time in the air. Only when the young roc has hatched is it carried to the nest.

Apart from a lot of flotsam and jetsam, my assistant, Dr Raymond Bentos, found fragments of a hatched egg of quite extraordinary size and thickness.

15 November, Manambato

After a tiring journey over dusty, rutted roads, we have at last set up camp in the Massif du Tsaratanana. Our guide, Didier, showed me a site known locally as the Elephant Graveyard, in the forest a few miles to the east. The name immediately caught my attention because elephants have never lived on this island.

We found a small clearing in the woods scattered withe all sorts of cracked and broken bones, many of them very old and very large. I am bringing back a large molar, which I suspect is from a hippo, How on earth did it get here? Marco Polo, writing in the early 14th century, provides a possible explanation. He

FRAGMENTS OF THICK ROC EGG FOUND ON THE BEACH NEAR CAP D'AMBRE.

Raymond with a roc egg and a 2-metre surveying rod for scale.

This is what I saw through my telescope: enormous eagle-like birds soaring high on thermals. Note the sharp hooked beak for tearing out chunks of flesh.

describes a roc
picking up an elephant
and carrying it high up in the air before
dropping it. It then descends to feed on
the smashed corpse, in much the same way as
song thrushes drop snails from a height to
crack their shells. The most surprising
find of the day was the skull of a dolphin
- a bizarre sight when you are 50 miles (80
km) from the coast and 2000 feet (609 m)
above sea level.

   Around the camp fire tonight, Raymond
speculated that the recent explosion of the
elephant population in Kenya and Tanzania
could well be a result of the depletion of
the roc population. Raymond even suggested
that the reintroduction of rocs might be an
effective method of elephant culling.

18 November, Maromokotro
My guides have taken me and Ray upstream
along the Mahavavy River to the foot of
Maromokotro, Madagascar's highest peak.
Various birds circled above us as we
walked, but their size is hard to discern
against the featureless blue sky. I have
come prepared, however, having paid well
over the odds for a couple of porters to
lug one of my heaviest and most powerful
telescopes through the forest. Set up camp
near a clump of trees which seems to be
home for an extended family of lemurs.

19 November, Maromokotro
After a restless night troubled by
marauding aye-ayes, I set up the telescope
early in the morning. By noon, the heat of
the sun had generated powerful thermals and
several large birds were circling low
overhead. At first I had difficulty
focussing on them, but then I realised that
they were actually flying at an extremely
high altitude, and were huge! It looks like
they have wingspans of at least 50 ft (15
m). They can only be rocs. I attempted to
attach my camera to the telescope, but the
wretched porters have managed to dent the
coupling ring. I observed these birds
for almost six hours without seeing a
single wing beat. This is to be
expected - even with their avian

IMMENSE TOOTH OF HIPPO OR ELEPHANT FOUND AT 'ELEPHANT'S GRAVEYARD'.

light, hollow bones and energy-efficient
metabolism, the rocs' massive bulk must
impose heavy demands on them. By skilfully
exploiting every updraft and air current,
they can save a lot of energy. It is easy
to see why the ancients believed that the
roc only ever touched the Earth at Mount
Gaf, the so-called 'axis of the world.'

23rd November, Maromokotro
After several days observation, all I have
seen is rocs in flight. I been unable to
observe them taking off or landing, and I
have no clue as to how they feed. Perhaps
they are feeding like osprey, scooping
large fish or whales out of the Indian
Ocean. This would explain the dolphin skull
at Manambato.

   Unfortunately our supplies are running
out, and we must head back to Antsiranana
and thence home. Hopefully, before too long
the Society will fund another expedition.
Next time they should take proper
functioning telephoto camera equipment, and
send some people with mountaineering
expertise.

PHOTOGRAPHS OF A DISTANT BIRD — POSSIBLY A ROC — AND OF A DOLPHIN'S SKULL, TAKEN BY RAYMOND BENTOS.

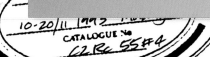

Simurgh

LATIN NAME
*Saena
senmurvia*

HABITAT
High mountains

LIFESPAN
100 years +

SIZE
*Wingspan up to
18 ft (5.5m)*

**INFORMATION
SOURCE**
Letter

DISTRIBUTION
Northern Iran

MEDICINAL
HERBS USED
BY SIMURGH.

Ali Asghar Barhamad
Ravanshad Institute
31 Esfahan Highway
Tehran 315
Islamic Republic of Iran

30th January, 1997

Dear James,

Warmest greetings to you and your family. It was a delight to see you last year after such a long time. Insh'Allah it will become easier for you to visit in the future. Enclosed is an intriguing find from the Alburz Mountains, north of Tehran, brought to me by a student. These striking plumes are not from any ordinary bird, my friend. They belong to one of Allah's most marvellous creations, the simurgh. Remembering your interest in such things, dear James, I have done some research on your behalf, and have learnt much.

The simurgh is a close relation of the phoenix (both are members of the Megafalconidae family), and it shares a similar level of intelligence, longevity and size. Like the phoenix, it was revered by pagan idolaters as a sacred bird. In ancient Persian myth it was a resident of Gaokerena, the Tree of All Seeds. Its wisdom and healing powers made it a popular figure, and it played a prominent part in many Persian folk tales and legends.

Many authorities described the simurgh as half-bird, half-dog (or lion). Indeed senmurv, the ancient Pahlavi name, means literally 'dog-bird'. This is probably caused by confusion with the griffon, a relatively common visitor in the northern mountains. In fact the simurgh is a large eagle-like bird, bigger than a man, with a wingspan that can reach up to 6 metres. Their plumage ranges from ordinary brown, through deepest crimson, to showy green and gold, with long, flowing tail feathers like those of a Bird of Paradise.

The simurgh is very long-lived, but matures slowly, at a similar rate to humans. The mother cares for her young for up to 20 years, and only reproduces once in her lifetime. As a result simurghs were, even in ancient times, very scarce, with only a few adult individuals who were restricted to the Alburz mountains.

Apart from the ability to speak, the simurgh's most prominent talents are its healing powers. With a wide knowledge of herbalism and medicine, it could prescribe herbal remedies and surgical procedures, make potions and even heal directly by touch. When the wife of Zal, a great Persian hero said to have been raised by a simurgh, was in danger during childbirth, the wise bird ordered a Caesarean section and concocted fabulous healing potions. When Zal's son Rustam was grievously injured in a battle she pulled six arrows from his body and healed his wounds by drawing her wings over them.

The simurgh has featured in Persian art, folklore and literature from the days of the ancient Zoroastrians (around 600 BCE) and remains a popular subject for modern qahveh khaneh (coffee house) art. It is best known for its role in the enormously popular Book of Kings, which is the lodestone of Iranian folklore and traditional culture. This epic work records how the simurgh helped several generations of the royal family, using its healing powers and great wisdom to save their lives and aid them in battle. In real life, the simurgh is as rare as ever.

There are a range of alternative names and spellings for the simurgh: symurgh, simurg, Saena (ancient Zoroastrian), senmurv (ancient Pahlavi), and in the Caucasus and Russia: sinam, simargl or simyr.

Insh'Allah this information will be of interest to you. Alas, my dear James, I do not believe that you will get permission to come to the Alburz mountains and conduct your own investigations. I long to hear your news. Please write soon, and if I can help you with any more information about the simurgh, you must only ask.

The blessings of Allah on you and your family,

Ali Asghar Barhamad

Ali Asghar Barhamad

CRIMSON SIMURGH FEATHER
FROM THE ALBURZ
MOUNTAINS.

LATIN NAME
Aesculapia alba

HABITAT
Urban and rural areas

LIFESPAN
15-20 years

SIZE
1–2 ft (30–60 cm) high; wingspan 4–7 ft (1.2–2.1 m)

INFORMATION SOURCE
Brother Evasio Radice, c.1250

DISTRIBUTION
Europe

OF PUREST WHITE IS THE NOBLE CALADRIUS that the ancients called an albinus for it hath no colour nor blackness either, not in its beak, nor in its wings, nor in its tail. This is truly the bird of Kings, and of a time was most welcome in the courts of all the Royal Houses of Europe, for it hath the power to divine sickness, yea and to cure it. Even jaundice can it cure, nor is blindness any impediment to it. In form it is like unto a Crow, but being somewhat larger, and of a solitary nature, not given to making its home in a Rookery nor where there are others of its kind, it is passing rare and few in number. And where the gluttonous Crow will eat of any meat or matter, the Caladrius is most particular in its habits, partaking only of those morsels such as would grace a King's table. Whereof there are many who do say that were the Royal courts to bar their doors agin the noble bird it would surely perish.

THE CALADRIUS IS LIKE UNTO CHRIST

who turneth his face from those who reject him but takes upon himself the sins of others. For if a man be sick, this sage bird can see the illness and all its course. If it doth turn away its face, then the man be fated to a certain death, but if he can be healed then the Caladrius will draw the sickness unto its own self and fly up to the heavens. Here the sun doth burn away the sickness and disperse it through the air.

There are certaine men of the new learning who cast doubt upon the Caladrius. These worldlie scholares in all their lights do make issue that the sick man follows the action of the Caladrius, and not vice versa. That is, if the sick man doth see the bird as it looks not upon him but turns its head away, he will despair and thus sicken unto death. But if he sees that it regards him he will be joyous and thus made strong. These men of science, followers of the venerable Greek doctor Galen, do then hold that the Caladrius is no more than a choosy Crow, which doth play upon the folly of men to secure a tasty repast. Alas these men have voices most powerful, and are now heard by many a Royal Ear. Should the Caladrius fall from favour it will go sore ill, and where once Kings and Princes both did set aside their Choicest Dishes, will this noble bird find no longer the welcome of the Court. Once it hath departed it returneth never, even unto the tenth generatioun.

ATALANTA THE HUNTRESS

by Nicholas Harris, MCSL

ATALANTA THE HUNTRESS

Atalanta, the only woman on board the legendary expedition of the Argo, *vanquished the cruel-beaked, sharp-clawed Stymphalian birds who attacked Jason and his Argonauts. The painting reproduced here and on the previous pages was commissioned by the Rothmarch Bequest as part of the refurbishment of the Smoking Room at 100 Piccadilly.*

THE FEMALE ARGONAUT

When Jason set forth in search of the Golden Fleece of Colchis, he filled his ship with the greatest, bravest heroes of ancient Greece. Only one woman was numbered amongst the Argonauts – Atalanta the Huntress.

Greek myth and legend featured a number of female warriors and heroines, but usually they were incidental to the main action of the stories. Atalanta of Arcadia, one of the greatest hunters, athletes and archers in all Greece, was a notable exception. According to legend she was the daughter of Zeus and Clymene, who abandoned her as an infant. She was suckled by a she-bear, and by the time Jason issued his call for recruits she had grown into a strong huntress, sharp-eyed, fleet of foot and as skilled at wrestling as she was with the bow.

Taking ship from Iolcos in Thessaly (modern Volos), the Argonauts set forth in their specially constructed vessel the *Argo*, the first longship ever built. After various adventures and storms they came ashore on the coast of Thrace where they encountered the blind seer Phineus. As a punishment from the Gods he was being plagued by a flock of harpies. Jason and the Argonauts made short work of them, helped in no small measure by the deadeye archery of Atalanta. In return, a grateful Phineus told them how to navigate through the Clashing Rocks (the Symplegades) in the Bosphorus.

Having successfully negotiated these, the *Argo* sailed forth into the Black Sea – for the ancient Greeks a wild and exotic region. After a few days travel they neared the Isle of Ares. It was in this relatively undisturbed locale that the Stymphalian birds had settled after their battle with Hercules. Though diminished by this previous encounter, the birds' brazen arrows that could be fired like deadly darts were still a formidable threat. As the birds rose up in a cloud and swooped upon the longship, Atalanta sprang into action. Fourteen arrows flew from her bow and fourteen Stymphalian birds fell from the sky. The flock scattered, pursued by Zetes and Calais, sons of the North Wind. This was Atalanta's finest day, and she receives scant mention in records of the Argonauts' subsequent adventures.

Some years after the Argosy, Atalanta took part in the famous Calydonian boar hunt. In the legend, Artemis had sent a great boar to plague the countryside, and a hunt was organised, with men and dogs, to kill it. In reality this legend probably records the antics of a rogue mutant boar of gigantic size, similar to the boar of Mount Erymanthus faced by Hercules in his fourth Labour. Although many of the pre-eminent hunters of Greece were assembled, it was Atalanta who scored the first hit, and who was later presented with the boar's skin as a trophy.

Atalanta has become an icon of modern feminism. Her strength and skill – and ability to outrun all her suitors – make her a symbol of female strength and independence.

Section 4

MAMMALS

Mammals are the most familiar of all animals.
We ourselves are mammals, nourishing our
young first in the womb, and then by suckling.
We even, unusually in the animal kingdom,
continue to drink milk for the rest of our lives.
We identify with our mammal pets such as
rabbits, cats and dogs, and the sheep and cows
seen on the farm. However, just beyond the
realm of the familiar lies the realm of the
unknown, where the animals that we know –
dogs, cats, horses, etc – take on fabulous, and
sometimes frightening aspects. It is with these
otherworldly mammals that cryptozoologists
concern themselves.

4

CSL R E V I E W

INSIDE CRYPTOZOOLOGY

Basic principles of cryptozoology explained in simple terms for schools, colleges and new readers. Created by the Education Department of the Cryptozoological Society of London.

Mammals

The most complex relationship between humans and the natural world is that with mammals, the creatures closest to us both biologically and psychologically. Our ability to identify with them tends to muddy the waters for serious scholars, because it can make observers lose the detached, dispassionate eye that ensures accurate reporting.

A common feature of many of the mammals studied by cryptozoologists, including the unicorn, *ki-lin*, the black dog and the chupacabras, is the complicated response they evoke in humans. The innocent *ki-lin*, for example, is virtually worshipped by the Chinese, while the chupacabras – scourge of wildlife and mankind – paradoxically is celebrated in popular song and modern folk legend.

Researchers have identified a confused relationship between literal and spiritual (or mystical) belief in the reality of these animals. Many observers believe this to be the result of an 'aura', a powerful energy or force field that surrounds the animal.

Roaring dogs

Witnesses to the black dog in England, for example, talk openly about its physical manifestations – how it makes a terrible roaring noise, or the way in which it knocks chunks out of masonry as it passes. But they nonetheless describe the animal as a spirit, ghost or manifestation of the Devil, probably as a result of its aura or atmosphere (see Fig 1).

In medieval times, few doubted the physical reality of the unicorn, but writers and artists were usually more interested in it as an allegory of Christ or a symbol of purity. The bestiaries, often our main source of information about fantastic creatures, were a mixture of zoological fact and didactic Christian allegory, and the two can be hard to separate.

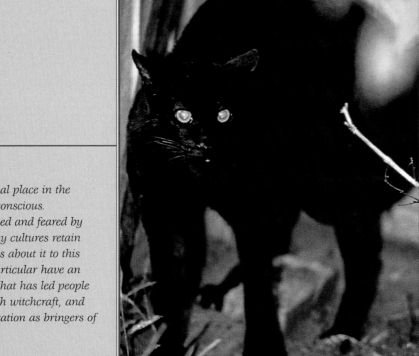

FIG 1 BLACK CAT

The cat holds a special place in the human collective unconscious. Alternately worshipped and feared by ancient peoples, many cultures retain powerful superstitions about it to this day. Black cats in particular have an aura of quiet power that has led people to associate them with witchcraft, and brought them a reputation as bringers of good or bad fortune.

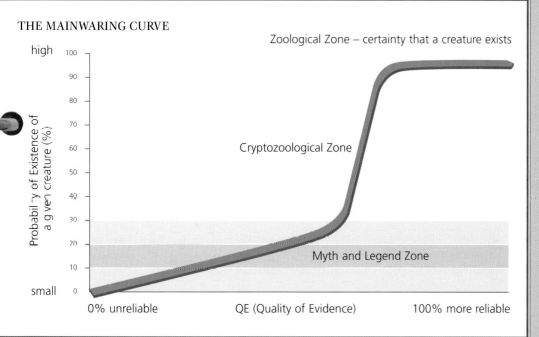

THE MAINWARING CURVE

Zoological Zone – certainty that a creature exists

Cryptozoological Zone

Myth and Legend Zone

Probability of Existence of a given creature (%)

high 100
90
80
70
60
50
40
30
20
10
small 0

0% unreliable   QE (Quality of Evidence)   100% more reliable

FIG 2 THE MAINWARING CURVE

The Australian cryptozoologist and statistician Audrey Mainwaring has provided a simple solution to cryptozoology's basic problem of inconclusive evidence. Reports and documentation for a given animal are cumulatively assessed for reliability (R) and quantity (Q). By multiplying Q by R, she arrives at a Quality of Evidence (QE) percentage that might, for example, give many unreliable oral reports the same credence as a single undoctored photograph. This percentage is then plotted against the probability of a creature's existence to create a graph. The resulting curve plots the increasing or decreasing likelihood of a creature existing: cryptozoologists will only consider beasts with a QE factor that puts them between myth and legend and 100% proven existence.

The same pattern emerges with the chupacabras (it can be hard to distinguish whether witnesses are talking about a real creature or a demonic spirit); the *ki-lin* (the mystical attributes of which are more significant to the Chinese than its physical reality) and the yeti, as Daniel Cohen reports in the *Encyclopaedia of Monsters*:

'...encounters reported by the natives of the Himalayan region ... are difficult to evaluate, for the people ... often do not make the same distinction between the material and spiritual worlds that is so important in the West today... A demon – even though it is not a material being – may be quite as "real" as an ape or a goat.'

Many researchers themselves are often less interested in the physical reality or otherwise of the creatures than in the social and psychological aspects of the human response to them. But for the serious cryptozoologist, assessing witness credibility is absolutely essential, since the bulk of evidence about strange creatures derives from witness reports – so-called anecdotal evidence.

The credibility gap

Serious cryptozoologists admit that there is a very real gap between the anecdotal evidence which usually sparks cryptozoological interest and the physical evidence which results from investigations. The latter, with alarmingly few exceptions, proves to be of a very low quality – for instance, almost all the carcasses attributed to black dogs or chupacabras prove to be the victims of perfectly natural causes such as dog attacks. Cryptozoologists are forced to accept a standard of evidence

that would by definition fail to convince a conventional scientist. At the same time, they have to exclude reports that are hallucinations or myths. A complicated formula (see Fig 2) is applied to make this judgement.

The problem is further complicated by the habitual enmity of officialdom, which generally blocks cryptozoological investigations, either through direct opposition, blank denial and stonewalling, or simple indifference. Such attempts to deter serious research are, of course, at once a signal that something may be being hidden which should be known and a vital spur to the keen instincts of any true cryptozoologist.

As with all genuine scientific enquiry, careful amassing and documentation of evidence lie at the heart of the cryptozoologist's method. The dispassionate eye and ear are the research tools which, above all, must never be left in the airport lounge, the sleeping bag or the hotel bar.

A sympathetic attitude towards the witnesses who are the source of anecdotal evidence, coupled with a healthy scepticism, are both equally essential. It should never be forgotten that encounters with the strange and unexpected will leave even the strongest of us disoriented, alarmed and perhaps given to inexplicable emotional outbursts.

Finally, the persistence of such encounters in the mind long after they have taken place also must be considered carefully. On the one hand, this very well can be an individual's response to the creature's aura. On the other, it can be the result of that muddled state of mind which is not recollection, but the combination of forgotten childhood legends with the desire for even transitory fame.

It is the difficult task of the dedicated cryptozoologist to weigh all these factors carefully when studying and reporting on the remarkable phenomena which are at the heart of this fascinating field of enquiry.

Pegasus

LATIN NAME
Equovolatus magnificens

HABITAT
Mountains and nearby plains

LIFESPAN
30–40 years

SIZE
c. 6 ft (1.8 m) high at shoulder; wingspan 18 ft (5.5 m)

INFORMATION SOURCE
Field Report

DISTRIBUTION
Previously the Balkan peninsula, now Atlas Mountains

LEFT: OLD QUARTER OF CASABLANCA, STARTING POINT FOR ELIOT'S TRIP.

The noble pegasus, or winged horse, is widely known thanks to the ancient Greek story of Bellerophon, the Corinthian hero who slew the deadly chimaera. As told by the Greek poet Pindar (522-440 BCE), Bellerophon's steed, Pegasus, was the child of the sea god Poseidon and the gorgon Medusa, and sprang from Medusa's blood when she was beheaded by Perseus. Bellerophon captured him using a golden bridle, a gift from the goddess Hera. Flying on the back of this marvellous creature, Bellerophon defeated the hideous hybrid monster, but was undone when pride overcame him and he tried to fly to the top of Mount Olympus to join the gods. Zeus sent a gadfly (or hornet in some accounts) to sting Pegasus, enraging him so that he threw Bellerophon, who plummeted to a messy end. Pegasus was subsequently captured by Zeus and forced to pull his storm chariot.

The ancient Greeks were not the only peoples to have encountered the winged horse. It figures in Mesopotamian art from the 13th century BCE, and on Carthaginian coins from 265 BCE. Pegasi were known as far afield as Russia, where the folk hero Ilya Muromets rode one. It still appears today as a commercial logo for many companies, including Reader's Digest and Columbia-Tristar, but all too few people see the real thing. Now extinct in its native Balkans, the only known surviving population lives in the high reaches of the Atlas Mountains in Morocco, where cryptozoologist Ben Daley has been making a long-term study of them. Our own John Eliot went to visit Ben in 1994. An extract from his report follows.

REPORT

The pegasus is the sole member of its genus, but is in the same family as the horse, zebra, unicorn, etc.

8 Jan. Haut Atlas, Morocco
Arrived at Ben Daley's camp here a few days ago. Today we trekked up towards what Ben calls the upper pastures. Ben has been studying the same herd for nearly three years, so he knows their habits well. He explained that the pegasi live in herds, graze their highland pastures and raise foals in much the same way as ordinary horses. Stallions compete for the favours of up to five mares, and fight each other for dominance during the mating season.

9 Jan. Haut Atlas
This morning we saw the herd – a beautiful and moving sight. I counted 31 pegasi in all, including stallions, mares and foals. They looked like large thoroughbreds, and although some were tan or pure black, most were a dazzling white. The huge wings, very like those of a giant bird, were their most striking

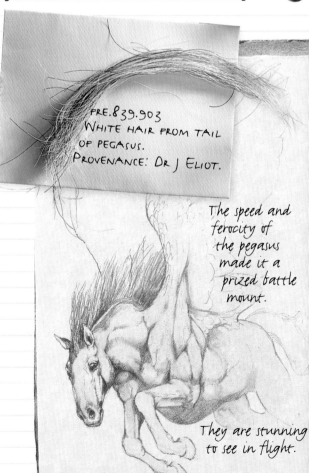

FRE.839.903 WHITE HAIR FROM TAIL OF PEGASUS. PROVENANCE: DR J ELIOT.

The speed and ferocity of the pegasus made it a prized battle mount.

They are stunning to see in flight.

features. Ben thinks some of the large
stallions have a span of 24 ft (7.3 m) or
more, and pointed out the muscular bulges
around their withers, shoulders, chest and
barrel (rib cage), where the flight
muscles anchor to the breast bone.

10 Jan.

We spent the day observing the herd's
five foals. Ben says these ones are about
six months old. Apparently they learn to
walk almost immediately after birth, but
do not develop flying skills until that
age. Like young birds, they spend weeks
flexing their wings and developing the
necessary muscles.

   All but one of the foals has managed
short flights. We watched the late
developer practising his flapping and
hopping energetically. He was clearly on
the verge of flight. Abruptly something
startled the herd and as one they
launched themselves skywards, the mothers
providing help and support for their
foals. It was a breathtaking sight.

FEATHERS FROM
A PEGASUS WING
— TAKEN FROM
BEN DALEY'S
CAMP.

HORSES ARE STILL VERY
MUCH PART OF DAILY
LIFE IN THE HAUT
ATLAS.

In rest, pegasi often stretch
and spread their
wings like this.

They are jumpy, but
amazingly graceful
creatures. How they
acquired such
spectacular wings is
still a mystery.

Bonnacon

LATIN NAME
Bubalis vitriolis

HABITAT
Steppes and grassland

LIFESPAN
5–10 years

SIZE
Equivalent to a buffalo; c. 5 ft (1.5 m) high at shoulder

INFORMATION SOURCE
Letter

DISTRIBUTION
Central Asia, occasionally China, India, Afghanistan

Bobac marmot (*Marmota bobac*).

saiga (*saiga tatarica*).

CROXLEY SENT THIS SNAP OF THE BONNACON JAW AND SEVERAL SKETCHES.

Dr Wilberforce Croxley, FCSL
Central Asian Wildlife Research Trust
Ulaanbaatur
Mongolia

15 August 1997

Dear Gentlemen and Fellows of the CSL,

It is my pleasure to be able to report on the presence here of a most peculiar beast, the bonnacon. Our work has generally focused on Przewalski's horse and the saiga, and on some of the smaller animals like the great bustard and the bobac marmot. But on a recent excursion to the plains around Lake Uvs, in the north-west, the local guides said they had something special to show me.

A two-day ride brought us to a small village. As is the custom, parts of a butchered animal had been hung on a line to dry. I assumed they were parts of a horse, but the guides urged me to look closer. I realised that they belonged to some sort of buffalo-like creature. On the bed of a nearby dry river gully lay a large jaw bone — again from some sort of buffalo. I followed my companions to a broad pasture near the lake. Here I beheld a buffalo-like creature with peculiar inwardly curved horns. When my guides described its unusual way of defending itself, I realised that I was looking at a real-life bonnacon.

This creature is a member of the <u>Bovidae</u> family, which includes the wildebeest and bison, and it is famous for its ability to discharge explosive, acrid secretions when threatened. Using a mechanism similar to the bombardier beetle, the bonnacon mixes two highly volatile chemicals in its specially lined and shielded lower intestine. These explode violently on contact, spraying a corrosive mixture from the animal's rear. Medieval and classical writers exaggerated the extent and potency of the bonnacon's noxious discharge, claiming that it could could cover three acres with a substance that set fire to everything it touched. But judging by what my guides tell me, the secretion is certainly highly caustic, and can strip vegetation of leaves and bark and burn holes in clothing.

Resisting temptation, I did not goad the creature into letting fly, but thought it best to leave this endangered animal as undisturbed as possible. A couple of days later my local contacts brought word that the villagers had shot and eaten it. Such are the trials of conservation work.

Hunters used to wield simple weapons like spears, bows and arrows when pursuing the bonnacon. Today, the high velocity rifle with telescopic gunsight renders its defences useless, but as long as the beast avoids humans it is fairly safe.

Yrs. wearily,

Wilberforce Croxley

Wilberforce Croxley

Przewalski's horse (*Equus przewalski*).

Local horse.

Typical Mongolian transport.

Bonnacon (*Bubalis vitriolis*).

Bustard.

A strange-looking, and weird-sounding, creature lives in the African savannah. Locals pretend it does not exist, and it never features on any safari tour, so it lives in glorious privacy.

THE CAT WITH THE CHAT

MAMMALS

Leucrota

LATIN NAME
Leucrota osseobucca

HABITAT
Savannah

LIFESPAN
10–15 years

SIZE
Equivalent to a large hyena; up to 5 ft (1.5 m) long

INFORMATION SOURCE
CSL Review

DISTRIBUTION
East and Southern Africa

HE LEUCROTA, WITH ITS STRANGE mouth and voice, is, in many ways, a living fossil or throwback. Probably the most ancient member of the hyena family (the *Hyaenidae*), it displays many feline characteristics. Although hyenas look more like dogs than cats, they are, in fact, more closely related to the big cats. The leucrota, then, may well be the nearest living descendant of the early 'proto-hyena' that lived 40 million years ago, betraying the feline ancestry of the hyena itself.

TOOTHLESS WONDER

The leucrota has an elegant, feline body, maned around the neck in the male animal, with a long canine head, much like a hyena's. Most striking, however, is the creature's mouth, which stretches fully back to its ears, and is filled not with teeth, but with interlocking horizontal bony ridges. This bizarre feeding adaptation is unique in higher terrestrial mammals, and has baffled zoologists who can only speculate on its function. Most argue that it is probably used in tandem with a sawing action of the jaw, used when eating carrion.

The strangest feature of the leucrota is its voice, which resembles high-pitched human chatter, as of many people talking all at once. While medieval naturalists were quick to ascribe supernatural powers to the creature, we now know that this bizarre vocal effect is simply a peculiar form of the hyena's laugh. The leucrota version of this call is probably very close to the noise that the hyena's Eocene forefather would have made.

OUT OF AFRICA

Humans have generally shied away from contact with the leucrota, finding its gaping mouth and unnatural voice disturbing. However, its specialised dentition and lack of proper biting teeth means that the leucrota poses little threat to living creatures, including man.

The traditional myths and folklore of many Eastern and Southern African tribes portray the leucrota as an evil or unclean creature, to be avoided at all costs. Even today, Kenyan guides never include the leucrota on the normal safari itinerary, with the result that few, if any, tourists are aware that it exists.

The leucrota's nearest relatives are the Laughing or Spotted Hyena (*Crocuta crocuta*), the Striped Hyena (*Hyaena hyaena*) and the Brown Hyena (*Hyaena brunnea*). Its more distant cousins include the *Felidae* – cats – and mongooses. An alternative spelling for leucrota, used by classical Roman naturalists, is leucrocotta.

 THE LEUCROTA'S STRONG JAWS CAN CRUSH ANY FOODSTUFF, MASHING IT UNTIL IT BECOMES A READILY-DIGESTIBLE PULP. THIS MAY HELP IT TO EXTRACT MORE PROTEIN AND MINERALS FROM BONES AND MARROW.

MAMMALS

Black Dogs

LATIN NAME
Canis diabolus

HABITAT
Heath and moorland; woodland; graveyards

LIFESPAN
Unknown

SIZE
4–5 ft (1.2–1.5m) high

INFORMATION SOURCE
Field Report

DISTRIBUTION
Western Europe

BACKGROUND

While hunting through the Society's archives, I came across a pamphlet written by Abraham Fleming in 1577. It describes an apparition in the form of a black dog that terrified residents of Bungay, Suffolk (a market town some 90 miles/145 km north-east of London). Fleming assumed that the beast was a manifestation of the Devil, but in practice black dogs are amongst the oldest and most widespread type of strange creature in the whole of Europe. They go by dozens of strange names, including barguest, gyrtrash and yell hound. As a long-standing dog-lover, I am determined to track one down.

FIELD NOTES

22 June. Bungay, Suffolk

Not much sign of the black dog (often called Black Shuck in these parts), although there is a striking dog-shaped weathervane in the market place. Spent the evening wandering round on the nearby fens in the hope of encountering a black dog. They typically appear out of the mist to either terrify or walk alongside lonely travellers. No luck.

24 June. Radford, Coventry

Though now a dreary suburb of this industrial city, this area is rich in suggestive place names. Here stood at one time the Black Dog Inn, which is near an old street called Dog Lane that leads into an area that was known as Dogland.

It was in this area, in the 19th century, that a lone horseman struck at a huge black hound with his riding crop. It promptly detonated, blowing the rider off his horse and into a ditch, from where he was later recovered with charred clothes and singed hair.

Next to Dogland is Shuckmoor, which borders on an area called Black Pad. To the north is Hounds Hill and a pumping station where a worker encountered a barguest in 1949. It had huge, saucer shaped eyes that glowed in the dark, a thick, shaggy coat of black fur and an ability to move with uncanny silence and extreme size. Barguests are reported to be the size of a pony; in this case the dog sitting on its haunches was nearly six feet (2 m) tall.

The area seems far too built up for black dogs now, however. They prefer lonely moorland, and are shy of traffic, settlements and groups of people.

26 June. Black Dog, nr Thelbridge, Devon

As if the name of this tiny hamlet were not enough, the local pub is called The Black Dog. The landlord is clearly not used to women drinking on their own in his pub, but he proudly showed me a peculiar and fierce-looking skull. He claimed that it had been in the pub for centuries. Here in the West Country, as elsewhere, black dogs seem to have two

My first sighting of the Black Dog as I walked past the Celtic cross near Torrington.

Thick black fur.

Big paws.

Left to right: The Black Dog in Thelbridge; Fleming's A Straunge and Terrible Wunder, describing the Bungay Black Dog; and my snap of the skull that the barman showed me.

functions. One is to protect lonely travellers, but the other is to herald a death in the family - often that of the person who sees it.

28th June. Torrington, Devon

Last night I went for a late evening walk on the lonely moors, following the route of an ancient pathway between Torrington and Copplestone. These old footpaths seem to attract black dogs.

It was a moonless night, very dark except for the starlight. The tiny rustlings of small animals and the whisperings of the countryside filled the air. As I came to a crossroads, marked by an old Celtic stone cross, there was a sudden silence. Nervously I continued up the road towards Down St Mary.

After a few steps the strangest sensation came over me, and I turned to see an enormous black shape keeping pace with me. It was a huge, shaggy black dog the size of a calf, with enormous eyes. I felt no fear - only a sense of calm. The great dog padded noiselessly alongside me for almost an hour, disappearing silently as I arrived back at my lodgings.

Does this foreshadow a gloomy fate for a member of my family, or even myself? Somehow I do not think so - the feeling I had was one of reassurance and protection.

SUPPLEMENTARY NOTES
The day after my return to London The Times carried the following article. It really does seem that despite its awesome appearance, the Black Dog is more of a friend than a fiend. Just like its domestic counterpart, in fact - as I am constantly reminded by Fifi, Otto and Hodge - my own beautiful, loving and loyal canine companions.

THE TIMES, 30 June 1984

DERANGED KILLER RECAPTURED

From Our West of England correspondent

A MASSIVE MANHUNT BY THE COMBINED DORSET AND Devonshire constabularies yesterday succeeded in recapturing psychotic axe murderer Denis "The Butcher" Kennedy. Kennedy, known to have brutally slaughtered at least six young women, escaped from Princeton Maximum Security Prison for the Criminally Insane three days ago. Chief Constable Finbar Smith hailed the operation as a major success, and promised a review of security measures at the jail. Kennedy was apprehended last night in a wood near Torrington, in North Devon.

Chupacabras

LATIN NAME
*Chupacabras
hispanicus*

HABITAT
*Varied – uses
caves as lairs*

LIFESPAN
Unknown

SIZE
*4–5 ft (1.2–
1.5 m) high*

**INFORMATION
SOURCE**
*Own Field
Report*

DISTRIBUTION
*Puerto Rico,
Florida, Texas,
Mexico*

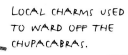

*LOCAL CHARMS USED
TO WARD OFF THE
CHUPACABRAS.*

Don Rogelio Cohénez de la Chingada
152 Avenída Coronel S de Bustamante
San José
COSTA RICA

Estimable Senores,

Two weeks ago I return from a two-month field trip in Brasil in search of the famous <u>minhocao</u> - a gigantic, violent worm which I am now certain does not exist. Ay cabron! While I am away el chupacabras, the crazy monster that sucks all the blood out of its victims, has been busy in Puerto Rico. Quickly I pack my bags again and fly to San Juan, el capital de Puerto Rico.

With mi viejo amigo Alberto Fiorito I travel to the Orocovis district in the centre of the island. It did not take long to find the tracks of the monster. Fiorito and I speak to many farmers who had lost their animals. They are angry with el gobierno, which treats them like idiotas y paysanos histericas. 'We are not idiotas,' one of them told me, 'we know the marks of the dogs and jungle gators. These killings are not the work of ordinary animales - there is something horrible here, and we are afraid.' I examine some of the cuerpos. All are without sangre, but also without any marks, except for holes no wider than a pajita - a straw for drinking!

The next day Fiorito and I speak to a veterinario who work for el gobierno. He say, 'when you see the evidencia it is not being convincing. Every body I see is having the bites from the dogs, the monkeys or it has been eaten after being dead.' We ask him about the drained animals we yesterday, but he just shrug and say he had not seen them.

Next we go to Aguas Buenas, near to San Juan, where there are many caves. We go into one cave very remote from the others. After 100 metres we see bones, and then a pollo muerto sin sangre - a dead chicken with no blood. We walk on for 15 minutas and it is getting very caliente , and in the air there is a un olor horrible de azufre - a sulphur smell. I want to go back, but Fiorito, he point with his luz to a shape near to us. Then el guia make a noise and the shape jump up, making a hissing sound. We yell: 'ai ai ai, la puta que lo pario!' - and for one second both torches are shining on el monster. It has red eyes and espinas on the back which stand up. Then it make a jump into the obscuridad and we all run for our lives. I have drawn you a pintura.

Rogelio

Guatemala Weekly News

Issue 3,206   26 JUNE, 1996

BEWARE OF THE CHUPACABRAS

IN MARCH 1995 REPORTS OF A STRANGE AND UNSETTLING phenomenon began to trickle out of central Puerto Rico. The corpses of chickens, sheep, cows and especially goats were being discovered, entirely drained of blood and marked only with a single puncture wound. These bloodless corpses started showing up all over the island, and the trickle became a flood. The first sightings followed in November: witnesses described a strange two-legged creature, about four or five feet high, which looked like a cross between an alien and a fanged kangaroo. The creature was named el chupacabras - Spanish for 'the goat sucker' - and chupacabras mania quickly became chu-

pacabras hysteria. 200-strong search parties combed farmland and jungle, while officials insisted that dogs and possibly feral rhesus monkeys were to blame. A spell of cold weather in early 1996 seemed to calm the situation, but by March the chupacabras bounced back. This time, though, it had apparently migrated. As the Hispanic media picked up on the story and disseminated it, so the rash of livestock mutilations and sightings spread to Florida, Texas and Mexico. By mid-April el chupacabras had claimed its first human victim, and the number of incidents and sightings soared. In just a few short months, this creature has become an established part of Latin-America's rich folklore.

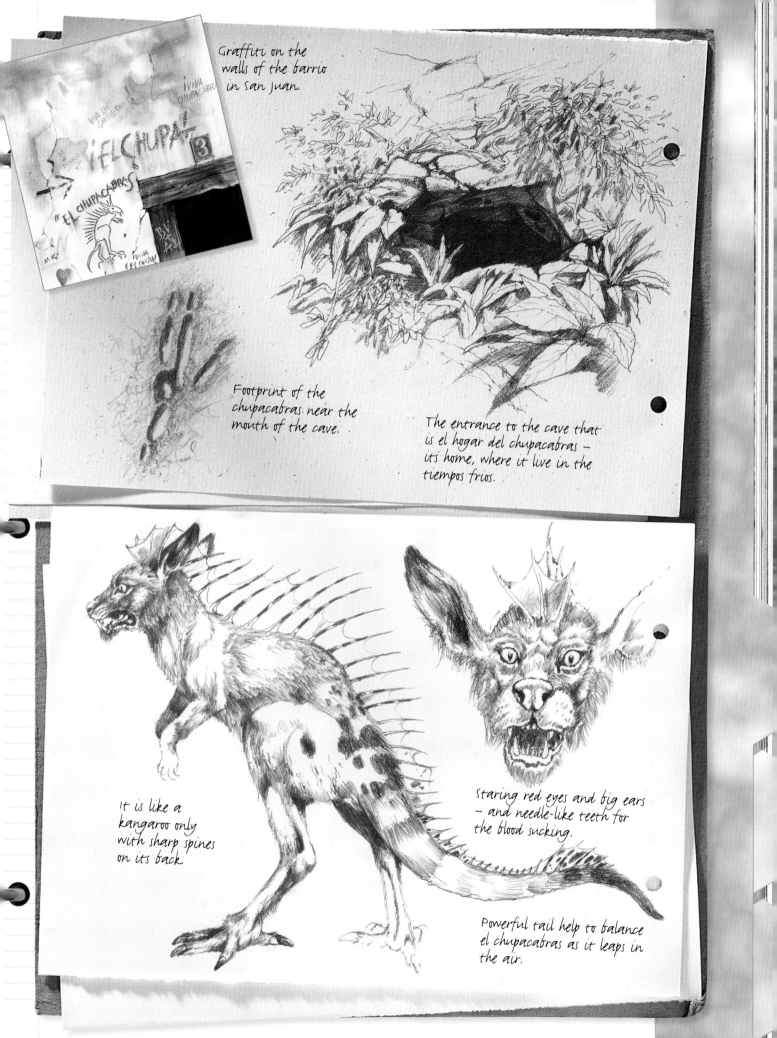

Graffiti on the walls of the barrio in San Juan.

Footprint of the chupacabras near the mouth of the cave.

The entrance to the cave that is el hogar del chupacabras — its home, where it live in the tiempos frios.

It is like a kangaroo only with sharp spines on its back.

Staring red eyes and big ears — and needle-like teeth for the blood sucking.

Powerful tail help to balance el chupacabras as it leaps in the air.

MAMMALS

Unicorn

LATIN NAME
Equus monoceros

HABITAT
Forest, light woodland

LIFESPAN
40–60 years

SIZE
Equivalent to a horse

INFORMATION SOURCE
CSL Review

DISTRIBUTION
Eurasia (especially India)

According to legend, unicorns disappeared when Noah forgot to take any on board his Ark. There is, however, plenty of evidence that they survived into the modern age before being hunted to extinction for the horns that make them unique.

ONE
FOR THE LADIES

 LONG WITH THE DRAGON, THE UNICORN is possibly the best known of the Earth's fabulous creatures. Yet, despite its universal fame, and the plethora of horns and horn fragments in the possession of Europe's noble houses, very few people have seen a unicorn. A common feature in heraldry, the unicorn has made regular appearances in bestiaries, natural histories, tapestries, paintings, jewellery, ornamentation and art of all kinds – depictions that are rarely made from direct observation.

WHITE AND WILD, PURE AND MILD

Cryptozoologists have long sought to explain the unicorn's high profile in the human imagination. Its beauty and grace are, no doubt, part of the equation. The sleek head and body of a horse, the strong legs of a buck, the tail of a lion and a single, sharp, horn make the unicorn an attractive beast. It is certainly a potent emblem of purity, thanks to its pure white coloration, its association with maidenhood and the anti-toxic properties of its horn. According to some scholars, the key lies in its archetypal contrast: fierce, wild and untameable by nature, it becomes meek and gentle with its young and in the presence of human virgins.

Much of what we know about unicorns and their habits comes from ancient and medieval sources. The environment has altered considerably since then and it is likely that the unicorn's habits may be

very different now. The classical unicorn, *Equus monoceros*, is the most common form, but many writers describe a much smaller variant, with a goat-like body. This is not a real animal at all, but a confused rendering of the original. One variety that may have existed in India in ancient and prehistoric times, but is now extinct, was the horned ass, *Equus assinoceros*. These were both members of the genus *Equus,* meaning that they could have interbred with horses and donkeys to give sterile hybrids. In other words, horned mules may have existed, or still exist, somewhere in the world.

As their wide distribution (from Scandinavia to India) suggests, unicorns can live in a comprehensive range of habitats. On the whole, however, they prefer woodland or forests, and the best place to catch a glimpse of one is in a shady forest glade or woodland clearing. Like horses, unicorns began as grazers, but have since become fairly specialised browsers, with a taste for the shoots and young leaves of selected saplings and young trees. This specialisation has made it very hard for them to adapt their diet and lifestyle to changing conditions.

HORSES FOR COURSES

As mentioned above, the unicorn can interbreed with horses, donkeys or any other species of the genus *Equus*. These unions, however, will only produce sterile hybrid offspring, and the unicorn is very choosy about mating anyway. Despite their solitary nature – they only come together with their

partners during the spring breeding season – unicorns are monogamous, mating for life. They are noted for their tender behaviour to one another, and particularly for being gentle with their young.

In the Far East, China and Japan have their own species of unicorn, the *ki-lin* or *ki-rin*, a more powerful yet gentler beast than the Eurasian unicorn.

HORN SECTION

Whatever the species, the unicorn's distinguishing mark is always the same: a straight horn with a spiral groove projecting from the middle of its forehead. The horn itself, normally about 18 inches (45 cm) long, is usually variegated – white at the base, black in the middle and crimson at the tip – but can be all black or light brown.

The Indian unicorn, observed in the 5th-century BCE by the Greek historian Ctesias, was more garishly coloured, with a purple head and dark blue eyes. Pliny the Elder (23–79 AD) quoted an early Greek ambassador to India, Megasthenes, who described a specimen with a splendid black horn almost 3 ft (1 m) long.

The fossil record of equine development is well-documented: the horse slowly evolved from the short, stumpy proto-horses of the Pliocene era, some 2 million years ago, to the majestic thoroughbreds we know today. The unicorn can be seen as another step in this development, with greater speed, strength and intelligence, and a fearsome weapon on its brow.

THE UNICORN'S ATTACHMENT TO YOUNG VIRGINS WAS ONE OF THE FEW SECULAR THEMES IN MEDIEVAL ART. LEFT: A COUPLE FROLIC ACROSS THE PAGES OF A 16TH-CENTURY ILLUMINATED MANUSCRIPT. RIGHT: A 15TH-CENTURY FRENCH TAPESTRY – ONE OF A SERIES ON THE THEME OF THE FIVE SENSES – ILLUSTRATES SIGHT BY SHOWING A UNICORN ENTHRALLED BY HIS OWN REFLECTION IN A MAIDEN'S MIRROR.

As herbivores, unicorns are natural prey for large predators like the lion or tiger (once found throughout the Near East and Southern Europe). Such predation pressure was probably the driving force behind the evolution of one of the unicorn's key characteristics: if left alone, it is a peaceable creature, but in battle, it is strong and ferocious. The ancient, perpetual conflict between lion and unicorn features in the coat of arms of the British royal family (where the shield is supported by an English lion and a Scottish unicorn) and in the well-known nursery rhyme:

The lion and the unicorn
Were fighting for the crown,
The lion beat the unicorn
All round the town.

The victory of the lion in the poem is, of course, a metaphor for the evolutionary triumph of the lion.

UNIVERSAL ANTIDOTE

The unicorn's horn is more than just a keratinised outgrowth. Composed of a remarkable and not yet fully understood material, the horn is stronger than any other organic substance known, and is also an

Unicorn

extremely potent anti-toxin. In medieval times, the unicorn was said to be able to purify entire rivers or lakes simply by dipping its horn into the water. Although this is an exaggeration, the horns were immensely valuable as antidotes to toxins as recently as the late 18th century. In 1641, an inventory of the Tower of London valued a unicorn's horn in the royal treasury at £40,000, the equivalent of well over £1 million ($1.6 million) today.

JAILBAIT, UNICORN-BAIT

Buyers of unicorn horn for antidote purposes had a major problem verifying its authenticity. England's King James I (1603–25) tested a purported horn by grinding it up and mixing it with poison. A servant was made to taste the concoction, and died – proving that the horn was a fake. There were, however,

less cruel and dangerous ways of doing this. One little-known characteristic feature of true unicorn horn was that it would stop silk wrapped around it being burnt by hot coals.

The astonishing speed and strength of the unicorn make it impossible to hunt it in any normal fashion, but the strength of its horn can also be the unicorn's undoing. The beast is much given to charging horn-first at all adversaries, secure in the knowledge that its weapon can pierce all armour. One old huntsman's trick was to stand in front of a tree and step aside, like a matador, at the last moment. The unicorn's horn would stick in the tree, leaving it vulnerable to attack.

The unicorn has other weaknesses. It is extremely devoted to its young, which means that it can be made to stand and fight if they are

'HUNTERS CAN CATCH THE
unicorn only by placing a young virgin in his haunts. No sooner does he see the damsel, than he runs towards her, and lies down at her feet, and so suffers himself to be captured.'

The Bestiary of Guillaume, Clerc de Normandie (13th century)

IN TIMES OF FAMINE, HUNGRY UNICORNS SOMETIMES RELIED ON MONASTERIES FOR THEIR FOOD.

THE 18TH-CENTURY NATURALIST NICOLAUS POSEN SPENT MONTHS OBSERVING WILDLIFE IN THE FORESTS OF POLAND. HE PRODUCED THESE DETAILED ENGRAVINGS OF THE FOREST ASS (TOP) AND THE UNICORN (BOTTOM) – MAGNIFICENT HORNED WOODLAND FORAGERS THAT ARE SADLY NOW EDGING TOWARDS EXTINCTION.

Onager Aldro: Wald Efel   Tab XIII

Monoceros feu Unicornu Iubatus
Einhorn mit Mahnen

was a re-enactment of Christ's annunciation, birth, and capture; the unicorn's surrender to a virgin, a reflection of Christ's surrender of his divinity to become man through the Virgin Mary; and the unicorn's death, a reminder of Christ's sacrifice.

This powerful symbolism turned unicorn horns into sacred relics. The cathedrals at St Denis (Paris), Westminster Abbey (London) and St Mark's (Venice) all had valuable unicorn horns, while kings and noblemen mounted their precious trophies in silver to become elaborate table ornaments for their banquets.

THE ZOOLOGICAL MUSEUM AT COPENHAGEN HOUSES THIS MAGNIFICENT STUFFED SPECIMEN OF AN UNUSUAL WIRE-HAIRED UNICORN. THE CREATURE IS THOUGHT TO HAVE BEEN CAUGHT IN THE 1920S NEAR VLADIKAVKAZ, IN THE CAUCASUS MOUNTAINS.

threatened. It is easily mesmerised by its own reflection. Above all, it is highly susceptible to the charms of young virgins, perhaps due to an accidental attraction exerted by the girls' pheromones. Shrewd hunters used to take young unmarried women along on hunting trips. A girl would entice a unicorn to emerge from hiding and encourage it to meekly lie on the ground, put its head in her lap and swoon in her embrace. The hunter would then seize the opportunity to kill the unicorn or simply saw off its horn. Without the horn to defend it, the unicorn was left vulnerable to all manner of predators. Using virgins to attract unicorns, which was largely responsible for decimating the unicorn population of Europe, had to be abandoned in the 17th century, when virgins suddenly became extremely rare.

CRUCIFIED CREATURE

Many medieval writers saw the unicorn as a living allegory of the life of Jesus. The single horn represented the unity of the Father and Son; the hunt

After the Renaissance, however, the horn trade suffered two grave blows. In 1563, the Council of Trent banned the use of the unicorn allegory in churches, and in 1638 the Danish zoologist Ole Worm claimed that all purported unicorns' horns were without value as they were, in fact, narwhal tusks. This was undoubtedly true in a number of cases, and some were probably rhino horn, but many valuable and unrecoverable artefacts were also thrown out as a result.

TOO LITTLE, TOO LATE

One benefit was that unicorn hunting more or less ceased, as demand for horn dropped. Numbers were drastically reduced, however, and most European populations were hunted out of existence. The few remaining unicorns continue to lead a lonely life in parts of Northern India, Central Asia and the Caucasus, untamed and unbowed.

Ki-lin

LATIN NAME
Equus orientalis

HABITAT
Unknown

LIFESPAN
1000 years

SIZE
*c. 5 ft (1.5 m)
tall*

**INFORMATION
SOURCE**
Letter

DISTRIBUTION
China, Japan

Prof Chow Yun
People's University of Beijing
Beijing
China

13 December 1994

John,

  Do you remember our chat in the lobby of the Shangri-La last year about the
Chinese ki-lin and the Japanese ki-rin? Well, yesterday I found this rather nice
postcard at the museum, and thought of you. It is a particularly lively depiction of
the ki-lin or ki-rin — a word, unless my memory fails me, that is usually better
known in your country as the brand name of a rather indifferent Japanese beer.

  As you know, the ki-lin is a beast of uncertain provenance, which may well stem
from a quite different branch of the Equidae family than the unicorn. It is usually
described as having a rainbow-coloured, stag-like body and a 12-inch (30-cm) long
horn made of flesh, rather than the unicorn's keratinous outgrowth.

  It is more powerful than the unicorn, being impossible to catch or kill, and is
only very rarely glimpsed, though it lives for a thousand years. The ki-lin is said
to be so gentle that it will not kill any living thing — it will not even tread on
an insect, and it eats only dead grass. Apparently it can talk, having a voice as
melodious as a gong. An expedition from the court of Genghis Khan was said to have
encountered one in the western deserts. The holy creature passed on a message of
peace and love to the great leader, who promptly called off one of his notoriously
bloody military campaigns.

  Like the Chinese dragon and the hōō (phoenix), its appearance often seems to be
associated with a momentous event: a ki-lin's visit is said to have presaged the
birth of Confucius. It has been incorporated into the traditional Chinese symbolic
system of correspondences between supernatural creatures and the elements. Where the
dragon represents air and the phoenix, water, the ki-lin symbolises earth, and was
held to have sprung from the centre of the planet.

  To be honest, not much is known about the specifics of the ki-lin's life cycle,
biology or habits. It is always going to be difficult to separate the mythical from
the factual when dealing with an animal which is held to be supernatural.

  Anyway, I hope that Margaret and the kids are well. All the best!

Yours affectionately,

Chow Yun

KDJ.094.043
'KI-LIN HORN
PURCHASED IN
SHANGHAI
MARKET.

THE CRYPTOZOOLOGICAL SOCIETY OF LONDON

Section 5

HYBRIDS

Some of the strangest beasts in creation are
mixtures of other, more conventional creatures.
There are animals with the tails of fish and the
heads of horses, monsters with bat's wings and
men's faces and other impossible combinations
that should not exist in the natural world.
Many of these hybrids strike fear into the
human heart – not just because they are fierce
or cruel, but because they seem somehow
to be against nature.

Basic principles of cryptozoology explained in simple terms for schools, colleges and new readers. Created by the Education Department of the Cryptozoological Society of London.

Hybrids

In the natural world, the term hybrid generally refers to the gradual adaptation of an existing species by natural means. Thoroughbred horses, domestic animals and many popular garden plants are hybrids bred for performance. Cryptozoological hybrids, by contrast, are essentially mongrel combinations of different creatures.

The cryptozoological menagerie is full of animals with the tails of fish and the heads of horses, monsters with bat's wings and men's faces and other impossible combinations that should not exist in the natural world. These are hybrid creatures – ones which combine the features and forms of different animals in one body.

Explaining the origins of these hybrids is one of the great challenges of modern cryptozoology. Scientists have identified five main mechanisms by which hybrid beasts may have been created, but this is by no means the complete picture. Some beasts almost certainly represent the outcome of two or more of these mechanisms acting together in concert.

Common ancestors

A Darwinian view, and one which is held by many cryptozoologists, is that some hybrids have descended from common ancestors of the groups whose characteristics they share. For instance, the amphisbaena, the basilisk and the couatl are all members of the family *Ophidioaves* – hybrids of snakes and bird. Paradoxically, this is a more logical combination of creatures than it might seem, for the genes of birds and reptiles can coexist very happily.

Ophidioavians are almost certainly descended from the theropods, a group of dinosaurs that lived about 100 million years ago and are thought to be the ancestors of today's birds. In evolutionary terms, birds and reptiles

FIG 1 BAT IN FLIGHT

Bats, birds, dolphins and humans have the same distant common ancestor, but have made different uses of their genetic inheritance. The wings of birds and bats, the dolphin's flipper and the human arm are homologous: they have a similar underlying structure, deriving from a common ancestral forelimb.

share common ancestors, and it is from these ancestors that today's amphisbaena and couatl, which have both reptilian and avian features, have evolved.

Analogous evolution

When creatures share a feature as the result of common evolutionary lineage – e.g., the basic four-limbed body plan of most higher vertebrates, or the flippers of seals and dolphins – the features are said to be homologous. That is, they all stem from one feature in a common ancestor (see Fig 1).

When creatures share features that appear similar but stem from quite different ancestral sources, like the wings of a bird and the wings of an insect, the features are said to be analogous. Cryptozoologists believe that analogous evolution explains many of the unusual features of hybrid creatures.

For example, the scaly skin of the chimaera closely resembles that of a snake, but has actually developed from mammalian skin as an adaptation to arid conditions. The 'human' face of the manticore is thought to have developed as a lure to help attract prey. In other words, it is not truly a human face, it simply looks like one – it is analogous to a human face. Other examples include the 'fur' on the front-quarters of the hippocampus, the wings of the manticore and the wings of a bat.

Mutations

Some substances, such as radioactive materials and some organic chemicals, are able to cause mutations in embryos or in creatures themselves (see Fig 2). Heavy doses of such substances are usually lethal or give rise to mutants which cannot survive, but occasionally a mutoid creature may survive and breed successfully. This might appear to the layman as the most obvious explanation for the origin of hybrids, but in fact mutations on such a large scale are very rare indeed. Nonetheless, in areas where mutagens (substances which tend to cause mutations in animal DNA) build up, local animals will be exposed to them for many generations and accumulate the materials in their own tissues. It is possible that mutoid creatures might be the result. For instance, the hideous catoblepas is believed to be a mutation caused by a build up of naturally-occuring mutagens in the swamps of its African homelands.

Lability of hybrid genomes

Lability is a term used by geneticists to describe the susceptibility of a given genome (the complement of genetic information) to change and rearrangement. This can happen accidentally: there are often glitches in the transfer of genetic information from one generation to the next. Hybrid creatures, such as the chimaera or the gorgon, have especially labile DNA, which means that their genes get shuffled and moved around more often than usual. At the same time, they remain perfectly viable in their rearranged form, so that they can give birth to similarly strange offspring. The increasingly complex permutations of interbreeding between these hybrids have resulted in some truly bizarre life forms.

This is reflected in Greek myth, where hybrid creatures are often said to be the offspring of other hybrids. The gorgon Medusa was said to have given birth to Pegasus, the basilisk and other creatures, while the sphinx was said to be the daughter of the chimaera. Such myths can be viewed in two ways. On the one hand, they provided the ancient Greeks with explanations for the origin of monsters whose parentage would otherwise have been a mystery. On the other hand they represent an accurate biological insight on the part of the ancients, who recognised that the genetic make-up of hybrid creatures was unstable and changeable.

Artificial hybridisation

These genetic factors may account for the genesis of most hybrid creatures, but the origin of others has defied explanation. One theory is that these beasts are the result of artificial hybridisations carried out by alchemists or witch doctors using methods that defy scientific explanation. Who performed these operations remains a matter of pure conjecture, but the fruits of their labours live on as some of the strangest beasts in creation.

Whatever created hybrid creatures, the complexity and variety of these marvellous creatures has made their study one of the most popular and rewarding fields in cryptozoology.

Basilisk

LATIN NAME
Ophidiogallus basiliscus

HABITAT
Prefers deserts, but found in any climate

LIFESPAN
20-30 years

SIZE
Under 2 ft (0.6 m) high

INFORMATION SOURCE
CSL Review

DISTRIBUTION
Europe, the Near East, parts of Africa

The basilisk is a creature no balanced person would want to see. In medieval times it spread destruction across Europe, but today it is restricted to desert regions.

IF LOOKS COULD

KILL...

ONE OF THE WORLD'S MOST INFAMOUS and feared beasts, the basilisk was generally held to be the offspring of an old cock's egg, hatched by a toad. This hybrid of snake and cockerel is one of the most lethal combinations nature has ever produced. Almost everything about it is reputed to be poison-ous, from its baneful gaze to the sound of its hiss. While some of the more extravagant claims must be discounted as hysteria, it is easy to see how the basilisk arouses such a powerful reaction.

KING OF THE SERPENTS

The basilisk has a snake's body and tail, with a cockerel's head, legs, wings and crest. Its skin is either yellow and black – the same warning coloration used by bees and wasps – or a khaki camouflage. Its crest is said to resemble a crown and this, with the deference shown to the creature by other beasts (who flee at its approach), has earned the basilisk the title 'King of the Serpents'. The name basilisk derives from the Greek *basilikos* (royal, or kingly). In the 14th century, the basilisk's relentless pursuit of its prey also earned it the name cockatrice, from the Latin *cocatris* (tracker).

The basilisk's closest relatives are the other members of the *Ophidioaves* family, such as the couatl (a feathered snake with human-like eyes) and the amphisbaena (a two-headed snake with a

☞ *THIS STATUE IN THE GRAND PALACE IN BANGKOK, THAILAND, IS A POOR RENDITION OF A BASILISK, PROBABLY BASED ON INACCURATE ACCOUNTS BROUGHT BACK BY TRAVELLERS TO THE WEST.*

bird's body). The South American iguana, also known as the basilisk (genus *Basiliscus*), is a harmless and very distant relative.

Like many other hybrid creatures, the basilisk's strange birth and parentage appear to defy scientific explanation. Pliny, one of the earliest authorities to write on the subject, described how elderly cockerels laid eggs which were incubated by a toad or a snake. Alternatively, the bird could simply lay his egg on a warm dunghill. In the Middle Ages old cockerels were regarded with suspicion. In the 15th century one was tried in a court and convicted of laying eggs in the Devil's service.

A WITHERING LOOK

Assessments of the basilisk's powers have varied widely, but all have agreed that it could be extremely deadly. There are reports that its gaze can fry birds in flight, and claims that it can wither vegetation, reducing whole areas to deserts. There is no proof of the latter, and it would seem the basilisk has simply become linked with the hot, arid areas that are its preferred habitat.

There is no doubt that it does have some highly toxic property that can kill by gaze, touch, bite, smell or noise. Anyone fixed by the basilisk's gaze

Bafilifcus.

is paralysed and then dies, while its bite induces hydrophobia and fatal convulsions. Its power can even travel through a weapon, so that anyone striking the monster will ensure his or her own doom.

DON'T FORGET YOUR WEASEL

The basilisk is so deadly that it needs few defences, but – perhaps unsurprisingly for a creature whose best form of defence is attack – under certain conditions it is extremely vulnerable. It dies instantly on hearing any cock crow, and it can be vanquished by a weasel, the only animal immune to the basilisk's deadly gaze, in much the same way that mongoose defeat snakes. These methods were well known in medieval times, when travellers across deserts would take a weasel or a rooster in a cage for protection. Some authorities claim that seeing a basilisk before it spots you will cause it to die, but this seems highly unlikely – and one would be foolish to try it. Finally, like gorgons, basilisks can be killed by their own reflection and they live in fear of mirrors and other reflective surfaces.

HERE COMES THE MIRROR MAN

Pliny the Elder (23–79 AD) described the basilisk in detail in his *Historia Naturalis (Natural History)*, and it duly became a regular feature of 12th- and 13th-century bestiaries. The authors of these works had little or no first-hand knowledge of the creatures they described, and were more interested in using basilisks as allegorical symbols of Satan and his evil works. In the 15th century, England was reputed to have suffered a plague of basilisks, which brought a savage reminder of reality. These beasts terrorised the country until one brave man donned a suit of mirrors and walked the length and breadth of the nation, until every basilisk was killed.

The above story has never been verified and in general the monsters were, and remain, restricted to hot, dry areas in North Africa and the Near East. The last recorded sighting in Europe was in Warsaw in 1587. Two girls and their nurse were killed in a gloomy basement, and the King's physician deduced that a basilisk was responsible. A convicted criminal was clothed in a suit of mirrors and sent to flush out the creature, emerging after a few minutes with a small snake-like animal that failed to impress a crowd of vengeful onlookers. Modern Europeans can count themselves fortunate to be free of the lethal basilisk.

EVERYONE WHO OBSERVED THE BASILISK PERISHED, SO ITS APPEARANCE HAS ALWAYS BEEN IN DISPUTE. IN HIS 1553 WORK, COSMOGRAPHIA UNIVERSALIS, SEBASTIAN MUNSTER GAVE THE CREATURE EIGHT LEGS BUT NO WINGS.

WRE.982.062 SKETCHES OF UNKNOWN DATE AND ORIGIN FOUND IN THE LIBRARY OF ST GALL MONASTERY, SWITZERLAND.

The wings appear to spring directly from the basilisk's rib cage.

The loosely jointed snake-like body is flexible, and the long tail may help the creature to keep its balance.

snake's tongue gives the creature a sharp sense of smell.

The viciously sharp claws are surely superfluous.

HYBRIDS

Amphisbaena

LATIN NAME
*Amphisbaena
janus*

HABITAT
*Most
environments*

LIFESPAN
5–10 years

SIZE
*c.4 ft (1.2 m)
long*

**INFORMATION
SOURCE**
Field Report

DISTRIBUTION
*Central
Balkans*

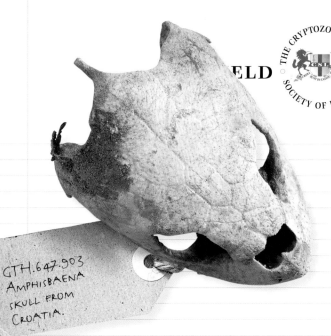

GTH.647.903
AMPHISBAENA
SKULL FROM
CROATIA.

midriff there appeared to be feathers! The ends of the skin were missing, but I was convinced that this was an amphisbaena. An old woodsman came past and explained that nailing the animal, or its skin, to a tree would make it easier to cut down, and in winter would protect him from the cold. I was reminded of something written by Pliny, in the 1st century AD. He said that the amphisbaena could be used as a cure for the common cold, and sufferers should wrap themselves in the skin of a dead specimen.

BACKGROUND NOTES

Two-headed snakes are not so very uncommon in nature, although they do not usually survive long. The amphisbaena is a different beast altogether. Firstly, it is a member of the <u>Ophidioaves</u> family – half-snake and half bird. Secondly, its dual heads are not both on the end of its neck – one is on the end of the creature's tail. This unique body form gives the amphisbaena several remarkable abilities.

FIELD REPORT

14th May: A three-mile trek from the station has brought me to the village of Banja Crdozja. The villagers I have questioned seem to recognise the pictures I've shown them, but their accounts differ slightly. It would appear that my best hope of a sighting lies to the south.

16th May: Have been working south through the foothills of the Kapaonik Mountains. The reports of the locals suggest that the amphisbaena is found throughout this area, and also further to the north and south. This wide distribution seems to confirm Professor King's theory that the <u>Ophidioaves</u> are warm-blooded, allowing them to exploit cooler regions which reptiles cannot colonise because of their cold-blooded nature.

23rd May: Approaching the border with Macedonia, I came across a peculiar sight. Nailed to a tree was a strange skin. It had black and white bands, and around the

AMPHISBAENA SKIN NAILED TO TREE
NEAR MACEDONIAN BORDER.

4th June: At last – a sighting! I have been tracking these elusive creatures for some days now, but have found it hard to get close to one. Legend has it that the amphisbaena's two heads allow it be alert all the time, since one head will remain awake while the other sleeps – this would certainly account for its alertness. But today I flushed one out of a small tree, and was amazed by its speed and agility. It had a serpentine body which thickened at the mid-point into a bird-like torso, with short, stubby wings and a pair of bird's legs. This one was banded like the skin I had seen earlier, but with

AMPHISBAENA SKIN.

alternating stripes of white and red. Perhaps coloration varies with region. At the end of the tail, which looked much like the neck, was a head identical to the one at the front end. It appeared able to move equally quickly in either direction.

6th June: Further sightings have led to some remarkable discoveries. For instance, to aid stability at high speeds the front head often seizes the rear one by the throat. Inevitably, falls sometimes occur, in which case it can roll along like a hoop until it recovers its footing. To see one of these beasts rolling along is a great thrill. I have also observed the creatures feeding on ants (their sole diet, according to Classical sources), but the locals tell me that amphisbaenae are highly venomous at both ends.

NB: The two-headed amphisbaena should not be confused with the sightless, limbless S. American lizard of the same name. The latter is a harmless burrowing creature.

BULGARIAN NECKLACE WITH A SNAKE SWALLOWING ITS OWN TAIL. WAS IT INSPIRED BY THE AMPISBAENA?

NORSE BRACELET WITH TWO-HEADED SNAKE.

Amphisbaena feathers serve no functional purpose – these snake-birds can't fly.

The 'rear' head often seems to keep a lookout while the 'front' head is busy doing other things.

Both heads have venomous fangs.

strong claws hold branches and prey in a tight grip.

Couatl

LATIN NAME
*Ophidiotrogon
queztlcouatlis*

HABITAT
*Jungle/
rainforest;
upland regions*

LIFESPAN
100–150 years

SIZE
*About 4 ft
(1.2 m) long;
wingspan
c.3 ft (0.9 m)*

**INFORMATION
SOURCE**
Letter

DISTRIBUTION
*Central America
from Mexico to
Costa Rica*

Fellows of the Cryptozoological
Society of London,
100 Piccadilly,

Don Rogelio Cohénez de la Chingada
152 Avenída Coronel Sanchez de
Bustamante
San José
Costa Rica

4 de febrero, 1974

Estimable Señores,

Exciting news from the Monteverde Cloud Forest! As you know I am for many years
searching for the couatl, the plumed serpent known to Mayans, Aztecs and Toltecs. One
of the main figures in the Aztec pantheon is Quetzlcouatl, a fantastic feathered serpent with dazzling emerald plumage and eyes of fire, como el couatl. The Mayans called
it kukulcan, and the greatest Toltec king, Topiltzin, claimed to be the living incar-
nación of the couatl.

Por supuesto the Mayans and Aztecs were based in Guatemala and Mexico, but the
range of the couatl extends as far south as Costa Rica. Last month I visit the
Monteverde Cloud Forest, una tierra bellissima con una majistad, where the lower slopes
are covered in thick rainforest, the couatl's natural habitat. Together with mis com-
pañeros, Miguel y Ciro I climb high into the montañas and enter the jungle, where only
the Indios live.

In the past I have found it hard to gather información about the couatl. The animal
is naturally wary and the Indios are not helpful. They have worshipped this creature
for over two thousand years, and they know it to be wise in the arts of science, nature
and magic. The invading conquistadores try to impose their own religion on the Indios,
dismissing the couatl as a myth, and since then the paysanos have been suspicious of
strangers.

Miguel is half-Indio, and with his help we secure the services of a guide who takes
us deep into the forest. After two days travelling el guia become muy agitada, pointing
to a tree ahead and telling us to keep silencio. We seea green flash amongst the tree-
tops and I take photographs como un hombre loco! But we soon see it is a bird –
Pharomacrus mocino, el bellissimo quetzal bird.

The next day we are muy fortunado. Shortly after siesta el guia lead us silently to
a gigante tree. On a low branch I see a strange créatura which seemed to be a reptile
and a bird at the same time – el couatl. It has a snake-like body – thick, muscular and
poderoso; a snake's head, with eyes like emeralds and teeth, sharp like the pantera. It
is mostly covered in bright green feathers, and has the small wings, like a bird, just
below its neck.

As we watch it glides noiselessly down to the forest floor and pounce on a small
bicho. At the last moment Ciro (el boludo) make a noise, and the couatl's prey escape.
El creatura turn and look at us, and I swear that in its eyes I could see the light of
an inteligencia inhumana. El guia whimper and cross himself, for los Indios believe
that the couatl has poderes magicales. Evidentemente his prayers were answered, for el
couatl turn and disappear into the forest like un fantasmo.

El guia refuse to take us any further, muttering "no voy a tener el riesgo de que-
mar en el infierno", and the next day we begin the long journey back to San José. I
wish that I take photograph for you, but I was too amazed. Fortunamente Miguel is a muy
buen artista, and he has made this dibujo. I send to you also this evidencio collected
from the floor of the forest. I think it is related to your European snake-birds, like
the amphisbaena and the basilisk, but probably separate from them hace
millónes de años.

Rogelio

Rogelio Cohénez de la Chingada

CIRO, MIGUEL AND ROGELIO ON
THEIR RETURN FROM THE JUNGLE,
AFTER SPOTTING A COUATL.

THE QUETZAL BIRD *Pharomacrus mocino* occupies the same habitat as the legendary couatl, and has very similar wings and feathers. Evolutionary biologists suggest that this bird, a member of the *Trogonidae* family, may have evolved to mimic the couatl, thus benefiting from the wide berth given the latter by predators of all kinds.

FEATHERS, TEETH AND A BITTEN LEAF RECOVERED FROM THE RAINFOREST.

THIS IS ONE OF THE WAYS THE COUATL IS PORTRAYED IN COSTA RICA. THIS IS A COPY OF A WALL DRAWING, BUT THE COUATL IS ALSO A POPULAR TATTOO.

This dibujo or sketch is by Miguel.

'Couatl' means 'snake' in the ancient Aztec tongue. The tail is certamente that of a serpent of some kind.

The couatl can strangle its prey, they say.

55

The tail helps this creatura to glide through the branches of the thick forest canopy.

sharp teeth and bright green ojos give the couatl a fearsome appearance.

some say that the couatl has claws.

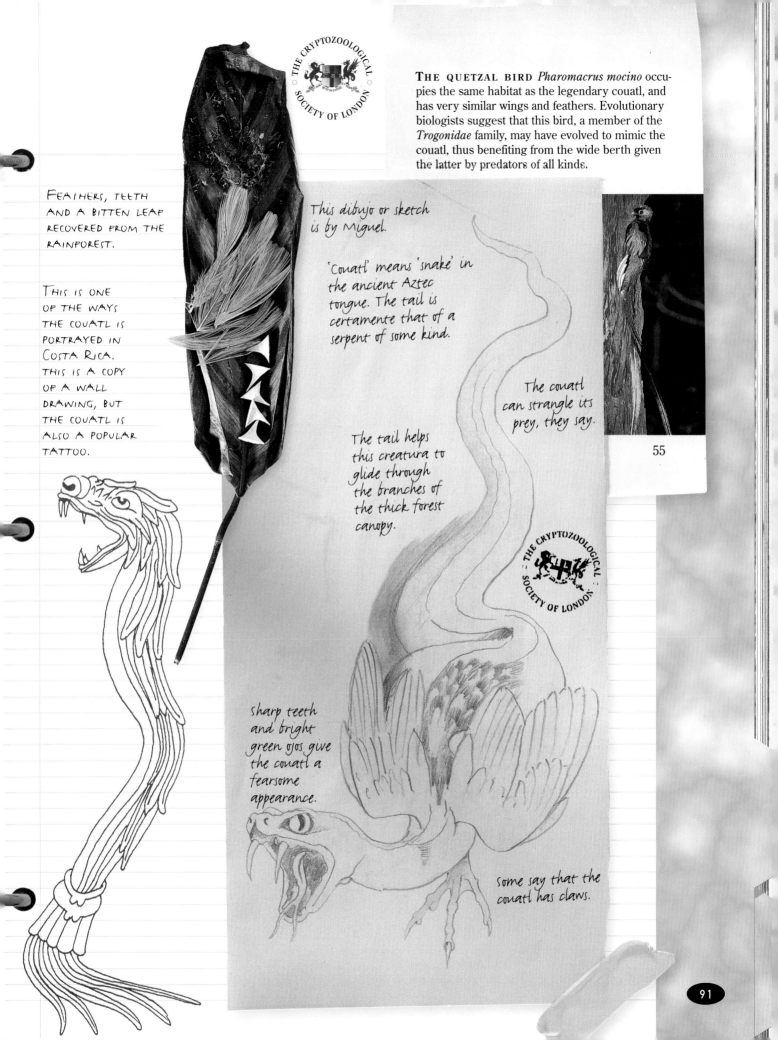

Manticore

LATIN NAME
Chiropanthera mantichora

HABITAT
Semi-arid mountainous regions

LIFESPAN
Unknown

SIZE
Like a large lion; wingspan c. 24 ft (7.3 m)

INFORMATION SOURCE
Colleague's Field Report

DISTRIBUTION
Near and Middle East, SE Europe

BACKGROUND TO THE FIELD TRIP

The manticore looks like a lion, but is equipped with a deadly tail, bat wings and most disconcertingly, an apparently human face. Its scorpion's tail is studded with poison-tipped, razor sharp quills. The name is derived from the Latin mantichora, from the Greek mantikhoras, a mis-transcription of two Ancient Persian words: martiya (man) and khvar (to eat) – i.e. 'man-eater'.

The manticore figured prominently in medieval bestiaries, and was often used as an allegory for the Devil. In the 13th century, Richard of Haldingham depicted one in his Mappa Mundi, now on show at Hereford Cathedral.

The manticore's range once extended through the semi-arid regions of Persia and Mesopotamia and as far West as Greece and the Atlas mountains of North Africa, but is now restricted to the inaccessible mountains of central Iran. The present expedition has been commissioned to visit the Kermān region, a sparsely populated, arid region of South-Central Iran. Luckily, the Shah of Iran has taken a close personal interest in our expedition, which has helped us to cut through a lot of red tape. We – me, Pip Diamond and an American journalist, Jody Friedman – will travel in a light aeroplane, generously loaned by the Shah.

FIELD NOTES

September 10th; Kermān, Kermān region, Iran
Spent the morning finalising arrangements at the aerodrome. The Shah has provided us with a six-seater Cessna and the services of one of his pilots, Hendi Zahedi.

September 11th; Bāft, Kermān region
Today we flew around some of the highest peaks in the area before landing near a small village to ask a few questions. My Persian is not what it used to be, but the villagers seemed to understand us. They were full of dire warnings about the manticore, and told us not to be taken in by its friendly smile. We drank coffee with the local headman, who proudly showed us a set of jaws from a manticore killed near Jiroft, further to the east. The jaw was huge and had three rows of sharp fangs. Jody took a Polaroid of it.

COULD THIS BE A MANTICORE'S JAW?

The manticore's friendly, wise facial expression is in stark contrast to the bat-like wings and deadly scorpion's tail.

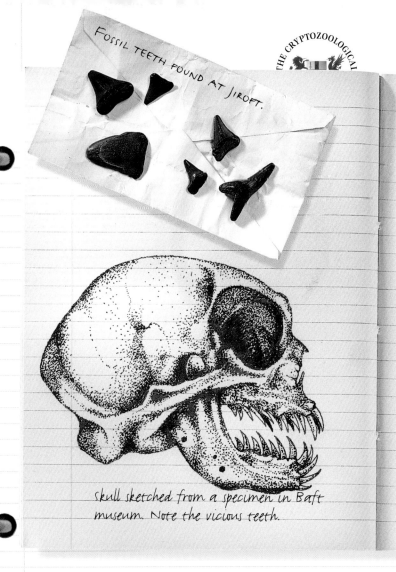

FOSSIL TEETH FOUND AT JIROFT.

Skull sketched from a specimen in Baft museum. Note the vicious teeth.

Cross-section of a manticore tail, showing the poison sac and the internal vessels that inject venom into the quills.

The hollow quills have very sharp, brittle tips. They snap off as they enter the flesh, delivering the poison.

The quills are fairly loosely attached – when the manticore thrashes his tail, they can fly off like darts.

September 15th; Jiroft, Kermān region
After several days fruitless searching we struck gold. This morning we were flying over low hills to the south. As we came over a ridge a shower of long black spines flashed in front of the windscreen. Hendi banked the plane and I found myself looking directly down at the ground, where a large, angry manticore crouched, its tail arched over its back, its wings pressed against its flanks and its startlingly human face staring up at me. It had clear blue eyes and an incongruously friendly expression, considering that it had just peppered us with poisonous quills.

We swung round for another look, but it had disappeared. We flew back to Jiroft, and plucked several evil-looking quills out of the fuselage. Tomorrow we intend to return to the area on foot.

September 17th; Jiroft
Yesterday was exciting but ultimately disappointing. We approached the area of our sighting by jeep, accompanied by several guides and fully equipped with helmets, body armour and the essential tranquillising darts. A few indistinct tracks and some scattered quills bore testament to the monster's passing, and we advanced cautiously on foot, only to be brought up short by the appearance of a human face around the side of a large rock. It smiled beguilingly and appeared to motion us over. I found myself strongly drawn to it.

Fortunately Pip had greater presence of mind. She was about to fire her dart gun when the guides panicked and opened fire with their rifles. The manticore roared and leapt at us, scattering quills in all directions. In the pandemonium my camera was crushed, Pip got shot through the leg and the monster escaped. Luckily, no-one was killed. Pip's injury meant an abrupt end to the expedition, as we had to return to base for medical treatment. With my camera destroyed, a few sketches and one or two things I picked up in the area are all I have to show for risking my life.

TRANQUILLISING DART.

MANTICORE QUILLS PICKED OUT OF THE FUSELAGE OF THE PLANE – SHARP AND DEADLY.

HYBRIDS

Griffon

LATIN NAME
*Raptopanthera
gryphos*

HABITAT
Mountains

LIFESPAN
50–60 years

SIZE
*About 8 ft
(2.4 m) high
at shoulder;
wingspan
c. 18 ft (5.5 m)*

**INFORMATION
SOURCE**
CSL Review

DISTRIBUTION
*India, Middle
East, Northern
Russia*

This decorative griffon, part of a Greek tripod from the 7th century bce, suggests that these fearsome animals may once have colonised the Mediterranean.

GRIFFONS LOVE GOLD AND GEMSTONES, which they steal, hoard and guard with savage strength and ferocity. In ancient times they were symbols of guardianship, protection and the retribution of justice, but in the 19th century assumed the mantle of harmless, and even gentle creatures. Modern readers should not be fooled, however, and anyone encountering a griffon would be well advised to remember that it is a highly dangerous wild creature and one of mankind's most implacable foes.

INDIAN OR HYPERBOREAN?

The vast majority of griffons belong to the one species, *Raptopanthera gryphos*. There are two main varieties: the Northern, or Hyperborean griffon, and the Indian griffon. The Northern griffon lives in the hilly forests and mountains of north-eastern Europe and Russia. These forested areas once extended deep into the Ukraine –

THEY EAT

HORSES

DON'T THEY?

much further south than they do today. The Indian griffon is found in mountainous regions of North-Eastern India and the Middle East. The only other species of the genus is the opinicus, *Raptopanthera opinicus*, recognisable by its feline, as opposed to aquiline, forelimbs. It was always rare and is now almost certainly extinct.

KNOW YOUR GRIFFONS

The griffon is a large, fierce looking creature, about 2 ft higher than a shire horse. It has the rear half of a lion, complete with long tail, but the front of its body is like an eagle, with upright, pointed ears and brightly glowing eyes. Sprouting from its back is a pair of wings strong enough to carry it at enormous speeds, and lift it off the ground bearing heavy prey. On the end of its eagle-like forelimbs are wickedly curved claws that match its cruel, hooked beak. Coloration varies, from the restrained dun of the Hyperborean sub-species, to the gaudy Indian

THE WORLD'S ONLY STUFFED GRIFFON – A FINE SPECIMEN OF THE HYPERBOREAN VARIETY SHOT DOWN OVER COPENHAGEN BY THE BELGIAN HUNTRESS NADINE LEGRAND – IS NOW PRESERVED IN A DANISH MUSEUM.

griffon, which has dark-blue variegated feathers at the neck, black feathers on its back, red feathers at the front and white wings.

THE YOLKS THAT LIVE ON THE HILL

Mountains – the less accessible the better – are the griffon's favourite home, and it prefers to live on particularly unscaleable crags and rock overhangs. Although many parts of the griffon's range lie in hot or tropical climatic zones, they are not fond of the heat and their nests are built high in the mountains, where the altitude ensures low temperatures.

died, the other would never re-mate. The egg-laying habits of the female were first properly described by St Hildegard of Bingen, a German nun writing in the 12th century. She outlined how the expectant mother would search out a cave with a very narrow entrance but plenty of room inside, sheltered from the elements. Here she would lay her eggs (about the size of ostrich eggs), and stand guard over them, especially protecting them against the mountain lions which then roamed the areas inhabited by the griffon. Some authorities claimed that griffons hatched out of chunks of the agate rather than eggs, but this can be dismissed as a medieval fancy.

Offspring remain with their parents for at least three years after hatching, while they shed their initial downy plumage, wait for their wings grow to their full extent and learn to fend for themselves.

The griffon's fierce, indomitable nature has inspired and terrified men for more than 5000 years. Its combination of lion and eagle, nature's most regal creations, has made it a potent emblem of rulers and empires.

Broody females seek out suitable caves, which offer extra shade and stable, cool temperatures, in which to lay their eggs.

The griffon is probably descended from an exotic branch of the avian (bird) family. Its unusual body plan has been the subject of much scientific study, for the griffon is a true six-limbed creature. The pegasus and the dragon evolved wings by developing the four-limbed skeleton that most vertebrates possess. But the griffon, like the manticore (p.92) and the lamassu (p.136), displays a true third limb pair. In the absence of a fossil record for the creature (apart from the discovery of a fossilised nest of eggs and claw fragments in the Gobi desert) it is hard to say how this body plan arose.

TILL DEATH US DO PART

The 9th century Irish writer Stephen Scotus asserted that griffons were highly monogamous. Not only did they mate for life, but if one partner

During this long adolescence the young griffons' are fed by their parents, who spend enormous amounts of time and energy foraging for them, often flying great distances to find food.

ELEPHANT? NO THANKS

Griffons are capable of grabbing all manner of prey, but they are particularly fond of horses, which they carry off whole – rider included. The Roman authority, Aelian (c.200 AD), said that the only animals that the griffon would not attack were the elephant and the lion. Several medieval bestiaries describe how they loved to tear humans up and rip out their inner organs on sight.

After eating, griffons' main preoccupations are gathering and hoarding gold and precious stones. Although classical and medieval writers were quick to impute base motives to the griffon, citing it as a symbol of greed, its motives are probably much nearer those of the magpie, which collects shiny

IT WAS NOT UNUSUAL FOR GREEDY GRIFFONS TO SWOOP DOWN ON KNIGHTS RIDING TO BATTLE. THE RIDER WOULD BE A TASTY APPETISER BEFORE THEY WENT ON TO MAKE A MEAL OF THE HORSE.

HYBRIDS

Griffon

☞ *AN ANCIENT ASSYRIAN BAS-RELIEF SHOWS A GRIFFON FLEEING FROM ARROWS. ADVANCES IN MILITARY TECHNOLOGY HAVE OCCASIONALLY GIVEN MAN THE EDGE IN THE UNEVEN FIGHT AGAINST THIS BEAST.*

objects. The griffon's nest, fabulously rich in gold, emeralds and stolen jewellery of all kinds has inevitably been the focus of much attention from avaricious treasure hunters.

FAMILY-MINDED FIENDS

The strength, speed, keen hearing and pin-sharp vision of the griffon are legendary. It can lift loads almost as heavy as itself, and rend its prey into pieces with its razor-like beak and claws, but it is best known for guarding its hoard with tremendous ferocity. Humans who attempt to steal this wealth usually pay with their lives, proving (according to Church moralists) that greed does not pay. In practice, though, the griffon's reputation has probably

bore the alternative title 'Mistress of Griffons'. Griffons were also known to the Minoan civilisation of ancient Crete in the second millennium BCE. Their images adorned the walls of the royal palace in Knossos, and a tiny golden model of a griffon was found in the Royal Tombs. Obviously the ancients were well acquainted with the vigilant and combative nature of griffons, depicting them in a guarding or protective role – defending the Tree of Life, perhaps, or as bodyguards to a king.

> **"THE GRIFFEN** ... *wyl bear to his nest flying ... two Oxen yoked togither as they go at plowgh, for he hath large nayles on his fete, as great as it were hornes of Oxen."*
>
> Sir John Mandeville, Travels, 1366

been distorted. It was Aelian who first suggested that the griffon was guarding its young, and not its treasure, and that its fierce protectiveness was a display of parental concern rather than greed. However, this view has only recently gained currency and is of little comfort to the treasure hunters, who suffer regardless.

The first recorded human encounters with the griffon appeared in *c.* 3000 BCE in Egypt and Mesopotamia, showing that the beast made an early impact across the civilised world. It was associated with deities like Negral, the Egyptian god of the afterlife, and Ishtar, who

The first authoritative source on their habits and habitats was the 5th century BCE Greek historian Herodotus. He tells of the land of the Hyperboreans, 'whose territory reaches the sea' in the far north of Russia. In these territories lived the Arimaspians, a race of one-eyed men, who were said to be in constant conflict with the griffons over the region's abundant gold and emerald reserves.

HERALDIC HEROES

Griffons continued to have religious significance for the Greeks, and later the Romans, well into the 4th century AD. Their reputation as noble guardians led to their adoption as symbols of Rome's imperial might and law-giving role. However, while classical art and religion portrayed them as creatures of lofty intent and virtue, in reality their struggle with mankind for possession of the world's riches continued undiminished. Aelian described how teams of Indians would make 3- or 4-year expeditions into the

🖎 *THE GRIFFON'S LIFE CYCLE FOLLOWS THE EAGLE RATHER THAN THE LION. THE UPPERMOST EGG HERE, THE GRIFFON'S, IS SHOWN FOR COMPARISON WITH THE EAGLE'S AND THE HEN'S.*

wilderness to prospect for griffon's gold. They would approach in dead of night, but the griffon's hearing is sharp, and their retribution swift and merciless. Few men would survive, but those that did became very wealthy men.

Griffons figured widely in medieval art, and were popular as decorative motifs in churches. They stare out from eaves, lurk in misericords and balance on the end of pews in innumerable churches and cathedrals. Medieval bestiaries waxed lyrical about the strength and ferocity of the griffon. Its reputation survived the Renaissance and Enlightenment, but the 19th century, however, saw a change in attitudes. Griffons were now so scarce that few Europeans had ever seen one except as an heraldic crest. The sleepy, amusing creature in *Alice in Wonderland* is typical of the 'loveable' image of the Victorian griffon.

The griffon might be rare, but it has not left us entirely. As recently as 1985, a flurry of excitement was caused by the appearance of one in Brentford, near London. How it got there, and what became of it, are mysteries that remain unsolved – perhaps it was blown off course by strong winds, or had escaped from a private collection. Such visits are rare, and only inhabitants of the sparse settlements of the Siberian taiga and the Persian and Afghan highlands still need to be on their guard.

0.5 HORSEPOWER

The griffon's only known relative is the hippogriff – the offspring of a horse and a griffon. Such unions are incredibly rare, since the relationship between the two species is usually one of predator and prey. Hippogriffs have the rear quarters of a horse instead of those of a lion, and large white or beige wings. Unlike griffons, hippogriffs could be tamed and used as aerial mounts, in which role they were immortalised in the Italian Renaissance poet Ariosto's famous saga, *Orlando Furioso*. Given the griffon's rarity, it seems extremely unlikely that there are any hippogriffs still alive today.

Long ears, sharp eyes and cruelly hooked bills make the griffon a fearsome beast.

The tail functions as a rudder in flight. When griffons eat, fight or make love, it lashes violently from side to side with pleasure, anger or lust.

The claws are like massive eagles' feet. As the griffon swoops on its quarry, the rear talon sinks into the flesh first. Then the front claws close in to form a deadly cage, firmly gripping the doomed creature.

The heavy rear paws help provide extra thrust during take-off and are used to hold prey down while the beak and claws do their worst.

HYBRIDS
Yale

LATIN NAME
*Equoaprinoceph-
alus mobiliceros*

HABITAT
*Savannah,
floodplain,
wet uplands*

LIFESPAN
20-25 years

SIZE
*6-7 ft
(1.8-2.1 m)
at shoulder*

**INFORMATION
SOURCE**
Letter

DISTRIBUTION
*East Africa; Nile
floodplains*

Herbert Smythe-Hawkins
Masai Mara
British East Africa

August 30th, 1892

Dear Hugh,

I write with news which is sure to be of interest to you and that collection of cads and bounders who pass as gentlemen. How is old Piccadilly? The high-stepping fillies in their fancy skirts still make their daily parade, I trust. It is all a long way removed from this savage land — I can scarcely get the blighters to keep their clothes on! I do my best to spread a civilising influence, though God knows it is hard.

I arrived at Kisangali Lodge about a fortnight ago and set to work making arrangements. The fellows at the Mess are decent enough, and help us best they can, but to get any real results you need a native foreman. I have one of the best — a fellow by the name of Osabo — just a little chap, mind, with skin as black as pitch, but by God when he hollers the natives jump to! Within two days we had our bearers, our supplies and our guides. Thus equipped I ventured forth in the name of Queen and Country.

To date, I have bagged four lions, two elephants, a half-dozen rhinos, a giraffe, ten zebra, a dozen wildebeest and a brace of antelopes (the Stebbings Automatic was working perfectly for the first week, and I obtained a number of fine pictures — I have enclosed two for your edification). Not bad for two weeks work! Of course none of this concerns you, and I am well aware of your prudish views about hunting. What does ccause me to write to you is the remarkable discovery I have made.

Three days ago I saw a strange beast at the waterhole — it looked very much like a large antelope, but had the jaws and tusks of a boar, the tail of an elephant and what looked like a goat's beard. Its most prominent features were two long, curved horns which were about 8 feet long. I promptly shot it. When I questioned Osabo he told me that it was known to his people as an 'eale'.

FGD.273.827
TUSK, BELIEVED TO BE FROM
YALE.
PROVENANCE: MARKET VENDOR
IN KHARTOUM, SUDAN.

STAMP ISSUED BY
BRITAIN'S ROYAL
MAIL SHOWING THE
FAMOUS HERALDIC YALE
OF BEAUFORT.

I trust that you recall our family's own coat of arms: the quartered chevron supported by eagle and yale rampant? It is derived from that of the Duke of Somerset, who was the first to portray the yale on his arms. I immediately realised that the beast which lay before me was, or rather had been, a living, breathing yale. What a place to run across a creature which I last encountered in the nursery. How clearly I remember reading about this strange, hybrid animal which could swivel its horns at will and wield them like lances. I determined to find another and photograph it on your behalf.

The next day we set out across the savannah towards another watering hole, passing a variety of game. I paused briefly to shoot an eagle but was damned unlucky. I assure you this is nothing like grouse shooting in Northumberland! Only men of breeding should challenge the mighty beasts of the Dark Continent.

Shortly after luncheon we reached the waterhole, and, advancing all the while unobserved, were able to view a most extraordinary spectacle — two yale fighting, or rather jousting (as it were). They swivelled their opposable horns with remarkable dexterity, fencing back and forth. Eventually one gained the upper hand and speared his rival through the heart — such is Nature's cruel pageant! I shot the victor, and would have photographed it for you but that the infernal Stebbings ceased to operate. Osabo made a sketch, and I intend to present the creature's horns to you as a trophy upon my return.

Pass on my regards to Mother and the girls, and God save the Queen!

Yrs, the Black Sheep of the Family (ad aeternam),

Herbert.

Osabo's sketch of
the creature — not
bad, eh? What
do you think?

Addendum
by Hugh Smythe-Hawkins, FRSL, dated December, 1892:

My brother returned to England in November of this year, but by a cruel twist of fate his baggage was lost at sea between the Azores and Southampton, including his entire collection of trophies. The yale was first described by Pliny in the 1st century AD, and although specimens may well have been captured and brought from Egypt to Europe at some point in the Middle Ages, there are none currently in civilised hands. This makes Herbert's 'regrettable' loss the Society's too — we would dearly have loved to obtain physical evidence of the existence of what was known as one of the 'Queen's Beasts'.

By way of an erratum I might point out that Henry IV's son John, Duke of Bedford, claimed to have introduced the yale to heraldic art previously to the Duke of Somerset.

HERBERT SMYTHE-
HAWKINS AND HIS
RETAINERS. OSABO IS
TO SMYTHE-HAWKINS'
LEFT.

HYBRIDS

Chimaera

LATIN NAME
Dracoprileo chimaera

HABITAT
Dry hills

LIFESPAN
Unknown

SIZE
Approx. 4 ft (1.2 m) high at shoulder

INFORMATION SOURCE
CSL Review

DISTRIBUTION
Turkey

AN ETRUSCAN BRONZE OF A CHIMAERA — WITH THREE HEADS.

REPORT

In ancient times, the chimaera, a hideous combination of lion, goat and serpent, terrorised the region of Lycia, in modern Turkey. The ancient philosophers waxed lyrical of its fearsome appearance and its ability to create a jet of intensely hot flame. Today, the chimaera is extinct, but many questions about this creature remain unanswered. This field trip was commissioned to search for evidence amongst the Lycian hills around modern-day Elmall, in SW Turkey.

FIELD NOTES
Sept 6th: Antalya
Arrived last night and met up with Osman Bayar, a local archaeologist currently excavating a site high in the arid Lycian hills.

Sept 7th: Elmall
The terrain is barren and dusty: weathered cliffs are pitted with caves that might have been occupied by huge lions. Osman adheres to the oldest description – Homer's – which tells of a creature with the head of a lion, the body of a goat and the tail of a serpent. Osman reasons that the chimaera's hybrid characteristics were the product of normal evolutionary adaptation, and explained his theory that the chimaera was a species of cat. He also drew me a rough sketch.

Sept 8th: Lycian hills
Today we looked at a cave which may have been visited by early Greek colonists foraging inland. The walls of the cave bore ancient scorchmarks, and we found an intriguing twisted glass bottle there.

SUPPLEMENTARY NOTES
Tests at the University of Ankara showed that the bottle bore heavy carbon deposits from the time of the earliest Lycian colonies. Dr Aziz argues that there was only ever a small population of chimaerae living in the Lycian hills. When the human population of the area expanded, conflict between the competing species became vicious. The torched bottle may well be the detritus of a chimaera's glass-melting breath, used in anger against a human foe.

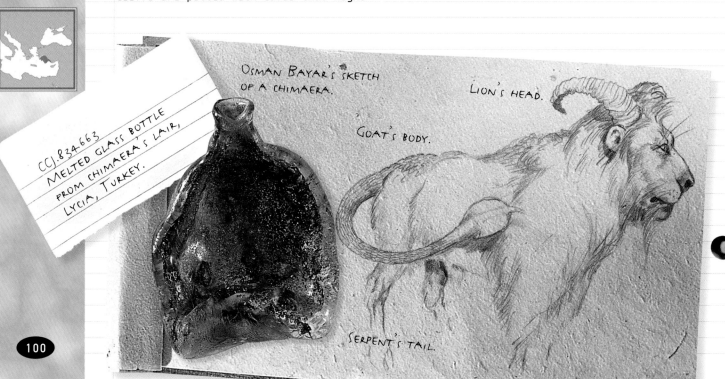

CCI.834.663 MELTED GLASS BOTTLE FROM CHIMAERA'S LAIR, LYCIA, TURKEY.

OSMAN BAYAR'S SKETCH OF A CHIMAERA.

LION'S HEAD.

GOAT'S BODY.

SERPENT'S TAIL.

The hippocampus or merhorse was to the undersea world what the horse is to our terrestrial one – a powerful steed, a valiant companion in battle and a creature of grace and beauty.

WET & WILD

THE WEBBED HOOVES AND FISH'S TAIL ARE JOINED TO A HORSE'S POWERFUL FORELEGS AND HEAD. THE OUTCOME IS A FAR CRY FROM THE SEA HORSE OF CONVENTIONAL ZOOLOGY.

THE FAVOURED MOUNT OF THE HALF-human denizens of the deeps, the hippocampus served as the mount of nereids and sea gods. Swift and powerful beneath the waves, hippocampi combined the speed, intelligence and loyalty of the horse with the undersea adaptation of the fish.

FISH TAILS AND FAKE FUR

The hippocampus has the head and front torso of a horse, narrowing into a long, serpentine, fish's tail. It has equine forelimbs that end in fins instead of hooves. The powerful tail can propel the hippocampus through the water at extremely high speeds, while the front legs provide fine control, a high degree of manoeuvrability and a rudimentary means of getting around on land.

Although the front halves appear to be mammalian, they are closer to fish in many respects. Their 'fur' is actually a covering of very fine scales (in contrast to the broad scales of their rear portions), and they breathe underwater using a form of modified gills. They do, however, give birth to live young, and reproduce much like a dolphin or similar marine mammal.

Like their terrestrial equivalents, wild merhorses roam the sea in herds, grazing on beds of seaweed. When threatened by sharks or other predators they will bunch together with the young in the centre of the group, and if possible the herd will take refuge in a kelp forest. They are difficult to tame, but if broken or raised in captivity they make excellent mounts – swift and agile, fierce in battle but docile with their masters.

SINDBAD AND THE SEA HORSES

Although they normally breed with their own kind, hippocampus stallions have the ability to inseminate terrestrial mares. The resulting fine, strong and speedy colts and fillies have always fetched enormous prices. Sindbad relates how, shipwrecked early in his first voyage, he came across the grooms of King Mahrajan. They had brought his finest mares to the shore so that they could be bred with wild 'sea horses'. The amorous hippocampi would charge out from the waves, mount the mares, and then try to drag them back into the sea. But the grooms would emerge at this point and scare them off, taking the impregnated mares back to the King's stables, where they bore offspring reported to be of 'inestimable worth'.

TEAMS OF HIPPOCAMPI PULLED THE CHARIOT OP THE SEA GOD POSEIDON – AS SEEN IN THIS 3RD-CENTURY MOSAIC PAVEMENT FROM A ROMAN VILLA IN TUNISIA.

HYBRIDS

Hippocampus

LATIN NAME
Equopisce hippocampi

HABITAT
Warm coastal waters

LIFESPAN
30–40 years

SIZE
4–5 ft (1.2–1.5 m) high at shoulder; 10–12 ft (3–3.6 m) long

INFORMATION SOURCE
CSL Review

DISTRIBUTION
Mediterranean, Red Sea, Indian Ocean

HYBRIDS

Catoblepas

LATIN NAME
Phacochaetes connochoerus

HABITAT
Swampland

LIFESPAN
500 years

SIZE
Equivalent to a buffalo or large wildebeest

INFORMATION SOURCE
Own Field Report

DISTRIBUTION
Sub-Saharan Africa

BACKGROUND

(Cyperus papyrus)

Deep in the heart of Africa, where two great sources of the Nile converge, lies the Sudd - a vast area of choked bogs where papyrus reeds reach 25 feet (8 m) high. A rich diversity of wildlife lives in and around this swamp, including the catoblepas. With the body of a buffalo, the legs of a hippo, a long neck and the head of a warthog, it is one of the most hideous creatures known to man. The catoblepas gives off a foul smell, and its face is so dreadful that a glance can kill. Although it is notorious in areas around its marshy home, it is not well-known in the developed world.

Due to reclamation of swampland for agricultural purposes, the catoblepas' habitat is in danger. In 1987 the CSL decided to send a fact-finding expedition to Sudan to learn more about the beast.

FIELD NOTES

1st September; Malakal, Southern Sudan
A seemingly endless drive following the course of the White Nile has brought us to Malakal, the gateway to the Sudd.

Catoblepas footprint near Fangak.

It's now late in the dry season and the temperature is often unbearable. The swamps are at their lowest ebb, but also their most accessible. As the surrounding plains and savannah dry out, animals draw closer to the wetlands, giving a high concentration of wildlife and providing a bonanza for carnivorous swamp dwellers.

*The f...
mask an...
perfume spr...
were essential t...
combat the sm...*

4th September; Fangak, As-Sudd, S. Sudan
We have penetrated the swamp. Fangak is small and smelly, but the people here tell me that the stench of the catoblepas is far worse. Most of them refuse to even talk about it, but one young man says he will lead us to his uncle's village deep in the swamp, where he says the 'old ones' will take us to the catoblepas.

6th September; South of Fangak
Two days of poling through increasingly impassable papyrus grass has brought us to a tiny, abandoned hamlet of crude huts raised on stilts. No-one can be seen, but there is an indescribable odour hanging on the air. It is very faint but extremely nauseating, and we can none of us keep down our food. Scouting the area has revealed nothing except some deep prints in the mud around the village. I have identified them as hippo prints, but the young native, whose name is Jubal, simply shook his head despairingly. Ahmed took a cast of one of the prints.

7th September; South of Fangak
Jubal has been disturbed since we left his uncle's village, but today he led us to a remarkable discovery. On an largish patch of dry land was a half-ruined building - remarkably it was built of stone. I recognised the architecture as New Kingdom Pharaonic, which would make it at least 3000 years old. The remains of two pylons and a shattered obelisk suggested that it may have been a temple.

Jubal reverently led us to a small pile of stones in one corner of the ruin, muttering about the 'old ones' under his breath. I have surmised that these old ones are ancient Egyptians who penetrated far down the course of the Nile, and

The Jonglei Canal in Sudan is a prime example. It cuts through the Sudd, linking the Bahr al-Jabal directly with the White Nile, and helping to reclaim millions of hectares of marshland for cotton farming.

The papyrus scroll (below) was found among papyrus reeds.

SKETCH MADE BY ANGUS MATHESON AFTER HIS RETURN.

transported stones here to build a shrine. From under the stones Jubal drew forth a scrap of ancient papyrus, its colours still astonishingly vivid. I suspect that acid soil and anaerobic conditions may have helped to preserve it.

The scrap shows Egyptian warriors attacking a hippo-like creature whose front portions are not visible. There are also some hieroglyphs - perhaps one of the other Egyptologists at the Society will be able to decipher it.

8th September; South of Fangak
This morning we were startled by a sudden onslaught of wildlife. Birds, antelope and even snakes rushed past us on either side. Jubal shifted uncomfortably and sniffed the air, but a strong breeze was blowing at our backs.

A little further on we saw a carcass - a dead hippo. Suddenly our senses were assaulted by an absolutely appalling stench, and there was a rustling in the reeds to our right. Emerging from the swamp was a large, heavy-bodied creature, its skin covered in boils and sores. It had a muscular, snaky tail and an equally sinuous neck. Its head trailed in the mud, but I could see that it was lumpy and disfigured. Slowly, ponderously, the creature raised its ugly head. We watched in horrified fascination, but at the last moment Jubal screamed and leapt between us and the

monster, blocking our view. It started, turned and ran, leaving Jubal lying face-down in the mud. The poor man was stone-cold dead, his face twisted into a rictus of horror and disgust.

Even now, several hours later, I cannot bring myself to attempt a sketch of the abomination. Let the farmers drain the swamp! I will not shed a tear.

SUPPLEMENTARY NOTES AND RESEARCH
The papyrus was successfully deciphered. Apparently the gaze of the catoblepas was fatal even to its own kind, so mating was a hurried affair, undertaken at night with the male approaching from the rear. The papyrus says that 'even the mother beast cannot bear the sight of her children, and abandons them at birth.'

Angus Matheson left the CSL after this expedition, citing 'personal reasons'. He retired to a rest home on the Firth of Clyde, where he is making good progress.

CATOBLEPAS TUSKS SENT TO THE CSL FROM YAOUNDE, CAMEROON.

Amemait

LATIN NAME
*Archomam-
malia
crocopotamus*

HABITAT
River

LIFESPAN
Up to 100 years

SIZE
*Up to 30 ft
(9 m) long*

**INFORMATION
SOURCE**
CSL Review

DISTRIBUTION
Lower Nile

👉 *A SCENE
FROM A 12TH-
CENTURY BCE
BOOK OF THE
DEAD SHOWS
WHAT APPEARS TO
BE AN AMEMAIT
ON THE FAR
RIGHT.*

DEATH IN THE NILE

This hybrid combines the ferocity and strength of the lion and the crocodile with the bulk and temperament of the hippopotamus.

MANY PEOPLE ARE KILLED ON THE NILE each year, and most of the deaths are attributed to hippos and crocodiles. Lurking in the vast reed beds and muddy bottoms of the Lower Nile, however, is a far deadlier predator. The amemait has been largely forgotten by the world at large, but the Egyptians know it well and fear it more than any hippo or crocodile. It has the massive, smooth-skinned torso of a hippo, with a long reptilian tail. It also has the legs, claws, mane and head of a lion, although its jaws are long and narrow, and full of sharp teeth, like a crocodile's.

MUD, GLORIOUS MUD

The habits and lifecycle of the amemait resemble those of both the crocodile and the hippo. It spends most of the day sleeping near the river bank, but it generally stays under cover of tall reeds or thick, cooling mud. It hunts mainly by waiting for unwary prey to come to the river to drink, grabbing them by the throats and dragging them into the river. Amemaits have been known to attack baby hippos, catch water birds and even capsize boats to prey on the humans within.

Amemaits tend to live in small groups, with a single male and three or four females with their young. In the pre-mating season, males fight for dominance of these mini-harems. Their savage contests make the Nile boil and churn, and humans are generally advised to keep out of the way at this time of year.

Amemaits are expert at blending in with their riverine habitats. Their muddy green and brown hides and frond-like manes camouflage them perfectly, so that when they strike, they have the advantage of total surprise.

GOD'S FEARSOME INSTRUMENT

The banks of the Nile have probably been settled for the whole history of human civilisation. Over the millenia, river dwellers have become attuned to the Nile's rhythms and ways of their habitat, and they are fully aware of the dangers posed by the wild animals that share their world. The power of the amemait to strike fear into the hearts of men impressed the authors of the medieval bestiaries, who used it as a symbol of retribution, an instrument of God's wrath on the sinner.

This power is also known in Asia. The Indian *makara* and *kalamakara* are also hybrids of various reptiles and mammals, including, in some of their many manifestations, the crocodile.

👆 *AS TODAY'S NILE-DWELLERS
KNOW ONLY TOO WELL,
THE AMEMAIT IS A
TERRIFYING MIX OF
HUMANITY'S
MOST DEADLY
NATURAL
ENEMIES.*

SUBMITTED BY
MARTINE LEMAITRE
LOCATION
CONGO
DATE
23/5/98
CATALOGUE №
CZWM 54#2
LONDON

THE CRYPTOZOOLOGICAL SOCIETY OF LONDON

HYBRIDS

Winged Monkey

LATIN NAME
Pan chiroptodytes

HABITAT
Rainforests and jungles

LIFESPAN
20–30 years

SIZE
c. 4 ft (1.2 m) tall

INFORMATION SOURCE
Field Report

DISTRIBUTION
Africa, India

BACKGROUND INFORMATION

Forests and jungles from West Africa to Northern India resound to the raucous calls of the winged monkey, an animal which is, in fact, a species of chimpanzee. Only one such species is known, and the following observations summarizing two years' observation of the monkeys and great apes of the Congo, were sent to the CSL by the renowned monkey behaviorist Martine Lemaitre.

FIELD NOTES

In many respects the winged chimpanzee is identical to its conventional cousin. It follows similar patterns of troop hierarchy, matriarchal family structure and promiscuous mating, as well as having similar social interactions, grooming habits and facial expressions. As with chimpanzees, males leave their group as young adults to allow 'foreign' males to take their places. Females stay put.

The main differences arise from the aerial capacity of Pan chiroptodytes, so named because their wings resemble those of the bats – the Chiroptera. For instance, while the chimpanzee's tastes range far and wide, it sticks mainly to shoots, leaves and grubs. The winged monkey enriches its diet withflying insects, small birds and bats which it catches on the wing, some carrion and small terrestrial animals such as frogs and mice.

When threatened or endangered, winged monkeys take to the air, flying in close formation if attacked by airborne predators. They like to taunt their assailants, staying just out of reach. Although the wings are not suited to high-speed or sustained flights, they do enable winged chimps to flit through the tangled upper branches of the rainforest, and swoop down on their prey.

At night the chimps wrap themselves in their own wings.

The wings are made of a leathery membrane.

Gliding from tree to tree.

Bony struts spring from the flying chimp's arms.

REMAINS OF CHIMP DIET COLLECTED IN THE JUNGLE.

Kappa

LATIN NAME
Circopithechelonia crurorana

HABITAT
Rivers, ponds, streams, pools

LIFESPAN
Up to 100 years

SIZE
Equivalent to small monkey; c. 1 ft (30 cm) long

INFORMATION SOURCE
Field Report

DISTRIBUTION
Japan

In fact, the kappa is so strong that it can drag both a horse and its rider under the surface.

BACKGROUND INFORMATION

The kappa is a peculiar hybrid: a monkey with a tortoise's shell and frog's legs that lives in the streams, lakes and ponds of Japan. It is an evil little creature, a murderous bloodsucker of supernatural strength that drowns and devours humans. But it also has some peculiarly Japanese characteristics: for example, it has impeccable manners.

I first heard of the kappa when I was posted to Japan as a British adviser to the occupying American forces. At the time I was sceptical, but since becoming involved with the CSL I have revised my opinions. Perhaps the persistent and popular folk tales about the kappa are based on reality. I intend to find out by visiting my friends Muneaki and Yuko Matsuda who live next to a National Park near Nikko, in Tochigi Prefecture.

FIELD NOTES

30th April. Nikko

Muneaki and Yuko have given me a warm welcome and promised to guide me to the most likely spots in the Park. We spent yesterday evening discussing 'river-children', as they call kappa – where they can be found; their

THE GROOVED TONGUE IS DESIGNED TO CHANNEL BLOOD TO THE KAPPA'S GULLET.

strengths and weaknesses. Apparently they have a shallow depression in the tops of their heads which is filled with a watery liquid. Without the liquid, they are helpless and harmless.

There was a time when you could find a kappa in any stream or river where the flow slackens or widens to give a pool or pond. Today, industrial pollution has restricted them to National Park areas, and Muneaki knows a few likely spots.

1st May. Kegon Ryokan, Nikko National Park

We spent the day scouting the waterways that flow from the foot of the 300-ft (91-m) high Kegon Falls. There are many placid pools where a kappa might lurk, waiting to pull a victim into the water with its superhuman strength. Once they are drowned the kappa can suck out their blood at leisure.

One way of avoiding this is to exploit the creature's fondness for cucumbers, which

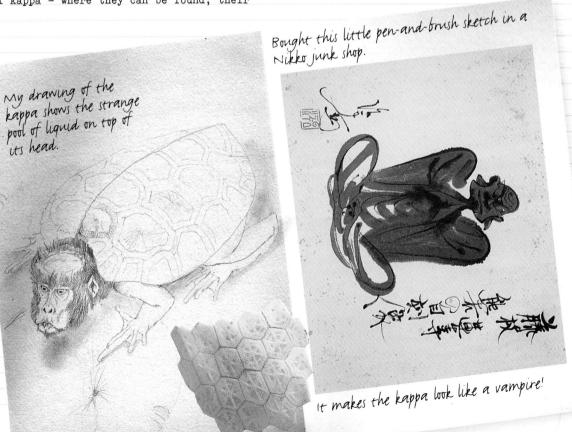

My drawing of the kappa shows the strange pool of liquid on top of its head.

Bought this little pen-and-brush sketch in a Nikko junk shop.

It makes the kappa look like a vampire!

POSTCARDS OF THE KEGON FALLS (LEFT) AND OF SUNSET OVER CHUZENJI LAKE.

it prefers to the taste of human flesh. If the names and ages of family members are inscribed on the fruit, they will be safe from the grateful kappa as long as it lives. Muneaki has brought along a good supply of cucumbers, each inscribed with the names and ages of himself, his wife and their children Munetoshi and Chikako.

The other way to defeat a kappa is to bow to it. Its extreme good manners mean that it will always bow in return, spilling the liquid from its head. Until it can refill the bowl, it will be utterly powerless. The nature of this liquid intrigues me - I hope to get a sample for analysis.

2nd May. Utagahama Ryokan, Nikko National Park

As we wandered around the beautiful Chuzenji Lake, peering into the shallow coves and creeks which fringe it, Muneaki and I became separated. No sooner had I noticed his absence than I heard a child-like voice calling to me from nearby. It pleaded with me to 'come and play pull-finger' - a simple game where you link fingers and try to break the other's grip.

Looking across the lake, I saw a monkey's face sticking out of the water and peering up at me. On the top of its head was a shallow indentation fringed with spiky red hair and filled with liquid. The creature had a tortoise's shell and yellowish-green frog's legs - Muneaki had the camera, but I made a sketch later on.
The kappa repeated its request, and then, alarmingly, sprang out of the water on to a floating lily pad and eyed me. Nervously I backed off, and then, remembering what

Muneaki had told me, I bowed politely to it. A flash of rage passed across its face, but it solemnly returned my bow. As it did so, the liquid on its head ran out onto the lily pad, and the kappa crumpled, sliding help-lessly into the water. Thinking quickly I leant over from the bank and scooped a few drops of the spilled liquid into a glass vial, and then beat a hasty retreat.

3rd May. Nikko
Muneaki tells me I had a lucky escape, and warns that the kappa is sure to be on its guard. Although they are very honourable and always keep their word, kappa can also har-bour a grudge, so he feels it would be best for us to cease our investigations. Tomorrow we leave for Osaka, to visit his aunt Ayako.

SUPPLEMENTARY REPORT
There was great excitement on my return to London with the physical evidence. I sent the vial of kappa liquid to the Naval research base at Portsmouth, but the results were disappointing - it appears to be nothing more than water. Obviously the supernatural powers are a property of the kappa, and not of the liquid in its head.

OTHER JAPANESE CREATURES INCLUDE BAKU P. 108 AND TENGU P. 131.

Dick,
Had that sample analysed as requested:

Mg/l: Na 3, K 0.5, Ca 3.5, Mg 1.3, Cl 5, SO4 6.5, NO3 1.9, HCO3 11, SiO2 7, pH 5.8

Basically old man, it's water.
Is this some sort of joke?
Anyway, chin up, you old leg-puller,
and don't let the buggers get
you down.

BTR 174.2
KAPPA TONGUE.

HYBRIDS

Baku

LATIN NAME
Taurelephans tigris

HABITAT
Marshy areas around human settlements

LIFESPAN
Unknown

SIZE
Large – size of a rhino or small elephant

INFORMATION SOURCE
Letter

DISTRIBUTION
Far East, mainly Japan

□□□-□□

The Cryptozoological
Society of London
100 Piccadilly

Richard Ogilvy, RN (retd.)
Osaka
Japan

10th May, 1960

Dear Fellows of the CSL,

Following the abrupt end to my field study in Nikko I have come to Osaka with my friend Muneaki to visit his aunt Ayako. A long time student of folklore, Ayako is a treasure trove of information on Japanese cryptozoologica. One beast I find particularly intriguing is the baku, a strange and little-understood beast given to haunting isolated rural settlements. Its overall form is somewhat nebulous, but the most striking features are an elephantine trunk, an ox's tail and a tiger's feet. I have drawn a quick sketch based on her description.

Despite its size and fierce appearance, the baku is a shy creature which goes to great lengths to avoid being seen. However, it needs to live close to human habitations. This is because it derives its sustenance from a most unusual source – negative psychic energy from the minds of troubled humans, particularly those suffering bad dreams or nightmares. At night, the baku emerges from its marshy home and roams the fringes of the nearest human village or hamlet, using its trunk to somehow harvest this negative energy. A few brave individuals occasionally venture near large towns or cities, where there is plenty of such food.

Paradoxically the Japanese regard the appearance of the baku as a good omen, especially when it appears at times of plague. It occurs to me that the concentration of negative psychic energy engendered by a plague might drive the baku into a sort of feeding frenzy, so that they become careless and allow themselves to be seen. If sightings coincide with the peak of a plague, then their appearance would signal the beginings of recovery. (It's a bit tenuous I know, but I can't think of any other explanation.)

I was all fired up to go hunting for baku, but Ayako tells me that it would be a wild-goose chase. These creatures are too timid to let themselves be seen, and are excellent at avoiding human contact. Still, I thought that the Society might be interested in knowing these few titbits.

You can expect my field report on the kappa when I return.

Best wishes from Japan,

Richard Ogilvy

Richard Ogilvy

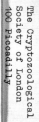

A feeding baku stretches out its trunk to suck in bad dreams and human misery.

This must be the only creature that is sustained by negative psychic energy.

Ayako assures me that this is actually quite a good sketch of this strange elephantine beast.

FROM THE CSL MUSEUM: A FINE BAKU TOOTH, FROM VLADIVOSTOCK.

Section 6

MANIMALS

Just because manimals – strange mixtures of
man and beast – haunt our collective
imagination does not mean they do not exist.
Some, like satyrs, fauns and centaurs, are either
extinct or nearly so. Others, like mermaids and
werewolves, still roam the Earth and seas, and
continue to pose a real danger to humans. The
Cryptozoological Society is particularly
interested in how manimals came into
existence. One school of thought argues that
manimals are one-off mutations; another theory
is that they are offshoots of mainstream
evolution. A third possibility is that they are
artificial hybrids, created by long-lost ancient
methods unknown to modern science.

Basic principles of cryptozoology explained in simple terms for schools, colleges and new readers. Created by the Education Department of the Cryptozoological Society of London.

Manimals

Creatures which combine human and animal forms in one body are technically known as semihominid hybrids. A simpler and more popular term is manimals.

In *Inside Cryptozoology No. 5* we explored the world of hybrids. One variety of hybrid, the union of humans and animals commonly called manimals, is currently an important area of study for cryptozoologists. The reason is that many aspects of manimal biology, not least the genetic basis of cross-breeding between humans and other species, continue to defy explanation.

Recent work has thrown some light onto the biology of manimals.

Cryptozoologists separate manimals into two broad classes: fully integrated and chimaeric. In integrated hybrids, such as the gorgon, *tengu* and werewolf, the genetic material of the constituent animals has become completely mixed. In chimaeric hybrids, the genetic material of the constituent animals has remained separate, giving the characteristic 'bolted together' appearance of, for example, the centaur and the mermaid (see Fig 1).

FIG 1 CHIMAERIC HYBRIDS

These creatures have two different kinds of cells, each of which have the pure characteristics of the component animals (see diagram adjoined). In a mermaid, for example, fish cells and human cells interface at waist level. A mechanism that is not fully understood, but is the subject of intense study, ensures that the two types of cell mesh together instead of rejecting each other. The Greeks believed that the legendary sorceress Circe (depicted left) used witchcraft to change men into beasts. It is now thought that she was an early biological engineer with a talent for creating chimaerae.

G. Doré

Integrated hybrids

Where a manimal looks and behaves like a new creature (while retaining identifiable traits of both man and animal), genetic material has somehow become intermingled (se Fig 2). This process could happen in several ways.

One area of investigation is in the way DNA, the molecule that stores genetic information, replicates and transcribes its sequences into RNA molecules, which then determine what kind of protein is formed. Errors in transcribing this DNA happen in nature, and it is possible that such an error might introduce genetic material from another species.

Some cryptozoologists are searching for viruses or bacteria that could act as natural 'molecular scissors', creating enzymes that splice sections of DNA together. The use of such gene-splicing enzymes is an established part of the recombinant DNA technology that produces genetically-engineered plants and laboratory animals.

Chimaeric hybrids

The term 'chimaera', derived from the lion-goat-monster of the same name, has been adopted by scientists to mean an organism containing two or more groups of cells with completely different genomes – the genetic materials that govern the appearance and other characteristics of an organism.

Modern biologists have created some simple chimaeras by grafting foreign cells onto embryo animals. For instance, adding some goat cells to a sheep embryo created a sheep with a patch of skin on its back which is composed of goat cells. The goat part of the creature remained separate from the sheep part, and the respective genomes of each organism remained discrete.

The chimaeric hybrids in cryptozoology are far more complicated. Entire body sections are replications of parts of different creatures. The front part of the centaur appears to be composed of cells which have human DNA, while the back half has the DNA of a horse.

This phenomenon is unknown in nature, and the real mystery is how such a remarkable situation arose in the first place. Human agency seems to be the only rational explanation, and there are some wild speculations as to who might be responsible. The suspects include Atlanteans, Hidden Masters in Tibet and visitors from outer space. Whoever they were, they had scientific capabilities superior to ours. Chimaeric hybrids themselves fall into two classes: creatures with human heads (e.g. harpies, sirens, mermaids, centaurs, lamassu, satyrs, sphinxes and lamiae); and creatures with the heads of animals and the bodies of humans (e.g. minotaurs and cynocephali). The latter might be expected to possess the brains and therefore the intelligence of animals, but the evidence is that they are much cleverer than this. Equally, many of the human-headed manimals display a fierce and bestial nature despite their humanoid brains.

The Greek manimal explosion

Manimal creatures are known to practically every culture, from the dog-headed men of India to the *tengu* of Japan. However, many of these beasts are familiar from Classical legend, and the Mediterranean region of ancient times seems to have been a particularly fertile breeding ground for these creatures. Special environmental conditions there might have helped to foster such creatures, but a more likely explanation, confirmed by the myths themselves, is that the social and moral attitudes of the time were more tolerant of sexual relations between humans and animals.

MANIMALS

Harpy

LATIN NAME
Gynaves harpa

HABITAT
Mountains

LIFESPAN
Unknown

SIZE
*5 ft (1.5 m)
high; wingspan
7 ft (2 m)*

**INFORMATION
SOURCE**
CSL Review

DISTRIBUTION
*Shores of the
Black Sea*

Of all the half-human creatures the harpy is probably the foulest and most repulsive known to man.

HELL HATH NO FURY...

THESE BIRD-WOMEN ARE EVIL, RAPA-cious, foul-smelling and stricken with unmentionable personal habits. For the ancient Greeks they confirmed all the worst stereotypes of the uncivilised female nature – wanton and unkempt. For the inhabitants of the shores of the Black Sea, they represent a menace to food stores, public health and lone travellers, particularly children.

NOT A PRETTY SIGHT

The harpy is often described as having the body of a bird and only the head and breasts of a woman. But this is probably the result of confusion with the closely related siren (see p.112). In fact the harpy has the breasts, head and forearms of an hideous, hag-like woman, and the wings, body and legs of a vulture. On the end of both its human and avian limbs are cruel talons. A harpy's hair is matted, her skin and feathers filthy and her claws covered in dirt. According to Virgil's description, harpies also suffer from constant diarrhoea, adding to their overpowering stench.

It is this odour that excites most comment. The smell precedes the screeching monsters, warning of their approach, and hangs around them like a miasma. It can cause nausea and retching, and thus functions as a useful weapon, disorienting enemies. Harpies can follow up with a raking pass of their talons. These are sharp enough to be lethal, and any wounds will invariably become rapidly infected, and may even be poisonous.

Usually harpies skulk around in flocks of 20–30 individuals, looking for unattended food stores,

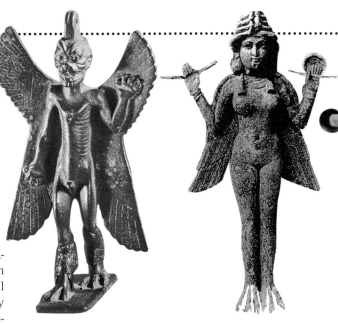

👆 *THE ANCIENT CULTURES OF THE MIDDLE EAST OFTEN ASSOCIATED HARPIES WITH DEMONS. ON THE LEFT IS THE ASSYRIAN WIND DEMON, PAZUZU, AND ON THE RIGHT IS THE SEMITIC DEMON LILITH – IN HEBREW MYTH THE FIRST WOMAN CREATED BY GOD.*

open-air banquets and even picnics. They will resort to scavenging from rubbish dumps when hungry, which is often. Observers from Classical times up to the present have noted their ravenous hunger – the Greeks believed that they were cursed by the gods to starve eternally. The truth is probably rather more prosaic. Flight requires an enormous amount of energy and, in order to maintain the necessary very high metabolic rate, harpies need fuel and plenty of it. Hence their constant hunger.

RIDERS ON THE STORM

Over the centuries harpies have been accorded a number of supernatural abilities (including prophetic powers) and roles. They have been seen as guardians/tormentors of the souls of suicides (in Dante's *Inferno*), or carriers of the spirits of the departed, transporting them to Hades. Homer said they were like the winds who snatch humans away, and they were widely associated with the storm-winds. This was probably due more to their role in many missing persons cases than to any divine provenance. Often cowardly, harpies will attack lone travellers, especially children, and carry them off to be devoured at leisure.

HUMANS AND HARPIES

The most famous documented human/harpy encounter is probably the harpies' battle with Jason and the Argonauts. The Thracian king Phineas was tormented by a flock of harpies who had infested his city, Salmydessus (near the modern Graeco-

✍ *A SAMPLE CULTURED ON A PETRI DISH SHOWS THE RANGE OF TOXIC BACTERIA THAT HARPIES HARBOUR BENEATH THEIR CLAWS, INCLUDING TETANUS AND NECROTISING FASCIITIS.*

Bulgarian border). According to the Ancients this was a punishment from the gods for revealing their secrets to mortal men, but more likely it was a result of poor public hygiene provision in the burgeoning city. The harpies had been stealing food and spreading disease until Jason and his shipload of heroes arrived. They drove off the monstrous bird-women, by strength of arms and skill with the bow, to the Strophades, in the Aegean Sea.

This colony later hounded Aeneas and the Trojans fleeing the fall of Troy, and eventually moved north-eastwards to the shores of the Black Sea. According to Pliny, they were sighted as far east as India by Clitarchus, a companion of Alexander the Great (c.340 BCE). Today the 'snatchers' (the literal translation of harpy) can only be found in mountainous regions of the former Communist bloc states that fringe the Black Sea, and possibly in parts of Turkey.

HARPIES AROUND THE WORLD

The harpies' relatives include the 'soul-birds' (*bai*) of ancient Egypt (extinct *c*.1300 BCE); the Islamic world's *murgh-i-adami*; the enormous *kura ngaituku* of the Maori, in New Zealand; the man-raping Australian *bagini*; and, closer to home, the Greek *Erinyes* – the Furies. The Norse Valkyrie may have been cousins of the harpy.

☞ *GUSTAVE DORÉ'S ILLUSTRATION FROM DANTE'S INFERNO SHOWS THE HARPIES PERCHED AMONGST THE TREES IN THE GROVE OF SUICIDES. NOTE THAT DORÉ HAS GIVEN THEM THE FORM OF SIRENS, A MISTAKE MADE BY ARTISTS SINCE ANCIENT TIMES.*

Their arms are scaly – almost reptilian.

Harpies glide a lot – possibly to conserve energy.

Harpies seem to prefer scavenging to actually hunting – This dominant female is claiming a carcass.

Individuals can be identified by ear shape.

Calculations suggest that harpies eat nearly half their own weight every day.

Sirens

LATIN NAME
*Gynaves
cantatrix*

HABITAT
*Meadows by
rocky shores*

LIFESPAN
Unknown

SIZE
6 ft (2 m) high

INFORMATION
SOURCE
CSL Review

DISTRIBUTION
*Tyrrhenian Sea
(West coast
of Italy)*

The scourge of Mediterranean sailors for centuries, if not millennia, the Sirens' beautiful and enticing song belies their evil nature.

"KILLING ME SOFTLY..."

I N 3000 YEARS OF RECORDED HISTORY the Sirens have been foiled only twice. Both Odysseus and the Argonauts escaped their clutches, but countless seamen have not been so lucky. Perhaps the real tragedy is that a few simple precautions can protect against their fatal lure.

SINGING FOR THEIR SUPPER

Each Siren has the head of a beautiful woman on the body of an eagle. Unlike the harpy she has no arms, breasts or other human characteristics. For the purposes of attack she relies on her sharp talons and her song (see below).

Sirens live in small colonies of between three and eight females. None of the sources ever refer to male Sirens, and it is perhaps this lack of male company that drives the Sirens' thirst for the blood of human men (although it may simply be that most sailors are men). The absence of males raises obvious questions about reproduction, and about the lifecycle of the Siren. For instance, their longevity is an unknown quantity. The ancient Greek sources span a number of centuries, but they all seem to refer to the same group of creatures, so it may be that Sirens are very long-lived.

Generally, Sirens favour small, rocky islands, well-equipped with reefs and shoals which can break up any ships that they attract. Once the half-drowned mariners wash up on shore they are attacked. There is a lack of consensus about exactly how the Sirens dispose of their prey (probably because few survive to tell the tale) but

🖎 *THIS ARTIST'S DEPICTION IS COMPILED FROM THE LIMITED FIRST-HAND SOURCES AVAILABLE. NOTE THE SIMILARITIES AND DIFFERENCES BETWEEN THE SIREN AND HER CLOSE RELATIVE, THE HARPY (SEE P. 112). PLUMAGE IS BELIEVED TO VARY WIDELY BETWEEN INDIVIDUALS.*

reports talk of island meadows strewn with bones and other ghastly debris.

SIREN SONG

The most prominent feature of the Sirens is their song. It is so irresistibly enticing that it has lured thousands of men to their deaths over the centuries, and it has entered our language as the epitome of fatal seductivity. The essential question, then, is: what does it sound like?

For obvious reasons, this information is hard to come by, but we can piece together an idea from a variety of ancient sources. Pindar said that the voices of the Sirens sound like flutes, and Francis Bacon, in *Wisdom of the Ancients*, argued that the power of the song derives from its complexity and intricate melodies. Both Homer and Cicero suggest that the attractiveness of the song lies in the knowledge which it offers – most writers would claim this meant carnal knowledge: the promise of exotic delights and unearthly pleasure. There is even an intriguing claim that the song was accompanied by instruments – Servius says that one of the Sirens played the pipes and one the lyre – but this would have been difficult given that Sirens do not have arms.

The ancient Greeks also attributed the gift of prophecy to the Sirens' song (similar claims were made for the closely related harpies).

GREEK TRAGEDIES

Most of our knowledge about the Sirens comes from ancient Greek sources. They are most famous for their role in the adventures of Odysseus and, later, the Argonauts. It seems certain that Greek legends mainly refer to one particularly notorious colony of Sirens, who dwelt off the coast of Italy, possibly on the Isle of Capri or somewhere between Italy and Sicily. They were said to be the offspring of one of the Muses (either Terpsichore or Melpomene) and the river god Achelous, and obtained their

☞ THIS DETAIL OF AN ATTIC RED-FIGURE STAMNOS FROM VULCI, C.450 BCE, SHOWS A SIREN – DISTRAUGHT BY ODYSSEUS' ESCAPE (HE IS TIED TO HIS MAST AT LEFT) – COMMITTING SUICIDE BY LEAPING FROM HER PERCH.

Devil and figured in medieval bestiaries, although there was a great deal of confusion between Sirens and mermaids, leading some experts to posit a link between the two. The most recent recorded sighting is that of a Mr Toupin of Exmouth, who, in 1812, saw a "mermaid" with "short, round feathers", who sang "wild melodies" – almost certainly a Siren. Why Mr Toupin was immune to her charms is not clear.

If Sirens still exist today they keep a low profile – a sensible adaptation in a world where would-be enemies no longer have to come within hearing range to attack. They probably hide on uninhabited islets off the coast of Italy, lying in wait for lone sailors and fishermen. There is evidence for this, because some 36 mariners still vanish without trace in the Mediterranean every year.

THE HARPY CONNECTION

The Siren is a close relative of the harpy, though with better hygiene. The Russian *rusalski* could be a rare northern variety of Siren. Reports speak of a water-dwelling female creature who lures men to their graves through song.

☞ THE 17TH-CENTURY BOOK, JOHNSTONE'S BIRDS, GIVES A FAIRLY ACCURATE PORTRAYAL OF A SIREN, BUT MISTAKENLY IDENTIFIES IT AS A HARPY. WRITERS AND ARTISTS HAVE OFTEN USED THE TERMS SIREN, HARPY AND MERMAID INTERCHANGEABLY. CRYPTO-ZOOLOGISTS SHOULD BE ON THEIR GUARD.

hybrid form after losing a singing competition with the Muses. A different legend has them as companions of Persephone, the Greek goddess of Spring who was carried off by Hades. In their grief the Sirens grew wings to search for her.

Whatever their origin, by the time of Odysseus Sirens had become a menace to the shipping lines of the Western Mediterranean. Forewarned by Circe, Odysseus was able to take the simple precaution of plugging the ears of his crew with wax. (More up-to-date protection can be provided by a set of headphones or ear-muffs.)

When the Argonauts passed by some years later, they were caught unawares and lost their youngest crew-member, Butes, before Orpheus drowned out the Sirens' song with a more attractive tune of his own. According to some accounts the Sirens were so depressed at this humiliation that they committed suicide. Obviously the Sirens are highly strung creatures, because ancient Greek art shows them having the same reaction to Odysseus.

In Christian times the Siren was an allegory for the temptations of the

☞ THE SIRENS ATTEMPT TO LURE ODYSSEUS TO A WATERY GRAVE. HERE THE SIRENS ARE DEPICTED AS MERMAIDS ALTHOUGH STILL POSSESSING WINGS.

Les Serenes en moftres.

ODYSSEUS AND THE CYCLOPS

by Nicholas Harris, MCSL

ODYSSEUS

Odysseus, 'the most cunning of men', played many roles in his long and active life. One of the Greeks' greatest generals, a wily leader, he was also, however, an unlucky traveller. During the years of his sea voyage home from Troy to Ithaca, recorded in Homer's epic, The Odyssey, he and his crew were exposed to many different perils. Along the way, however, he had the chance to observe at first hand perhaps more cryptozoological phenomena than many investigators. His pioneering experience of the Sirens' normally fatal arias, for example, must rank as one of the earliest and most courageous cryptozoological field investigations.

ODYSSEUS' TRAVELS

His translation of *The Odyssey* (1904) was the last work of Lord Harris of Marbourne, former President of the Royal Academy and Secretary of the CSL 1884-1890. Lord Harris, whose great-grandson, Nicholas, has carried out many commissions for the Society in recent years, died in 1905 of syphilis.

Modelling himself after Richard Burton, the great Arabist and fellow translator, Harris was renowned as one of the most profligate rakes of his generation. He won international notoriety for his part in the Affair of the Nepalese Jewel Maidens. On his release from prison he famously announced that he would rather 'bed down with the Queen Mother than spend one night sober'. The notes which follow are drawn from the Harris *Odyssey*.

1 THE TROJAN HORSE

Odysseus, King of Ithaca, served with the Greek army that for over a decade besieged Troy. He broke the deadlock with a clever ruse: the Trojan Horse – a gigantic hollow statue filled with Greek soldiers that the Trojans mistook for an offering to the goddess Athena. The siege over, Odysseus set sail for Ithaca with a fleet of twelve ships.

2 THE ISLAND OF THE LOTUS EATERS

Blown off course to a mysterious island, Odysseus' men ate the fruit of the lotus, which caused them to sink into a torpor. He managed to rouse them, and they continued on their way.

3 POLYPHEMUS THE CYCLOPS

On their next landfall, Odysseus and his men took shelter in a cave, which proved to be the home of a cannibalistic one-eyed giant, the cyclops Polyphemus. The monster ate some of Odysseus' crew and shut the remainder in the cave. Odysseus then succeeded in blinding him with a heated stake and the survivors slipped past the enraged giant by hanging from the bellies of his sheep.

4 AEOLUS AND THE BAG OF WINDS

Aeolus was the God of Winds and aided Odysseus by confining contrary winds in a magical bag. When Odysseus' sailors foolishly opened the bag the fleet was blown hundreds of miles off course.

5 THE LAESTRYGONES

Blown far to the north, the fleet passed Telepylus, home of the Laestrygones – a group of fearsome cannibalistic giants. Like their cousins throughout the world, these giants enjoyed tossing huge boulders, as Odysseus' fleet learned to its dismay. The angry giants managed to sink eleven ships before the remaining one escaped.

interests of cryptozoological experimentation, to expose himself to the Sirens' song. While the crew had their ears filled with wax, Odysseus was tied to the mast. As the ship passed the island of the Sirens the evil bird-women struck up their compelling tune, and Odysseus began to struggle with his bonds and rage at the crew to set him loose. But they rowed on obliviously, and soon passed beyond range of the Sirens, who were so upset, according to some sources, that they committed suicide.

8 SCYLLA AND CHARYBDIS

Charybdis is a treacherous whirlpool on one side of the Straits of Messina. Opposite lurked the monster Scylla, depicted in ancient art with six heads and a ring of barking dogs around her belly. In practice, Scylla was probably a rare Mediterranean specimen of a giant octopus (see p. 20) that was threatening shipping in the area. Odysseus success-fully steered clear of Charybdis but Scylla devoured six of his crewmen, for which dire crime she was subsequently turned into a rock.

6 CIRCE THE ENCHANTRESS

On the next island the travellers encountered an enchantress who transformed Odysseus' men into pigs, and in some versions a host of other animals. The trans-formations described are reminiscent of those undergone by were-beings, suggesting that Homer's 'enchantress' was actually infecting the sailors with a virus along the lines of the Lyc-V virus which is thought to cause lycan-thropy (see pp. 146–147). In the story Odysseus forces Circe to undo the sorcery, which suggests that in ancient times, at least, there was a cure for Lyc-V infection.

7 THE SIRENS

Forewarned of the dangers of the Sirens, Odysseus prepared his crew for the encounter but decided, in the

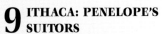

9 ITHACA: PENELOPE'S SUITORS

On his eventual return home, Odysseus faced problems of a more human kind, namely a large band of suitors for his wife Penelope. With his usual cunning, he invited them all to a banquet. As part of the enter-tainment the guests were invited to string a special bow. None succeeded, so Odysseus showed them how, rounding off the celebra-tions by using them all for target practice. As Homer says, 'There are no free lunches in Ithaca'.

MANIMALS

Mermaids

LATIN NAME
Pischomina nympha

HABITAT
Mainly coastal waters

LIFESPAN
75–150 years

SIZE
*4½–5½ ft
(1.3–1.6 m)*

INFORMATION SOURCE
Field Report submitted by Dr P. Beardmore

DISTRIBUTION
Oceans and seas of the world

Archive notes

Mermaids (and mermen) have perplexed and beguiled their landbound cousins for millennia, and even today what we know of them is an uneasy mix of folklore and fact, superstition and science. Few of the creatures that we study at the CSL have been so often sighted, and even fewer are represented by specimens in the collections of major museums, yet we lack the answers to basic questions about biology, inter-species compatibility and sociocultural practices. The mermaid – beautiful, alluring human above the waist, silvery-scaled fish below – calls out from her ocean home, taunting us with her mastery of the seas, and tempting us with the promise of erotic and material pleasures. In days gone by she was feared and respected – what can we learn from her ilk today?

   The CSL has sponsored a number of expeditions in search of mermaids, as well as extensive research and the collation of a mass of sightings and reports. Here we have reproduced the original field report of one such expedition.

**100 PICCADILLY
LONDON W1**

Field Report No
CZMm 14#6

Date
2nd–22nd April, 1957

Archivist
Joel Levy

Signature
Joel Levy

6th March, 1957
Eric de Bisschop, Port Moresby

Cher Johnathan,
An amusing card, non? One of my crew picked it up in Aden—they have the dugong making the masquerade comme une sirène. Mais ca c'est rien - in January we are three days out of Vanuatu when Jacques is seeing the real thing! When he went near it, it began to glow, comme une feu diabolique!
Then it leapt from the boat, and there was n...
q'une ...
seawe...
hair ...
incro...
immed...

Natur...
thoug...
fello...
Now e...
kind ...
Alors...
ce qu...
Parce...
Faste...
than ...
Au re...

" SOUVENIR "

Mermaid, Sirenian, Manatus ADEN

BACKGROUND NOTES
In March of this year the CSL received a report from the South Pacific, which has set my colleagues abuzz with excitement. Captain Eric de Bisschop writes that, on the 3rd of January, a member of his crew saw a mermaid on the deck of the ship. It had seaweed for hair, and began to glow when approached. It then leapt over the side, leaving only a fishy odour. This is believed to be the first well-attested sighting for some years, and has caused us to re-open our mermaid files. I have been set the task of launching a new expedition. A trip to the South Pacific being somewhat beyond our resources, I have resolved to begin closer to home - at the British Museum in Bloomsbury.

FIELD REPORT
2nd April: The collection at the British Museum includes a fascinating mermaid specimen of the kind sometimes mistakenly termed a 'Jenny Hanniver' (true Jenny Hannivers are skate or rays which have been altered to look like dragons or strange sea monsters). Accepted scientific wisdom dismisses these as fakes, made by stitching together the top half of a monkey with the lower portion of a fish. Closer study by an expert cryptozoologist (myself) revealed the specimen to be genuine! Although desiccated and wizened it was clearly the body of a young Pischomina nympha, a 'mer-child'. This particular specimen was caught off the coast

of Japan in the 18th century, and later presented to HRH Prince Arthur of Connaught. There have been a number of sightings of live juveniles in the wild – most notably a 3 ft (1 m) long mermaid seen off the Hebrides in 1830. It was said to be the size of a 4 year-old, but with 'an abnormally developed breast'. Most mermaid sightings in British waters have occurred off the Scottish, Welsh or Cornish coasts, particularly near islands. I intend to take the Flying Scotsman north, and investigate the Western Isles for myself.

4th April: I reached Edinburgh last night, and have spent the day at the Royal Scottish Museum, examining their extensive collection of preserved mermaids. Why are the only specimens in human possession those of juveniles? My research indicates that adult mermaids have been captured several times. The Speculum Mundi of John Swan reports that, in 1403, a mermaid was swept through a broken dike in the Dutch town of Haarlem, near Edam. She lived in captivity for some 15 years and was taught to spin wool and kneel in front of a crucifix. She was never heard to speak, and made many attempts to escape (mermaids trapped on land by one means or another always long to return to the sea). Another well-known example is the mermaid of Amboina. She was captured off the coast of Borneo in the early 18th century and kept in a tank of water. She had blue

eyes and webbed hands, squeaked like a mouse and had excrement that resembled a cat's. However, she would not eat any fish, and died after 4 days and 7 hours.
Tomorrow I will travel to Oban, and there take ship for the Hebrides.

6th April: I am now on board the Ceasg, an old mail-packet named after the Highland word for mermaid. Captain McArdles, an old sea-salt if ever there was one, seems to be well versed in mermaid lore. He tells me that the ceasg (pronounced keeask) is considered an ill omen by seafarers. To see one heralds shipwreck and disaster, especially since mermaids have control over storms, and seem to take great pleasure in drowning sailors. At the same time, men cannot help but desire them, and the beauty

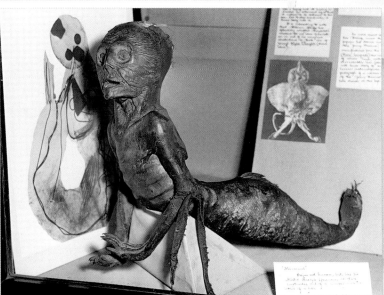

A COMMON MOTIF IN CELTIC FOLK TALES ABOUT MERMAIDS, SELKIES AND ROANES

LEFT IS A SNAPSHOT OF THE JUVENILE Pischomina SPECIMEN FROM THE ROYAL SCOTTISH MUSEUM. COMPARE IT WITH THE SPECIMEN FROM THE BRITISH MUSEUM ABOVE.

Mermaids

ACTUALLY, DATES VARY FOR THIS SIGHTING – ACCORDING TO ONE ACCOUNT THE SIGHTING HAPPENED IN 1625, 14 YEARS AFTER HUDSON DIE

and siren song of the mermaid are her best-known features. This immediately raises one of the fundamental issues about mermaids and their relations with humans. There are many tales where mermaids marry human men (and a few where mermen, or tritons, marry human women), and even have children – but given their piscine lower halves, how is this possible? Captain McArdles claims descent from one such union. He says that many generations ago one of his forebears married a ceasg, producing sons gifted with extraordinary maritime skills. I hope there is some substance to his story, since the weather is closing in.

11th April: I have come ashore at the tiny village of Hynish, on Tiree. Several of the villagers claim to have seen mermaids and mermen cavorting amidst the waves or sunning themselves on rocks. The females are described as beautiful and well-endowed, with golden hair. I am curious about this hair – several reports describe mermaid's hair as being more similar to seaweed, and its colour seems to vary with locality. In 1610, Sir Richard Whitburne saw a mermaid with 'blue streaks resembling hair', during his voyage of discovery to Newfoundland; in 1614, Captain John Smith saw a mermaid off

the West Indies with 'long green hair'; while in 1608 members of Henry Hudson's expedition saw a mermaid with long black hair off Nova Zembla. It seems that, as human characteristics vary, so do mermaids'.

The local people have suggested one solution for the problem of inter-species mating. They – in common with most other Celtic lore on mermaids – describe mermaids as shape-shifters, capable of adopting human form, complete with legs (and presumably other organs). Mermaids, with their love of music, are often attracted to village dances, where they can be identified by their long dresses which are always wet at the hems. Communities like Hynish sometimes bartered with mermaids. In return for golden combs and mirrors, the villagers might benefit from the mermaid's powers of weather control and foretelling.

These precognitive powers seem to me be

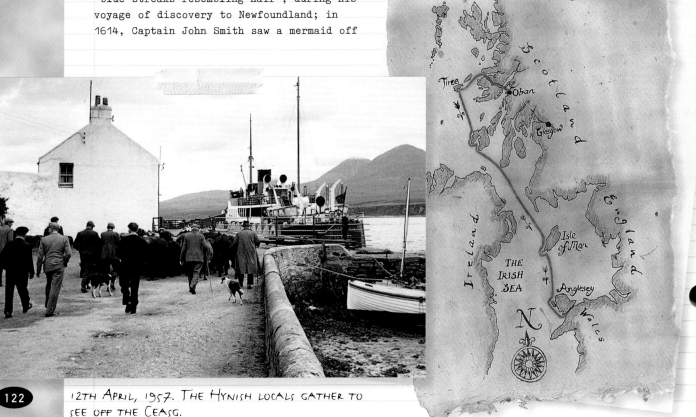

The TY GWYN Hotel
LLANFAIRPWLLGWYNGYLLGOGERYCHWYRNDROBWLLLLANTYSILIOGOGOGOCH
ANGLESEY, North WALES

12TH APRIL, 1957. THE HYNISH LOCALS GATHER TO SEE OFF THE CEASG.

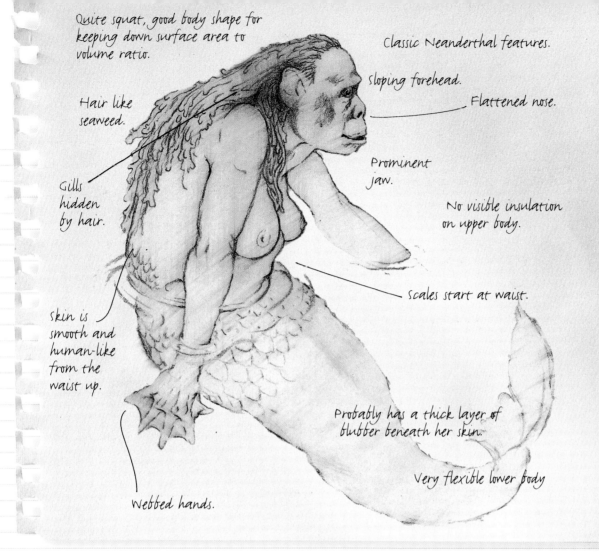

Quite squat, good body shape for keeping down surface area to volume ratio.

Classic Neanderthal features.

Sloping forehead.

Flattened nose.

Hair like seaweed.

Prominent jaw.

No visible insulation on upper body.

Gills hidden by hair.

Scales start at waist.

Skin is smooth and human-like from the waist up.

Probably has a thick layer of blubber beneath her skin.

Very flexible lower body

Webbed hands.

another link between mermaids and Sirens. They both lure sailors to their deaths with erotic enticements, they both have the power to see the future, and they are both said to sing. Some of the earliest reports of mermaids talk of this singing – for instance Pliny, in 77 AD, describes the cantum tristem ('sad song') of a mermaid washed up on the coast of Southern Spain. Perhaps there is an evolutionary link between the two species, with mermaids representing sirens who have taken to an aquatic lifestyle, rather as penguins have taken to the sea. It may be that mermaids are more like penguins than fish.

18th April: Several days sailing south has brought us close to the rocky shores of the Isle of Man, where mermaids are known as ben-varreys. At eight bells the lookout claimed to have heard a strange melody, almost like

Note the resemblance to a monkey, with the heavy brows and muzzle.

singing, off to starboard. Captain McArdles was too canny to change course, and the dawn revealed a wrecker's coast to the East. The crew are relieved at their narrow escape, but I am excited. I have asked the captain to sail back and forth in this area.
4:00PM: I believe I have seen a genuine Pischomina nympha. As I scanned the waves I noticed a flash of gold and then silver off to port. Looking harder I was startled to see an apparently neanderthal face looking back at me. It was crowned with what looked like yellow seaweed, and there was something disturbingly fish-like about its eyes. In all other respects it looked like a primitive woman, but I noticed what might have been gills at the sides of the neck. This would certainly explain how mermaids are able to breathe underwater, and ties in with reports which describe something strange about their ears – some medieval reports speak of ears like those of a bear. The creature raised itself some way out of the

Mermaids

I fished this out of the sea soon after seeing the mermaid. A crewman told me it was a mermaid's purse. This strikes me as singularly odd. Why would a mermaid need a purse? They are said to have fondness for trinkets – perhaps they keep them in handy carriers such as this

ES : 3333769 L 3323019

water, revealing a pair of handsome breasts, and then disappeared beneath the waves with a flash of silvery tail-fin.

21st April: We have put into port near Anglesey, in North Wales, and I have bid farewell to Captain McArdles and the crew of the Ceasg. I am not far from the spot where, in the 6th century, a mermaid was caught and baptised. She subsequently became St Murgen, which would certainly indicate a degree of assimilation with her human captors. Tales like this seem to contradict the reports about the mermaids of Haarlem and Amboina, Those suggest a low level of intelligence, placing mermaids at the intellectual level of an ape. Certainly all the specimens held by museums more closely resemble monkeys than humans, and my own sighting bears this out. So does the sighting of a more illustrious seaman than myself – Columbus. He reported seeing three mermaids (he called them serenas) off the coast of Haiti, saying they were "not as pretty as they are depicted, for somehow in the face they look like men". Pliny describes mermaids as being hairy all over – even their upper parts. Both these observations accord with an apelike appearance.

   I would theorise that mermaids have, in effect, been glamorised. Over the bare bones of fact – that a creature closer to a

Fish-like eyes with nictitating membranes.

The webbed hands are clearly an adaptation to marine life.

neanderthal-fish hybrid than a human-fish hybrid exists in the oceans and seas of the world – has been laid the flesh of folklore and the misty veil of legend. Out of respect for the strange powers that mermaids may possess has arisen a body of lore that portrays them as beautiful and alluring – beings who can bridge the gap between man and nature.

SUPPLEMENTARY NOTES AND RESEARCH:
The merman, or triton, is much neglected in contemporary mermaid research and under-represented in recent sightings. He has figured more prominently in the past. The first record of a mer-being of either gender is that of the Akkadian sage Oannes, who lived in 5000 BCE, and was a teacher of men (the ancient Chaldeans revered him as a sea-god). North American Indians tell of a merman who led their people across the ocean from Asia. Pliny, at one time commander of the Roman fleet, recorded a number of sightings in his Natural History (77 AD). These included a triton seen playing a conch shell (a favourite pastime for tritons, who were said to use shells to influence the weather), and a number of Roman merchants who saw one climb onto a ship in the Gulf of Cadiz.

   In Greek myth tritons accompanied the chariot of Poseidon, god of the seas, announcing his progress with blasts on their conch shells and tending to the hippocampi that pulled it. They were said to be lusty, violent and ill-tempered. In 596 AD, a pair of tritons were seen in the Nile, where they sported for a whole day. They became a favourite subject for illustration, with later examples showing a mixed-gender couple. In practice, male and female merfolk seem rarely, if ever, to have been sighted together. This, and other clues from

The broad caudal fin and muscular lower parts provide a lot of power through the water.

THE CRYPTOZOOLOGICAL SOCIETY OF LONDON

A full list of sightings is beyond the scope of this report - I would refer researchers to the CSL archives, files MMMXCIII-MMMCCLXXIV.

sightings, allow us to make some deductions about the lifecycle of mermaids. They are mostly solitary creatures, occasionally gathering in same-sex groups of between two and four. An exception is the remarkable case of Vasco da Gama's fleet - according to Camoen's 16th-century work, The Lusiads, the fleet was saved from attack off the coast of Africa by an entire army of mermaids. They generally stay close to shore, but occasionally venture into the open sea. They feed on raw fish (mermaids who are trapped on shore are renowned as terrible cooks). Contact between male and female is rare, and probably only ever happens far beneath the waves. The young are left to fend for themselves from an early age, and mature quickly in form but only very slowly in size, hence the sightings of small mermaids with adult 'features'.

VARIANTS AND RELATED CREATURES

Mermaids may be related to sirens and harpies. They are known by different names around the globe. In the Scottish Highlands, ceasg or maighdean na tuinne ('maiden of the wave'); in Manx, ben-varrey; in Ireland, merrow, murdhuacha or merucha; in Scandinavia, havmand (mermen); in Estonia, nakh or nakinein; in Armenia, nhang; in parts of India, matysa; and in Melanesia, adaro (mermen who are said to ride on rainbows).

she was roughly 5 ft (1.5 m) in length.

Note the fish-like eyes, seaweed-like hair and gills.

I couldn't help but think of all those stories where the mermaid is beautiful and alluring.

The ears do look strange, one can see how they could be confused with a bear's.

125

MANIMALS

Gorgons

LATIN NAME
Gynophidia gorgo

HABITAT
Dry, upland regions

LIFESPAN
Immortal

SIZE
*8–9 ft
(2.4–2.7 m)
high*

INFORMATION SOURCE
CSL Review

DISTRIBUTION
Libya, Japan

Famously fearsome females, the gorgons were well known for their withering looks and slithering locks.

HAVING A BAD-HAIR DAY?

O N THE WHOLE THE GORGONS are a mystery. What we know of them is found mainly in the Perseus legend, and their origins and eventual fates are uncertain.

Only three gorgons are known from ancient sources – Stheno and Euryale, who were immortal, and Medusa, who famously wasn't.

SISTERS OF NO MERCY

A gorgon has a monstrous and powerful human female body with the addition of wings on her back, claws on her feet, and greenish skin. She also has a massive head, which is round and flat-featured, with a broad nose, protruding teeth (like a boar's) and a lolling forked tongue. Her eyes are a burning red and, most hideous of all, her hair is a writhing mass of venomous serpents (an even 100 according to one version). Homer mentions only one gorgon, and Hesiod only three. Three individuals does not constitute a viable breeding population, but since two of the gorgons were widely supposed to be immortal, they may not have needed to reproduce. This conclusion is supported by the fact that only

GRISLY EVIDENCE OF THE GORGONS' DEADLY GAZE CAN BE FOUND IN THE SHAPE OF PETRIFIED HUMAN REMAINS LIKE THIS INDIVIDUAL, RECOVERED FROM A CAVE NEAR AL-QATRUN, IN SOUTHERN LIBYA.

☞ *DETAIL FROM THE WEST PEDIMENT OF THE TEMPLE OF ARTEMIS IN CORFU, C.580 BCE.*

☞ *A LOCK OF THE GORGON'S SERPENTINE HAIR IS SAID TO PROTECT THE BEARER FROM HER DEADLY GAZE, BUT BE WARNED – THE SNAKES ARE HIGHLY POISONOUS.*

female gorgons are mentioned by the ancient Greeks, who left precious few indications about their natural history.

In Greek myth Medusa was said to have slept with the sea-god Poseidon, and to have been the mother of Pegasus and the warrior Chrysaor. Another myth says that from a single drop of the gorgon's blood, all the serpents of Libya sprang forth. Some slightly salacious versions of the Medusa story say that she had the body of a beautiful young maiden; Pindar (218-438 BCE) even says that her face was beautiful. These myths should not be taken literally, but they indicate that the Greeks attributed a sex life of some kind to the gorgons.

Around 1400 BCE the gorgons lived in Libya, where they dwelt in dry, upland regions (probably in the south or west of the country). However, some accounts place them in regions at the very edge of human ken, such as Hyperborea, in the far north of the world, or beyond the western ocean, in a land toward the realm of night. This may indicate that they originally dwelt in a distant land, or (and this is supported by evidence from Japan – see below)

There are few depictions of the gorgons in flight, suggesting that the wings are not functional, and are possibly even vestigial.

that they left Libya and migrated to a place beyond the Hellenic sphere of experience.

As for the origin of the gorgons, Greek myth offers several explanations. In one version Medusa (from the Greek *medousa*, meaning ruler or queen) was a Libyan princess who was transformed by Athene, Goddess of Wisdom, either as punishment for her beauty, or for sleeping with Poseidon. In another version the gorgons were offspring of the sea-god Phorcys and his sister Ceto. They had sisters – the Graiae – although this could be interpreted as a reference to a related species.

DROP-DEAD GORGEOUS

The gorgon's most powerful weapon is her deadly face, which literally petrifies its victims if gazed upon directly. However, she can be looked at in a mirror. It is her face, and not her gaze that is deadly – hence Medusa's severed head still had the power to petrify. The area around where they lived was surrounded by the stony forms of their victims, frozen like statues.

SPLITTING HEADACHES

Early records indicate that Medusa had established herself as a ruler in Libya at one point, but the gorgons were principally known for their encounter with Perseus, grandfather of Hercules, and one of the earliest Greek heroes.

But what of the real gorgons: Medusa's remaining – and immortal – siblings? It seems likely that they fled soon after Perseus' attack, and the Greeks placed them in far-off realms in the borderlands of the known world. A clue to their whereabouts comes from Japanese legend, which speaks of the

With the help of a mirrored shield Perseus was able to decapitate Medusa, the only mortal amongst the three gorgons. He escaped with her head in a bag, hotly pursued by her sisters.

yama-uba, a hideous mountain-dwelling ogress with snakes for hair. Perhaps Stheno and Euryale made their way across Asia and settled in the farthest possible spot from the scene of their sister's demise. Travellers in the mountains of Japan are advised to take care, and perhaps to carry a mirror.

The Japanese *yama-uba* is the only occurrence of the gorgon in the non-Hellenic world of which I am aware. Many cultures around the world speak of hideous and dangerous female monsters, ogres, giantesses and the like, and it may be that some of these legends and folk tales represent visits from the gorgons.

Medusa and the gorgons have now become bywords for ugliness, and particularly for unpleasant women. In the past few decades, however, feminist writers have used them as a symbol of feminine power and even lesbian separatism.

Perseus gave Medusa's head to Athene, who placed it on her aegis, or shield, to terrify her enemies.

MANIMALS

Satyrs & Fauns

LATIN NAME
Homocapri pan

HABITAT
*Woodlands, hills
and mountains,
wild land
anywhere*

LIFESPAN
20–120 years

SIZE
*4–6 ft
(1.2–1.8 m) tall*

**INFORMATION
SOURCE**
CSL Review

DISTRIBUTION
*Europe and the
Near East*

Satyrs & Fauns

were numerous in ancient times, but are now rare to
the point of extinction. Today's Homocapri do not
present the organised threat that they did in ancient
times, but their spirit is present at many raucous
gatherings (from football matches to wild
parties) and they retain the power
to induce fear and havoc in
humans and animals – indeed
the word 'panic' stems from the
god Pan, usually pictured as a
satyr or faun..

The silenus has heavy fat
deposits, dense auxiliary hair.
Its horns are shorter and its
ears are bigger than satyrs'.

In the Classical world, satyrs' love of
wine, parties and sex appealed to
the wilder side of human
nature, but they could easily
erupt into violence. Their
revelries were just a
step removed from
savage frenzies. The
cosy, image of fauns
today, like the amiable
Mr Tumnus of C.S.
Lewis's Narnia books, is far
from reality.

Hands are
hairy, and are
always poised
to make a
lecherous grab
for female
flesh.

The horns take a
long time to grow. The curve starts
to develop after about two years.

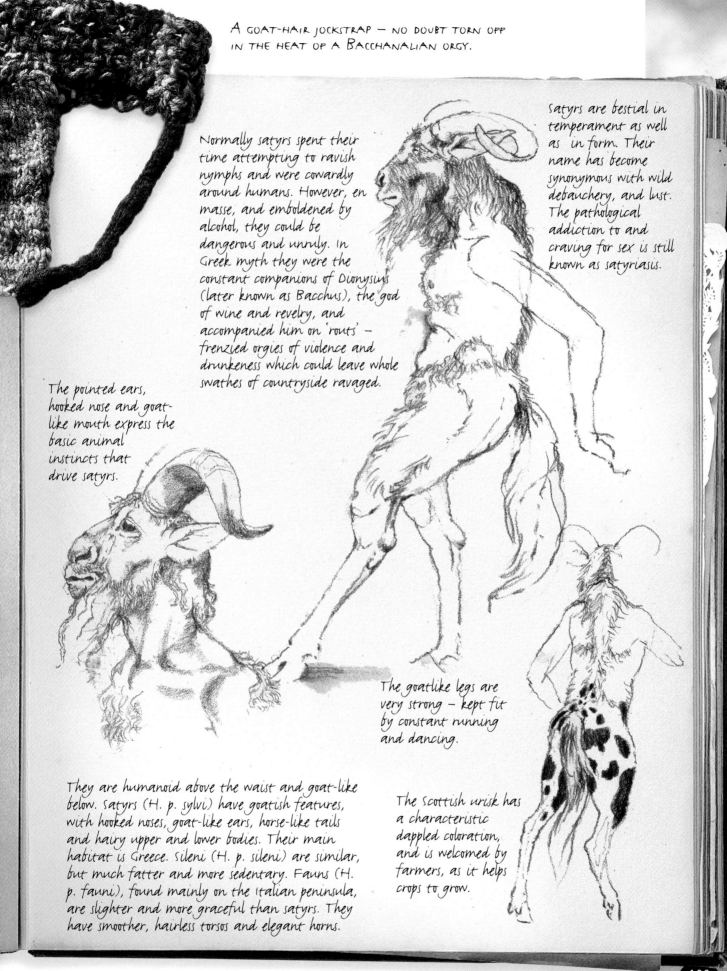

Normally satyrs spent their time attempting to ravish nymphs and were cowardly around humans. However, en masse, and emboldened by alcohol, they could be dangerous and unruly. In Greek myth they were the constant companions of Dionysius (later known as Bacchus), the god of wine and revelry, and accompanied him on 'routs' — frenzied orgies of violence and drunkeness which could leave whole swathes of countryside ravaged.

Satyrs are bestial in temperament as well as in form. Their name has become synonymous with wild debauchery, and lust. The pathological addiction to and craving for sex is still known as satyriasis.

The pointed ears, hooked nose and goat-like mouth express the basic animal instincts that drive satyrs.

The goatlike legs are very strong — kept fit by constant running and dancing.

They are humanoid above the waist and goat-like below. Satyrs (H. p. sylvi) have goatish features, with hooked noses, goat-like ears, horse-like tails and hairy upper and lower bodies. Their main habitat is Greece. Sileni (H. p. sileni) are similar, but much fatter and more sedentary. Fauns (H. p. fauni), found mainly on the Italian peninsula, are slighter and more graceful than satyrs. They have smoother, hairless torsos and elegant horns.

The Scottish urisk has a characteristic dappled coloration, and is welcomed by farmers, as it helps crops to grow.

Cynocephalus

LATIN NAME
*Cynocephalus
indica*

HABITAT
Rural areas

LIFESPAN
40–50 years

HEIGHT
*5–6 ft
(1.5–1.8 m)*

**INFORMATION
SOURCE**
Correspondence

DISTRIBUTION
*Northern and
Central India*

THIS IS A 16TH-CENTURY GREEK IMAGE OF A DOG-HEADED HUNTSMAN. COULD THESE DOG-MEN HAVE LIVED IN GREECE, TOO?

From the desk of Dr R. S. Rajirashwan,
Oudh Institute of Ethnography,
Lucknow, U.P.,
INDIA.

23rd September 1973

Dear Esteemed Friends,

I write with news of a most stimulating nature. Recently I have been most studious in my perusal of Il Milione, Marco Polo's 13th-century account of his journey across India en route, as the expression goes, to China.

This most admirable of travellers describes some of the strange peoples and creatures which he observed on his travels. Many of these we can most easily dismiss as fabrications and works of the utmost fancy, but I noted his description of the men known as cynocephali (dog-headed) who possessed the heads of dogs. They were quite incapable of normal speech, and could only be barking and howling like canine creatures.

I was very stunned and interested by the remarkable similarity of this report to that made by Ctesias, physician to Artaxerxes Mnemon in the 4th century BC. Both sources are frustratingly vague over the whereabouts of the cynocephali, but one of the mediaeval illustrations is clearly shows the dog-men bartering over sacks of grain in a wooded and hilly landscape. This landscape put me in mind of the country to the north-east of here, in the environs of Gorakhpur.

Seeking further enlightenment, I travelled to this area, and engaged the local farmers and brahmins in most stimulating discussions. Certainly, they assured me, there was no-one of this nature currently residing in the area, but one venerable sadhu told me that he recognised the dog-men from legends his grandfather had told him.

This is all that I have learned at present, but I found this very intriguing. Clearly these creatures were present in the time of Ctesias, some two thousand and three hundred years ago, and still survived in the 13th century and quite possibly even longer, according to the local oral tradition. I am sending with this epistle the illustration of which I have spoken.

With my warmest regards,

Dr R. S.

FURTHER SEARCHES IN THE ARCHIVES OF THE CSL HAVE REVEALED THAT THE CYNOCEPHALI MAY ONCE HAVE LIVED AS FAR WEST AS GEORGIA OR NORTHERN TURKEY. IN THE RECORDS, THERE ARE SEVERAL MENTIONS OF 'HEMICYNES': MEN AND WOMEN WHO HAD THE HEADS AND VOICES OF DOGS AND LIVED ON THE SHORES OF THE BLACK SEA. IT SEEMS LIKELY THAT THESE BELONGED TO THE SAME RACE AS THE CYNOCEPHALI.

THIS WAS THE ILLUSTRATION CONTAINED IN DR RAJIRASHWAN'S LETTER. IT SEEMS T BE AN ENGRAVING BASED ON A MINIATURE IN THE 14TH-CENTURY LIVRE DES MERVEILLES DU MONDE.

AN EPAULETTE OR SHOULDER
COVERING.

T. Yamamoto
Associate Fellow of the CSL
Maebashi,
Gumma prefecture,
Japan.

1995/November/10

Gentlemen!

Further to your letter of November 1st, I enclose the relevant portion of
Field Report CZTn 281 4, together with a brief summary of background
information:

The tengu are one of the oldest species of the Japanese archipelago, and
there is evidence that they lived here for several millennia before the
arrival of humans. They are half-human and half-bird, with the appearance of
proud and fierce warriors. Their faces have long, beak-like noses (which are
sometimes red) and instead of hair they have feathers running down their
necks, along their shoulders and along the backs of their arms. At the end

of all their limbs they have the claws of eagles. The tengu's eyes are said
to have a fierce glitter. They are renowned as master swordsmen, and have a
reputation for vanity, boastfulness, mischief and occasional vandalism. Tengu
are associated with Japan's ancient Shinto religion, and seem to harbour
some prejudice or grudge against Buddhism, for they delight in destroying
Buddhist temples. They live in mountainous regions.

I hope that you find this report informative. I know that you are familiar
with the netsuke carved in the form of tengu at the National Museum in
Tokyo, so I enclose my sketchbook for your archive. Forgive my clumsy
drawing. There are no photographs. I had used up all my film on the way to
Sennokura-yama, and there was none in the village.

T. Yamamoto

ARMLETS AND
BRACELETS, LIKE
ALL TENGU
CLOTHING, ARE
MADE OF LEAVES.

A TENGU
BREASTPLATE.

Tengu

LATIN NAME
Aquilahomo
saevus

HABITAT
Wooded
mountains

LIFESPAN
100–150 years

HEIGHT
5–6 ft
(1.5–1.8 m)

INFORMATION
SOURCE
Field Report

DISTRIBUTION
Japan

Gentlemen! Kindly accept this account of my recent expedition in search of further information about the <u>tengu</u>.

FIELD REPORT (EXCERPT)

October/6:   After six days of fruitless searching I have reached the foot of Sennokura-yama, a peak more than 2000 ft (610 m) high. I stayed overnight in an inn which occupies the site of an old Buddhist temple which mysteriously burned down two hundred years ago. The inn-keeper told me that <u>tengu</u> were responsible. He explained that they lived high on the mountain, but were rarely seen. He said that there are two types of <u>tengu</u>. First, nobles and kings who live in gold-roofed palaces. Second, their servants and henchmen the <u>koppa tengu</u> who live in trees, especially pine and Japanese cedar.

October/7:   Today I climbed up Sennokura-yama through thick woods, checking the pine and cedar trees that grow thickly on its slopes. Eventually, near the tree-line, I caught sight of a strange figure high up in the branches. It seemed to be clothed in leaves or feathers, and its hair was tied up in a topknot. As it moved with agility through the canopy, I could see that it was practising with the long sword we call the <u>katana</u>. I made some rapid sketches with my brush before the creature caught sight of me. It gave me a furious stare before running off across the canopy and vanished from sight. I sketched on until dusk, then returned to the inn.

Strange ear jewellery.

A typical warlike pose.

TRH.943.093
DETRITUS FROM
TENGU NEST.

A TENGU'S BELT.

THIS IS THE MOST POLISHED OF MR YAMAMOTO'S SKETCHES, AND MUST HAVE BEEN FINISHED
AT HIS DESK WELL AFTER HE SIGHTED THE TENGU — SO IT MAY NOT BE AS RELIABLE AS HIS
LIGHTNING SKETCHES.

MANIMALS

Sphinx

LATIN NAME
Sphinx aegyptus
and *Sphinx*
orientalis

HABITAT
Arid, rocky
regions

LIFESPAN
50–70 years, but
some much
longer

SIZE
5–10 ft
(1.5–3 m) at
the shoulder,
12–24 ft
(3.6–7.5 m) long

INFORMATION
SOURCE
CSL Review

DISTRIBUTION
Egypt, Near and
Middle East

S PHINXES ARE NOW ALMOST RELEGATED to the league of mythical and non-existent creatures. As late as the 4th century BCE, however, sphinxes were fairly common in much of the Near and Middle East and even on European soil. In the few centuries since then, however, the sphinx has vanished into the realms of imagination and art.

DOMESTIC PUSSYCATS

There are two species of sphinx – the Egyptian and the Oriental sphinx. The fomer has the head of a human and the body of a great lion. The Oriental sphinx of the Near and Middle East also has wings like an eagle's. Egyptian sphinxes tend to live longer than their Oriental cousins, but are less active, spending up to three-quarters of the day asleep. When roused, however, both species can be formidable hunters, leaping on their prey and using their great claws to seize their prey and tear them into chunks small enough for their human mouths. Both species are wise, serious and independently-minded, with a tendency to be self-sufficient and inscrutable.

☞ *THE FRENCH PAINTER INGRES CAPTURED THE MOMENT OF TENSION BEFORE OEDIPUS SOLVED THE RIDDLE OF THE THEBAN SPHINX.*

MOST PEOPLE ARE FAMILIAR WITH THE GREAT SPHINX AT GIZA, AND WITH MANY OTHER PICTURES OF SPHINXES FROM DIFFERENT CULTURES AND ERAS.

Sphinxes were domesticated in around 3000 BCE by both the great civilisations of the age, the Egyptians and the Mesopotamians. Starting with Menes (c.3100 BCE), the Old Kingdom pharaohs first began to use male sphinxes (androsphinxes) as palace and temple guardians, a role well suited to their feline temperaments. In about 2000 BCE, the Egyptians realised that female sphinxes were easier to domesticate than males, but just as capable.

THEY'RE IN THE BIBLE

Egyptian influence spread the sphinx further afield – for instance, pharaoh Amenemhet III (1844–1797 BCE) sent a pair to guard the entrance of the temple of Baal at Ras Shamra, in Syria. In the 10th century BCE, Egyptian sphinxes were used, together with lamassu, to guard the entrance to the king's great palace compound at Susa.

It is even possible that sphinxes were used to guard the great Temple of Solomon. The 1st Book of Kings suggests that Hiram, King of Tyre, sent a pair to Jerusalem. The Oriental sphinx, more agile and active than the Egyptian, could also be used in an offensive capacity. Chariot decorations from this time show rampant winged sphinxes crushing foreign enemies.

Sphinxes set foot in Europe thanks to the ancient Minoans of Crete, who imported Oriental sphinxes.

RIDDLE OF THE

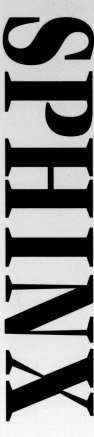

SPHINX

By the 8th century BCE, the Greeks were using sphinxes to guard temples and tombs – reflecting the fact that the sphinx was probably the only exotic creature that could be trusted not to eat carrion. Careful selective breeding meant that Hellenistic sphinxes began to diverge from their Oriental progenitors.

TRICKY QUESTION

In around 700 BCE, a sphinx escaped from central Thebes and terrorised travellers on the road into town by asking them a fiendish riddle; when they failed, she would kill them. Oedipus, the long-lost son of the King of Thebes, was returning to the place of his birth when the Sphinx sprang out and blocked his path.

'Halt! Answer my riddle, or die!' she cried. 'What creatures start life with four legs, then have two and end their life with three?' Oedipus replied without hesitating: 'The answer is, human beings. As babies, they crawl on all fours; as adults, they walk upright; when they are old, they use a stick as a third leg.' The sphinx, her power destroyed, promptly committed suicide by throwing herself off a mountain.

When Rome added Greece and Egypt to its empire, sphinxes became a familiar sight in Italy. A pair of Egyptian

A BAS-RELIEF OF THE GUARD-SPHINXES OF THE PALACE AT SUSA, ANCIENT CAPITAL OF MESOPOTAMIA.

sphinxes were brought to guard the Temple of Isis in Rome's Iseum Campanese around the 1st century BCE, and their remains were unearthed in 1856 behind the Church of Santa Maria Sopra Minerva. The Emperors Hadrian and Diocletian regularly employed sphinxes to guard imperial residences. The pair imported in around 300 AD by Diocletian for his palace at Split (in what is now Croatia) were probably the last live sphinxes in Europe.

LAST HIDEOUT

With the ascendancy of Christianity in the Roman world, and Islam in the East, the old traditions died out, and with them the capture and breeding of sphinxes. They have remained a popular subject for artists and designers, but the real thing is now seldom, if ever, seen. The last survivors of this magnificent species cling on to existence in the mountain and desert wastes of Arabia.

Everyone has heard of it, and most people could recognise one if they saw it. But what is the mysterious sphinx really like?

Lamassu

LATIN NAME
Homocephalus bos

HABITAT
Deserts and arid mountains

LIFESPAN
75–150 years

SIZE
Up to 16 ft (4.8 m) high at the shoulder

INFORMATION SOURCE
Field Report

DISTRIBUTION
Iraq/Iran

This is one of the lamassu droppings Aziz found. It was at least 2 ft (0.6 m) long.

ARCHIVE NOTE

Lamassu are colossal winged bulls with the heads of men. Like the sphinx, they are members of the genus <u>homocephali</u>. Bred as guardians of Assyrian palaces and temples, they may still survive in small pockets along the Turkish/Iraqi border. About 50 years ago, the future Shah of Iran was saved from certain death in a lamassu attack by the intervention of one of the Society's fellows. Unfortunately, no written record ws made of the event. Now Government rhetoric is directed against foreigners so, as a last-ditch attempt to see if any still exist, we've asked local aid worker Tallulah Harper to investigate.

3rd December: Mosul, N. Iraq

Arrived by train from Baghdad last night. Great to get away from the clinic, but the atmosphere here is very tense. Westerners are not popular. I'm sure I'm being followed. Spent today arranging transport and a guide. Much generous gift-giving (OK, ordinary bribery) needed.

4th December: Nimrud, S of Mosul

Visit the colossal statues of lamassu guards at the palace of the great Assyrian king Assurnasirpal II (883-859 BCE) - a distant echo of the king's awe-inspiring power and authority. Assyrians clearly preferred lamassu to sphinxes as

royal guardians. I wonder why? Leave disappointed - there are no clues here to the whereabouts of living lamassu.

6th December: Nineveh, NW of Mosul

This great city was the centre of the Assyrian empire from the reign of Sennacherib (704-681 BCE). There are breathtaking ruins here, and many teams of archaeologists have given the place a good going over. They have uncovered evidence of a library containing hundreds of clay tablets, including some of the Epic of Gilgamesh, the legendary Sumerian king. In one passage, Gilgamesh fights a bull-like creature - possibly a lamassu.

Gazing at a lamassu statue in one of the excavated areas, I noticed an old man standing in the shadows. He had a knowing look about him. When my guide questioned him about the lamassu, he grinned, cackled toothlessly and pointed to the north.

11th December: Dahuk, N Iraq

Baksheesh, baksheesh, baksheesh. Had to spend most of my funds on bribes and wasted two days hanging around dingy government offices, but finally got the permits necessary to get here, close to where the borders of Turkey, Syria and Iraq meet. This is a weird place - you can almost smell the tension. Aziz, my new guide, says that everyone here thinks I'm a spy. He explodes with laughter when he says it really doesn't matter - just about everyone round here is a spy too.

14th December: Near the Turkish border

Making camp last night, we heard a strange bellowing from the hills to the north, so this morning we searched the area. Aziz

THE RUGGED TERRAIN NEAR THE BORDER OF IRAQ AND TURKEY, WHERE LAMASSU DWELL.

DCG.456.900 .50 ARMOUR-PIERCING SHELLS USED ON THE HARPER EXPEDITION.

called me over in a highly excited state, to show me what he claimed were lamassu spoor. They looked like cowpats to me, but they were undeniably huge. Nearby we found some hoof prints, each nearly two feet long. Tomorrow we'll look further.

Ms HARPER'S GUIDE AZIZ, DRYING HIS SOCKS AND WARMING HIS FEET OVER A BRAZIER IN DAHUK.

16th December: Mardin, Turkey

Disaster struck yesterday as we were closing in on our goal, a large cave which seemed to be the source of the mysterious bellowing. We had no intention of harming or killing the lamassu, but with a monster that may weigh up to two tons, it is better safe than sorry. I and the two Iraqi porters were armed with tranquillising dart guns, and Aziz was carrying a huge hunting gun.

In our excitement, we did not realise that we had crossed the border. A patrol of Turkish soldiers caught sight of us – a band of armed Iraqis on Turkish soil – and shouted. We froze, terrified, and the soldiers opened fire. I couldn't believe what was happening. Aziz was killed almost immediately. I'll never forget the expression on his face as he died. The rest of us were arrested and brought by truck to this border post. The British consul has secured my release, and tomorrow I am being deported. I fear the Iraqis may not be so lucky. I will never forgive myself for what happened to Aziz, and fear that the others face a series of cruel interrogations. What a fool I was.

Lamassu statues at Nimrud.

ISTANBUL
Citymap
patentfolded

ISTANBUL

5. EDITION

Lamassu hoof, Nimrud.

24" (60 cm).

16" (40 cm)

SUBMITTED BY
Tallulah Harper
DATE
23/12 1989
CATALOGUE
CZLm 24 #46

Minotaur

LATIN NAME
*Buhomo
minotaurus*

HABITAT
*Subterranean
caverns*

LIFESPAN
40–50 years

SIZE
*up to 10 ft
(3 m) tall*

**INFORMATION
SOURCE**
CSL Review

DISTRIBUTION
Crete

☞ *IN THIS GREEK VASE-PAINTING, BLOOD SPEWS FROM THE MINOTAUR'S WOUNDS AS THESEUS PREPARES TO DELIVER THE COUP DE GRACE.*

TAURUS! TAURUS! TAURUS!

According to Greek myth, there was only one Minotaur – the child of Pasiphae, Queen of Crete, and a white bull sent by the sea god Poseidon. New evidence, however, suggests there was in fact an entire race of these horrible man-eating monsters.

ALTHOUGH IN CLASSICAL MYTH THE Minotaur was slain by the great Athenian hero Theseus, two centuries of remarkable archaeological discoveries on the island of Crete have revealed that the myth of Theseus and the Minotaur almost certainly hides a darker, more terrifying truth.

The enchanting frescoes and murals of the great palace at Knossos show that at its height around 1600 BCE, the Minoan civilisation of Bronze Age Crete was vibrant and carefree. But older remains hint at more sinister preoccupations – twisted labyrinths, cruel animal gods, and human sacrifices. Could it be that the tale of the Minotaur, who dwelt within the famous Labyrinth, represents an echo or archetype of a terrible lost race of hybrid monsters, who dwelt in darkness underground and fed on human flesh? Consider the evidence: bulls are a prominent motif in Minoan art; the Minoans practiced regular blood sacrifices; and the crumbling remains of stygian labyrinths lie beneath the ancient Cretan palaces of Knossos, Phaestus, Mallia and Zakron.

A LOAD OF BULL

If, as seems likely, there was in fact a whole subterranean race of minotaurs on the island of Crete, what information do the ancient sources tell us about these creatures ?

The Minotaur had the body of an enormous human, with the head and shoulders of a bull. His body – particularly the animal parts – was covered in brown hair, and his horns were wickedly sharp, with a span wider than a man's outstretched arms. Given his fearsome reputation, it seems likely that the Minotaur was an especially large example of his species, but it seems likely that males – or 'bulls' – were around 10 ft (3 m) high, while females – 'heifers' or 'cows', who presumably had women's bodies and cow's heads – were smaller, around 6 ft (1.8 m).

Minotaurs grow quickly, attaining sexual maturity by the age of 12 or 13, by which time they have attained nearly their full height. By this time they have also developed a taste for meat – human meat. King Minos kept the Minotaur satisfied by feeding him 14 young men and women exacted as tribute from the Athenians. According to one version of the legend, this tribute was made every nine years, suggesting that minotaurs can live off stockpiled nutrient reserves for long periods of time. However, other versions say that the tribute was annual, or that Minoans were slaughtered instead of Athenians eight years out of nine.

GET THE HORN

The Minotaur was probably about 30 when Theseus killed him, and was at his physical prime. This suggests a total lifespan of around 50 years.

Many observers said that the Minotaur was invulnerable to any weapon but his own horn driven through his brain. This is probably an exaggeration, although a minotaur's size, speed, strength and ferocity, combined with a pair of deadly horns, must have made it a formidable adversary.

The Minoans had a complex relationship with the creatures which lurked below their land. On the one hand they loathed and feared them, placating them with blood sacrifices to stop them from growing hungry and launching devastating raids on the world above. Yet many murals and archaeological artefacts suggest that sporting with minotaurs (similar to a modern bull fight) was an important part of Minoan initiation into adulthood – a way for young men to demonstrate their virility.

FLOODED OUT

Knossos was destroyed by some form of cataclysm around 1450 BCE. Barbarian invasion from the mainland was once the favoured explanation, but now a volcanic eruption and subsequent tidal wave are thought to have been responsible. By 1100 BCE, the Minoan civilisation had faded. With their subterranean homes flooded and their prey dwindling, it seems certain the Minotaur declined simultaneously.

A ROMAN MOSAIC OF THE 1ST CENTURY AD DEPICTS THE MINOTAUR AT THE CENTRE OF A COMPLEX MAZE, PARTS OF WHICH STILL SURVIVE.

In art and myth, at least, the Minotaur lived on. Theseus and the Minotaur were favourite subjects for painters and craftsmen of ancient Greece. The tale continues to be one of the most popular of ancient legends. In the Middle Ages, Dante imagined the Minotaur as the brutal guardian of the Seventh Circle of Hell, a symbol of perversion.

DIET OF WORMS

In the real world, however, the minotaur is probably extinct, since there have been no recent sightings. However, the full extent of the labyrinths beneath the Minoan palaces is unknown, and there may be many more caverns and tunnels beneath the soil of Crete. Perhaps a few hardy minotaur eke out an existence on a diet of rodents, worms and the occasional potholer.

Related species may linger on in isolated pockets. The bucentaur is a reverse minotaur, with the head, arms and torso of a human attached to the body of a bull. The nearest relation to the minotaur is probably the dog-man, or *Cynocephalus* – part of a different family, but the same order (see p. 130).

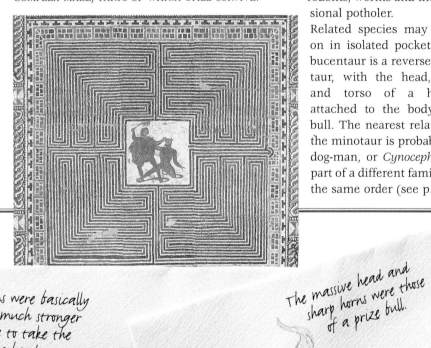

The torso and arms were basically human, but with much stronger shoulders and spine to take the extra weight of the head.

The eyes were more human than bovine, set at the front of the face for stereo vision.

The massive head and sharp horns were those of a prize bull.

No man could survive attack from the sword-like horns until Theseus, who managed to wrench one off and

use it to stab the Minotaur.

The Minotaur had the tail of a bull and very hairy, muscular legs.

Centaur

LATIN NAME
*Sagittarius
centaurus*

HABITAT
*Wooded
mountainous
regions, steppes*

LIFESPAN
*Usually 30–40
years, occasion-
ally 100 +*

SIZE
Equine

**INFORMATION
SOURCE**
CSL Review

DISTRIBUTION
*Asian steppes
(prev. Greece)*

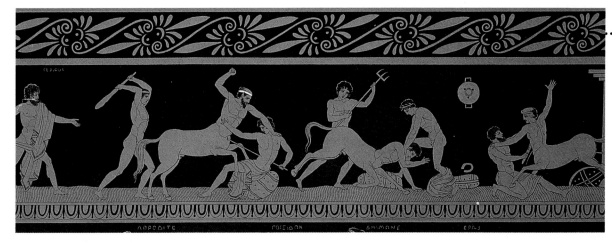

BASIC INSTINCTS

Once a familiar member of the Greek fauna, centaurs were a mixed blessing. Although a few were noble creatures, the majority were violent and lecherous, the yobs and hooligans of the ancient world.

HUMAN FROM THE WAIST UP, AND HORSE below, centaurs are naturally strong and powerful athletes. Their great flaw, however, is their fondness for strong drink, which they cannot hold, quickly becoming drunk, violent and lecherous. The ancient world, especially in rural areas, was occasionally terrorised by groups of foraging centaurs, who were usually out to make trouble.

THE INVISIBLE WOMAN

Centaurs live in tribes, each of which bases itself around a central cave with a communal wine jar. Guardianship of this jar is equivalent to leadership of the tribe. Female centaurs – *Empusäe* – are very rarely seen. It is thought that they prefer to stay in the cave or in thick woods nearby, raising their foals peacefully while the males rampage elsewhere. Centaurs mature at a

☞ *THE CENTAUR IS A FEARSOME WARRIOR, WITH THE SPEED AND STAMINA OF A HORSE AND A STRONG HUMAN TORSO IDEAL FOR ARCHERY AND SPEAR THROWING. ITS HEAD IS HUMAN, EXCEPT FOR THE EARS, WHICH ARE POINTED LIKE THOSE OF A SATYR, REFLECTING ITS WILD AND LUSTY NATURE.*

rate between humans and horses: adulthood starts at about 13 years old, and their life expectancy is probably about 55 years. Most, however, are dead by the time they reach forty – either killed or fatally injured in one of the many fights in which they become involved.

The origin of the centaurs is uncertain. It seems likely that they came into Greece from Scythia, to the north, settling in the wooded mountain regions of Thessaly (in Northern Greece) and Arcadia (on the Peloponnese). Centaurs reached Scythia from the vast steppes of Southern Russia, the Ukraine and Kazakhstan, which is probably where they evolved, and now thought to be the only place they survive in any numbers.

There are two tribes of centaurs. One (the Centaur proper) is descended from Chronus, and is marginally more gentle than the brutal

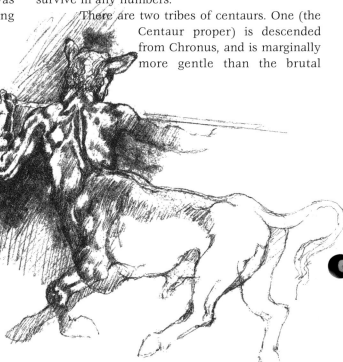

Lapiths. The latter are descended from Ixion, the first man to murder a blood relative, who tried to seduce the goddess Hera. She tricked him into making love to a cloud, and the offspring of this union was the first of the Lapiths.

MEDICAL CENTAUR

Centaurs have a well-deserved reputation for having more brawn than brain. As a rule, centaurs are not very intelligent, although they have fearsome reserves of raw strength. A few, however, were cultured and sophisticated. Chiron, educated by Apollo and Artemis, was a skilled musician, gymnast and doctor, tutor to Hercules, Jason and Achilles. Chiron was an immortal and had great wisdom, powers of prophecy and healing. He left Earth only after being wounded by one of Hercules' poisoned arrows. Rather than see immortal Chiron suffer for an eternity, Zeus took pity on him and turned him into the zodiacal constellation of Sagittarius, the archer.

☞ *A POMPEIIAN MURAL DEPICTS A CENTAUR CAROUSING WITH A MAENAD. IRONICALLY, THE LUSTY CENTAUR WAS THE ONLY CREATURE WHO COULD RESIST THE CHARMS OF THE SIRENS.*

The notoriously rowdy centaurs of Greece made their greatest mark in history at the marriage of the Lapith king, Peirithous, to Hippodamia. Several centaurs got very drunk at the wedding feast and attempted to rape the bride. The Lapiths defended Hippodamia and an enormous battle, or *centauromachy*, ensued. The Lapith wedding, as the incident became known, was memorably depicted in several classical Greek masterpieces, including carvings at the Parthenon and the Temple of Zeus at Olympia. Eventually the centaurs were defeated and forced to leave Thessaly. The remnants of the tribe later tangled with Hercules, who killed many of them.

FULL-TIME YOBS

Many centaurs joined the satyrs in becoming followers of Dionysus, the Greek god of wine known to the Romans as Bacchus. They were renowned for spreading mayhem, and for being at the forefront of any general hooliganism.

By the time of the Romans, there were very few centaurs left in Mediterranean lands. In the 1st century AD, Pliny claimed to have seen one

☞ *A CENTAUR WIELDS SOME CENTAURY – THE BITTER HERB PRESCRIBED BY THE LEARNED CENTAUR CHIRON AS A DIGESTIVE TONIC.*

embalmed in honey, brought from Egypt to Rome. Their evil reputation, however, survived in Europe until the Middle Ages. There are now only a few isolated groups of centaurs living in the remote steppes of central Asia, practising thieir traditional skills of hunting and brewing.

There are several other species of centaur. The onocentaur (*Sagittarius onocentaurus*) has the body of an ass, and is said to be even more stupid and gluttonous than its equine cousin. The bucentaur (*Sagittarius bucentaurus*) has the body and strength of a bull, and although surly and irritable, it is very slow-moving. Several writers testify to the existence of what seems to have been an ichthyocentaur (*Sagittarius ichthyocentaurus*) an extraordinary creature with the head and torso of a man, the front legs of a horse and the tail of a large dolphin or fish.

☞ *THERE ARE SEVERAL COMBINATIONS OF MAN AND BULL, INCLUDING THE MINOTAUR AND THE LAMASSU. THE BUCENTAUR IS ONE OF THE RAREST. IT WOULD BE DANGEROUS IF IT WERE NOT VERY HEAVY AND SLOW ON ITS FEET, MAKING IT EASY TO RUN AWAY FROM.*

Werewolf

LATIN NAME
Varied

HABITAT
Any

LIFESPAN
Human

SIZE
Human

**INFORMATION
SOURCE**
Field Report

DISTRIBUTION
Worldwide

ARCHIVE NOTE: THIS
FIELD REPORT WAS
COMMISSIONED AND
JOINTLY FUNDED BY
THE CSL AND THE
BALKAN WEREWOLF
COMMITTEE, SOFIA.

FIELD REPORT

THE CRYPTOZOOLOGICAL
SOCIETY OF LONDON

*Sir Arthur Bentley Fox
SUBMITTED BY
DATE 4/6 - 7/9 1995 LOCATION Bulgaria/London
CATALOGUE No. LZWw 2275
LONDON*

Mutilated sheep — a victim of the beast.

August 4: Sofia, Bulgaria

We have come to Bulgaria, in the heart of
Southeastern Europe, because this is one
of the last corners of Europe with any
detectable werewolf activity. The team
consists of myself, my assistant Nick
Jenkins, Dr Mercedes Jerez, Colonel Lewis
Farley-Runkin DSO and our Bulgarian fixer,
Georgi Bissirov. We will be heading north,
to the foothills of the Balkan Mountains,
a rural area rich in folklore.

August 7: Mihajlovgrad

Arrived at this scruffy little town early
in the morning and called on the local
newspaper to chase up reports from
outlying rural areas of mutilated
livestock and missing children. We decide
to move on to Dolni Lom, further NE.
The moon is gibbous, and getting fuller.

August 8: Dolni Lom

This normally sleepy settlement is up in
arms. Fear and suspicion are visible on
everyone's face, and the lintels and sills
of every house are covered with a
profusion of wolfsbane (<u>aconitum</u>), a herb
believed to be proof against werewolves.
We have interviewed a number of people.
Maria, an elderly widow, scrutinised us
carefully before she would talk. She
explained that she was checking to see
whether our eyebrows met in the middle,

our index fingers were the same length as
our middle fingers or our palms were
hairy — all certain signs of lycanthropy.
Petar has moved his family into town
after finding the savaged carcasses of
four sheep on his nearby farm. He said
that he'd seen the results of attacks by
wild dogs, and that the marks on his
sheep were far worse, and made by
something much bigger. Four sheep would
not long satisfy the werewolf's hunger, he
told us, and in any case they were known
to prefer the taste of human flesh.

August 9: Dolni Lom

The local policeman, an affable fellow
named Todor, approached us to suggest we
accompany him on a trip to Petar's farm.
We have returned to our inn to pick up
our equipment, including the dart guns,
the Winchester and the Uzi. Georgi insists
that we need silver bullets for the
rifle, but I am convinced that this is
simply superstition.

August 10: Dolni Lom

A bright, moonlit night filled with
action! Staking out a single sheep as
bait, we lured the creature into the
open. We surrounded it as it started to
attack the sheep. It was huge, and looked
like a cross between a gorilla and a
wolf. It broke through our cordon,
slashing Jenkins' shoulder, and ran off
into the night — but not before Farley-
Runkin managed to wing the creature.

This woman told me that she lost
three goats to a 'wolfman'.

The werewolf's head has vicious fangs and staring eyes.

Before eating, the werewolf stands and howls over its slaughtered prey.

WOLFSBANE — IN THE FORM OF A HERB OR AN EXTRACT — IS A POPULAR WEREWOLF DETERRENT.

It left a trail of blood, clearly visible in the bright moonlight. We followed it to a shepherd's hut, and discovered an unconscious man within. He was naked and extremely hairy, with a nasty bullet wound in his side. Dr Jerez examined him briefly, and took a sample of blood, but there was nothing she could do. The man never regained consciousness.

The town has greeted us with cheers and celebration, but we have other things on our minds. Jenkins' wound has gone septic, and he is weak and feverish. It is essential that we get back to London as soon as possible.

<u>August 20: CSL Headquarters, London</u>
Jenkins appears to have recovered from his wound, but Dr Jerez is troubled by the results of tests on blood samples from the werewolf and Jenkins. Both samples show similar changes, and Jenkins apparently has an elevated T-cell count — a key sign of a viral infection. If our

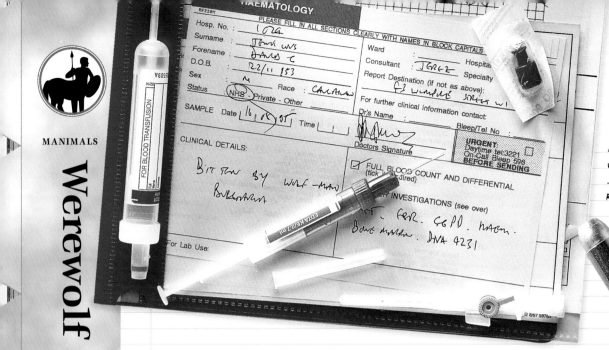

SAMPLES OF JENKINS' BLOOD WERE SENT FOR ANALYSIS BEFORE HE WAS KILLED BY THESE .50 AE SILVER-TIPPED ROUNDS.

theory that werewolfism is caused by a virus turns out to be correct, Jenkins could be in danger.

August 29: CSL Headquarters

More worrying symptoms from Jenkins. His eyebrows are definitely closer together, and careful measurements have shown that his index finger is getting longer! He has agreed to stay under guard in the research cells in the basement. The guards are ex-Special Operations men armed with Desert Eagle semi-automatic pistols.

September 7: CSL Headquarters

A terrible day. At about 9:00 PM Dr Jerez came into the Smoking Room in a state of high excitement, claiming to have isolated viral particles from the werewolf's blood. Preliminary analysis showed that the virus is similar to the HIV virus, and contains a high level of wolf DNA.

As she was telling me this, a terrible roar came from the basement. Instinctively I looked out of the window, and saw that there was a full moon. As we ran down the stairs we heard loud crashes, the breaking of glass and a volley of shots. Then silence. Rounding the corner we saw the broken body of Jenkins, lying in a spreading pool of his own blood.

RESEARCH AND SUPPLEMENTARY INFORMATION

Dr Jerez's findings have led to the discovery of a virus which we believe causes lycanthropy. We have named it Lyc-V. This virus transfers between wolves and humans, as well from human to human, and we believe that it picks up wolf DNA and copies it into the DNA of its human host. Normally the wolf genes are dormant, and there are only minor physical signs, such as hairy palms, that infection has occurred. When the wolf genes are activated - for instance under stress, or when there is a full moon - the victim transforms into a wolf, or wolf-human hybrid.

Lyc-V is a particularly virulent organism that can be passed on in the saliva or blood, or even by contact. This explains why infection can be caused by a bite or scratch, by contact with a werewolf's blood or even by eating an animal killed by a werewolf.

In different parts of the world the Lyc-V virus will transfer to species other than wolves - generally carnivorous mammals. Depending what this animal is, the virus will incorporate the DNA of different animal species, explaining the range of were-beasts around the globe. At the moment Lyc-V infection is, tragically, incurable. It seems there was nothing that we could have done for poor Jenkins anyway, God rest his soul.

VARIANTS AND RELATED CREATURES

I have already discussed the range of were-beasts reported in other parts of the world. Another possible example of a transmogrifying virus in action is the seal-maiden of Celtic tradition - the selkie or roane. These were women who could change into seals and back again. They were classified as fairy creatures, but their shape-shifting suggests a relation to the werewolf.

ATTACHED ARTICLE FROM SCIENCE TODAY EXPLORES THE LYC-V VIRUS IN GREATER DEPTH.

T O DAY

Science

VOLUME 68 OCTOBER 1998

Lycanthropy:
THE EVIDENCE

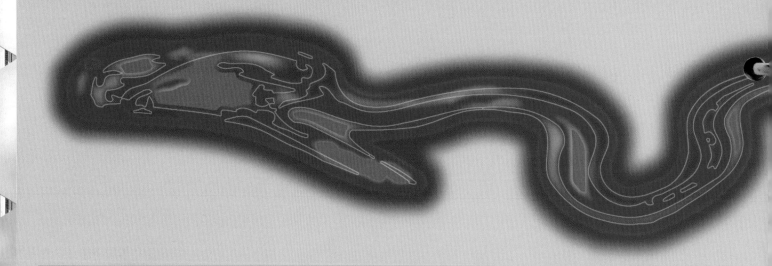

Retrovirus

implicated in lycanthropic transformations

Research carried out into the Human Immunodeficiency Virus (HIV), the organism that causes AIDS, has expanded our knowledge of how viruses work. Work carried out by the Cryptozoological Society of London shows that a similar virus causes lycanthropy – the bizarre disease that turns humans into wolves.

LIKE THE DEADLY HIV VIRUS, THE LYC-V virus belongs to a class known as retroviruses. These microscopic organisms are characterised by a sequence of genetic code which allows them to hijack the host cell's resources and manufacture an enzyme called reverse transcriptase, which copies and incorporates the virus's own sequence of RNA into that of the host cell's DNA.

Infection with Lyc-V means that the genetic makeup of the host cell is permanently altered. When the cells multiply, they reproduce not just the genes in their own DNA, but also those of the invading virus. These genes, of course, contain code for more copies of the virus, which means in effect that the host cells have been subverted to become a rapidly-expanding virus factory.

This is all that the HIV virus needs to do to survive and multiply. Lyc-V has some peculiar side-effects, however, caused by an unusual feature of its lifecycle. Human HIV retroviruses are believed to be variants of a simian virus, long endemic in the ape population, that have now vectored into the human population. They make use of intimate (usually sexual) contact to move from one human to another, but stay within the one host species. By contrast, Lyc-V has what is known as a reservoir population: for parts of its lifecycle it lives in the cells of animals of a different species. Lyc-V seems to favour whichever species of large carnivore is dominant in the locality; in Europe, for instance, this has historically meant wolves.

This split lifecycle results in the Lyc-V virus picking up genetic material from its secondary host population, which is then packaged in the viral particle along with the virus' own genes. When Lyc-V invades a human body and copies itself into the human DNA, it incorporates some wolf DNA into the host cell's genes. As with the HIV virus, there is normally a dormant period following initial

by Dr Arthur Bentley FCSL

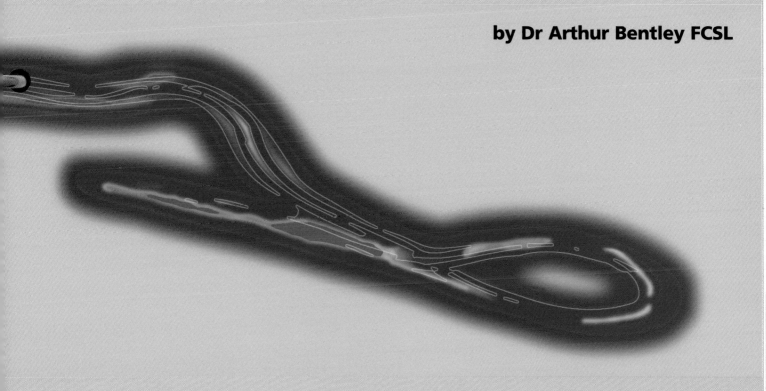

infection, as the body's immune defences (such as the T-cells) can kill off infected cells faster than Lyc-V can produce them. Elevated T-cell counts in the blood are a sign that infection is in progress.

Unfortunately Lyc-V soon overwhelms these defences and lurks, waiting to be activated – apparently by the gravitational field of a full moon.

Understanding the way that the virus spreads explains a problem that has long troubled scientists: why does the degree of transformation vary? Some sufferers become fully-fledged wolf-beings, while others become hybrid wolf-men. Current thinking is that the difference arises from two sources:

a) the amount of wolf DNA carried by the particular strain of Lyc-V in question

b) the 'penetration' of the Lyc-V infection, or the extent to which the virus infects the victim's cells. If only 50% of the victims' cells are infected, then only 50% can be affected by the expression of wolf DNA when the moon catalyses the virus into action.

For more on lycanthropy, see Science Today *no. 6374.*

HIV and the virus that turns people into werewolves work in much the same way

A 17th-century German engraving depicts the werewolf that terrorised the residents of Eschenbach in 1685. Medical science at that time knew nothing of the way diseases transmit themselves.

MANIMALS

Lamia & naga

LATIN NAME
*Homophidia
indica*

HABITAT
*Lamiae: deserts,
naga: aquatic*

LIFESPAN
Up to 400 years

SIZE
*Up to 15 ft
(4.6 m) long*

**INFORMATION
SOURCE**
Letter

DISTRIBUTION
*Northern
Sahara, India,
South Asia*

Editor's note: Trawling through the CSL archives during the compilation of this book, I came across a fascinating piece of correspondence from the early days of the Society. This letter, dated 26th February, 1852, is from Lord Alfred Faversham, the 13th Marquis of Gravesdowne, and one of the Society's founding members. It is addressed to C. Penforth Wright, another founding member, but was probably intended as an open monograph for the Society's journal. The original document is reproduced here in its entirety, together with an enclosed sketch.

THE CRYPTOZOOLOGICAL
SOCIETY OF LONDON

*From the Desk of
Lord Faversham, KB
Gravesdowne House,
Gravesdowne, Herefordshire*

Dear Wright,

Thank you for the splendid leatherbound edition of Keats's Lamia. A dark and fascinating tale indeed! Keats has, of course, made the classic Romantic error of confusing Fact with Phantasy. For him the lamia is simply a symbol — the locus classicus, as it were, of a universal Psychologic Phenomenon. In practice the lamiae were all too real: the unpleasant European arm of a once widespread race of human-serpent hybrids — the naga.

In Greek myth Lamia was a queen who committed an indiscretion with Zeus. Hera punished her by killing her children, and in the madness of her grief Lamia became a monster who sought out children and men to destroy — her name meant 'devourer'. The main population of lamiae lived in the deserts of North Africa, preying on lone travellers. They were said to be unable to talk, but could whistle with siren-like beauty to lure men to their doom.

There were noble lamiae, such as King Erichthonius of Athens, who were much closer in nature to their Eastern brethren the naga. The latter once covered much of Southern and Southeastern Asia, where they lived in rivers and lakes, and in their magnificent capital — the wondrous Bhogavati, buried deep beneath the Himalayas. This underground citadel was hewn from the living rock and filled with marvellous treasures, and the naga and their consorts, the nagini, dwelt there amidst dancing and feasting. Curiously, it seems that unions between nagini and humans were fertile, for many of the noble families of the subcontinent claim descent from these creatures. Do you recall our stay in Indochina, Penforth, and that strutting bantam of a Khmer princeling? It seems that he too is the scion of a line founded by the noble naga.*

Affectionately,

Alfred.

* *Cambodian*

HOMINIDS

The natural history of the unnatural world
would be incomplete if it did not include the
dominant species on the earth: human beings.
Just as there are giant insects, strange birds and
bizarre reptiles, there are many variations on the
human theme. Some, like fairies and
leprechauns, are usually harmless; others, like
vampires and trolls, are malicious and evil. The
bewildering range of hominids is more than a
simple evolutionary response to local conditions
such as environment and society. It is also a
true reflection of hominids' close relationship to
Homo sapiens, an echo of the physical and
psychological variety of humanity itself.

Basic principles of cryptozoology explained in simple terms for schools, colleges and new readers. Created by the Education Department of the Cryptozoological Society of London.

Hominids

In the same way as it seems that Earth is not the only planet with life, it seems ever more likely that humans are not the only hominid species on Earth. In more ways than one, we are not alone.

From the point of view of the conventional zoologist, *Homo sapiens* is something of a mystery. The scientific establishment believes human beings to be the only living species in their genus (the hominids), which would be a highly unusual state of affairs in the animal kingdom.

Cryptozoologists believe that this is almost certainly not the case. Robert Foley, a bioanthropologist at Cambridge University, has used the speciation patterns (numbers and characteristics of species) of other

mammals to calculate that there should be between two and ten other hominid species alive in the world today. The accepted view in cryptozoology is that there are at least six extant species of hominid, but that the world of conventional zoology has been too hidebound and blinkered to observe the diversity of its own species (see Fig 1).

A confusion of faeries

Traditionally, there has been little consensus in the field of cryptozoology about the grouping and naming of

different types of fairies, goblins, leprechauns and so on. This has, at times, hampered research.

There are several reasons for the welter of confusion that surrounds the naming and classification of hominids. One of the most obvious is the difference between 'faerie' and 'fairy'. The latter refers specifically to the specific sub-species *Homo fata vulgaris*, while the former is variously: the collective term for nearly all unknown hominids; the collective term for fairies, pixies, elves and so on; an adjective; and the term for the mysterious parallel realm in which these beings live.

Bewitched, bothered, bewildered

This is just the tip of the iceberg, however. Faery folk are rarely seen, having either learned to steer clear of humans or to gain an advantage from living invisibly in houses alongside their human counterparts.

Many hominids can change shape or cast 'glamours' – use magical powers to confuse observers. Witnesses, therefore, often have their senses addled; just as often, they are not taken seriously by those who listen to them. Finally, different countries and cultural groups have different repsonses to the presence of faeries in their communities. The same phenomenon could be reported as demonic in one country and benevolent in another.

We are all homos

It is generally accepted that the wide range of hominid creatures known across the globe, from fairies to yetis, are all species of the genus *Homo*, and have shared a common ancestor with each other and ourselves within the last 2 million years. Recent discoveries by palaeoanthropologists have caused a perfect hubbub within the closely related discipline of palaeo-cryptoanthropology. The current debate rages over exactly when this common ancestor lived. Is it so, as the traditionalists argue, that human and demi-human lineages diverged around 2 million years ago, thus making *Homo ergaster* the last candidate for the title 'Father of all Hominids?'

FIG 1 A GALLERY OF THE GROTESQUE

The human species alone produces extraordinary individuals who could easily qualify as cryptozoological specimens. They have often cashed in on their unusual appearance and become popular attractions at 'freak shows' and even international celebrities. Today, medical advances mean that such bizarre human specimens are very rare indeed.

Far left *Tom Thumb and Minnie Warren, two well-known dwarves of the 19th century, are married.*

Centre left *a 'rat-person' of Pakistan. These creatures begin their lives as normal children, but grow up with a rat-like head, and earn their living by aggressive begging.*

Centre right *Joseph Merrick (1862–90), the 'Elephant Man' immortalised in David Lynch's 1980 film of the same name. Merrick's condition baffled doctors at the time, but is now thought to have been a rare viral disorder.*

Right *Two Burmese dwarves, slightly over 3 ft (1 m) tall, exhibited at a Berlin fair in 1898.*

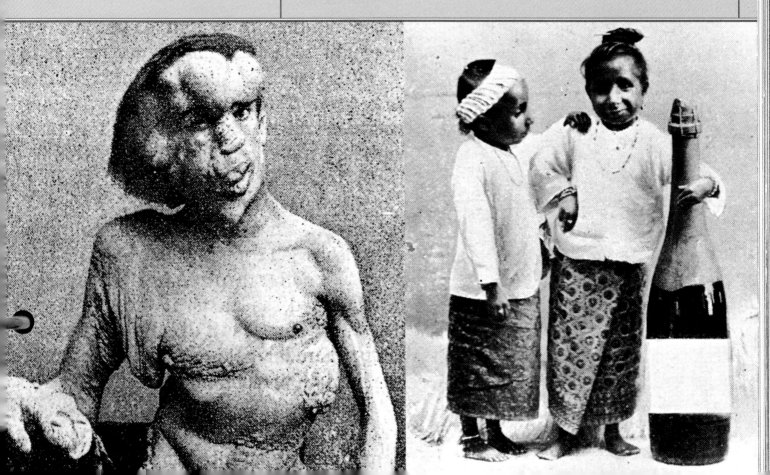

Challengers of this view point to well-known evidence about Neanderthals and recent finds indicating a divergence between 1 million and 500,000 years ago in human ancestry, with the newly unearthed *Homo heidelbergensis* as our distant, common progenitor.

The most likely scenario may well be a compromise between these positions, with different species of hominid diverging at different stages along the evolutionary tree (see Fig 2). Close relations such as elves and halflings may be relatively recent divergences,

while the imp or sasquatch may share a more distant ancestor.

To koboldly go ...

One branch of the evolutionary tree gave rise to the species *Homo sapiens*, and several other branches evolved into

FIG 2 EVOLUTION: THE HOMINID RACES

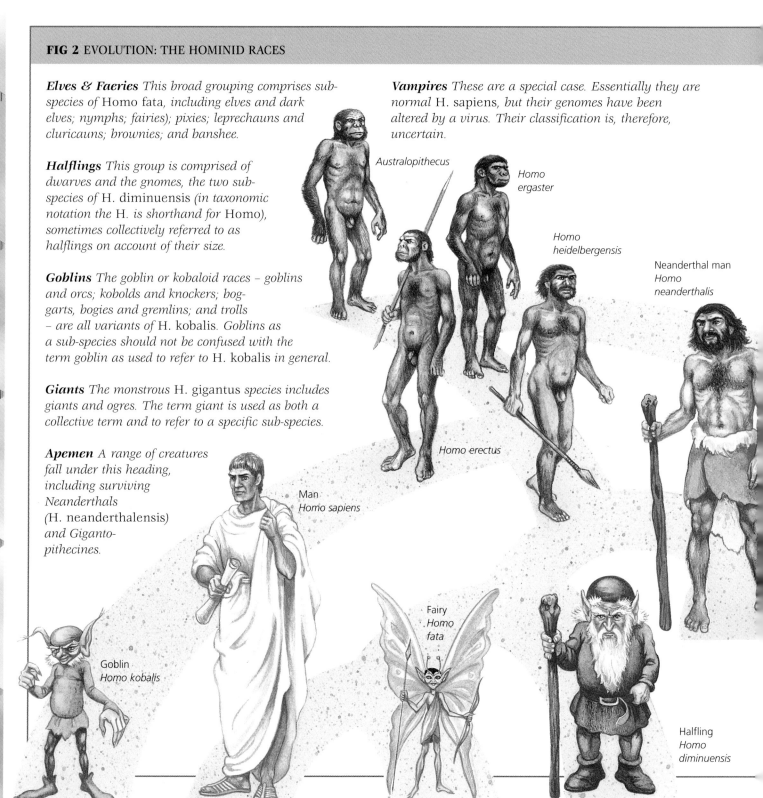

Elves & Faeries This broad grouping comprises sub-species of Homo fata, *including elves and dark elves; nymphs; fairies); pixies; leprechauns and cluricauns; brownies; and banshee.*

Halflings *This group is comprised of dwarves and the gnomes, the two sub-species of* H. diminuensis *(in taxonomic notation the* H. *is shorthand for* Homo)*, sometimes collectively referred to as halflings on account of their size.*

Goblins *The goblin or kobaloid races – goblins and orcs; kobolds and knockers; boggarts, bogies and gremlins; and trolls – are all variants of* H. kobalis. *Goblins as a sub-species should not be confused with the term goblin as used to refer to* H. kobalis *in general.*

Giants *The monstrous* H. gigantus *species includes giants and ogres. The term giant is used as both a collective term and to refer to a specific sub-species.*

Apemen *A range of creatures fall under this heading, including surviving Neanderthals (*H. neanderthalensis*) and Giganto-pithecines.*

Vampires *These are a special case. Essentially they are normal H. sapiens,* but their genomes have been altered by a virus. Their classification is, therefore, uncertain.*

Australopithecus

Homo ergaster

Homo heidelbergensis

Neanderthal man
Homo neanderthalis

Homo erectus

Man
Homo sapiens

Goblin
Homo kobalis

Fairy
Homo fata

Halfling
Homo diminuensis

the shadowy and elusive denizens of the worlds of folklore and myth. Not all of these branches produced wondrous or magical fruit, such as mermaids or leprechauns – some have produced loathsome, repellent creatures of crude design, such as ogres.

One such group comprises the variants of the species *Homo kobalis*, the goblin races. This heading subsumes the goblin proper (*H. k. scrofa*), his immediate relative the orc (*H. k. orcus*), and closely related groups like the kobold (*H. k. kobalis*), the troglodytes (*H. k. troglodytes*), the boggarts and bogies (*H. k. bugge*) and the gremlin (*H. k. vexus*). Goblin, the common (or vernacular) name for *H. k. scrofa*, is a bastardisation of the German 'kobold', itself derived from the Greek 'kobalos', meaning 'mischievous spirit'. This has led to much confusion: the common observer often assumes, improperly, that goblins and kobolds are one and the same species.

Humanoid horrors

The kobaloid races do, however, share many common traits, most of them unpleasant. They are generally ugly, coarse-grained creatures, often grotesquely misshapen and they are universally dirty, exuding a rank odour which is immediately repellent to even the least fastidious. They tend also to have malignant intent towards humans and other species of hominid.

Kobaloids were almost ubiquitous in Europe and Western Asia in prehistoric times, but they are now confined to remote wilderness regions. Some types, however, mainly gremlins and boggarts, did manage to spread to the New World. Their high levels of fertility and omnivorous and undiscerning nature might have made them as successful as the rat or the cockroach, but they have a natural tendency to argue amongst themselves, often fighting to the death. Some goblins are thought to practice cannibalism. The very high death rate, and their almost universal hatred of sunlight, mean that only rare and unlucky travellers ever have the extreme bad luck to encounter these unpleasant creatures.

Just like us?

Fairies, goblins, and yetis are unlike the other strange creatures in cryptozoology. The human response to them is complex, perhaps because they somehow reflect aspects of our inner selves. Some say that is all they are, but the evidence suggests otherwise.

Giant
Homo gigantus

Apeman
Gigantopithecus

Elves

LATIN NAME
Homo fata alfar

HABITAT
Woodland and underground

LIFESPAN
400 + years

SIZE
c. 6 ft (1.8 m) – some very small

INFORMATION SOURCE
Artist's sketchbook

DISTRIBUTION
Northern Europe (esp. Scandinavia)

Elves

Elves evolved in the mountains and forests of Scandinavia, where they are known as the alfar or the huldre folk. There are two main types of elf – dark (svartalfar) and light (liosalfar) – together with some regional varieties. Dark elves have black hair and black eyes, and sometimes black skin. Light elves are typically Scandinavian-looking, with blond hair, pale skin and blue eyes. They are generally tall and slim, with sharp, delicate features and pointed ears, although some British and German elves can be very tiny, and are often mistaken for fairies.

A high northern elf, dressed for battle. In legend, the elves fought with the Gods against the evil giants.

Elves crop up in some surprising places and guises. Some types only exist in the imagination.

some dark elves have adopted the dress of Kenyan Masai people.

A GALLERY OF ELVES

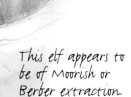

This elf appears to be of Moorish or Berber extraction.

A Saxon elf, showing the Germanic elves' love of ostentatious jewels.

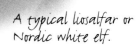

A typical liosalfar or Nordic white elf.

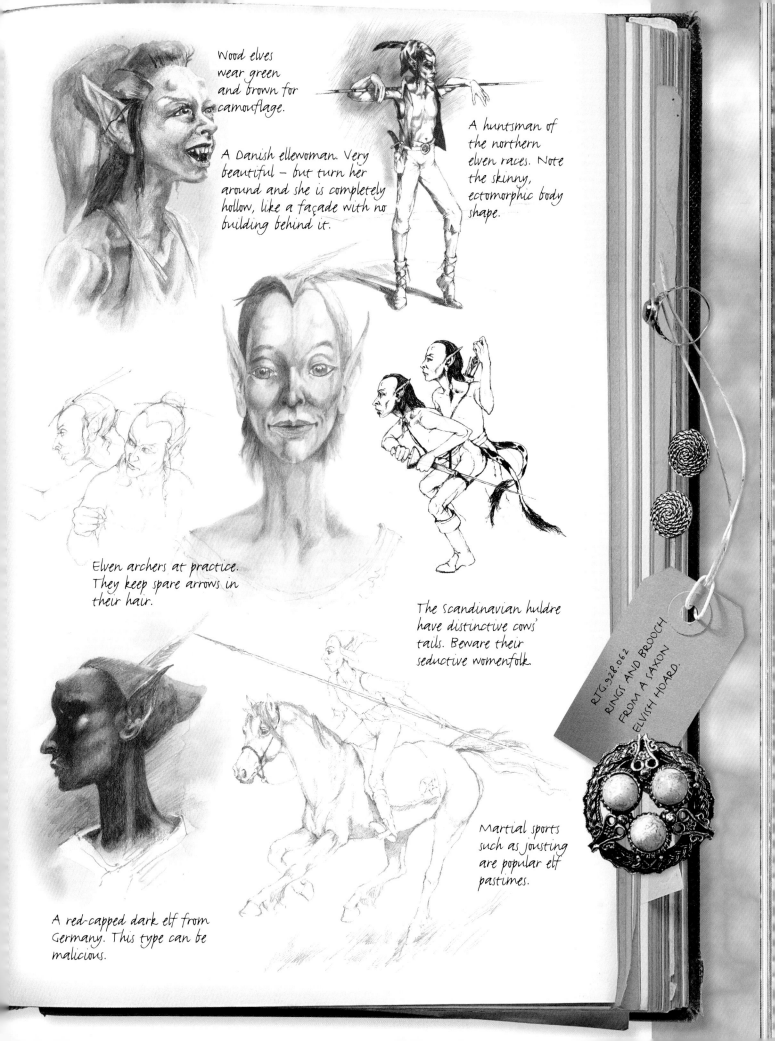

Wood elves wear green and brown for camouflage.

A huntsman of the northern elven races. Note the skinny, ectomorphic body shape.

A Danish ellewoman. Very beautiful – but turn her around and she is completely hollow, like a façade with no building behind it.

Elven archers at practice. They keep spare arrows in their hair.

The scandinavian huldre have distinctive cows' tails. Beware their seductive womenfolk.

Martial sports such as jousting are popular elf pastimes.

A red-capped dark elf from Germany. This type can be malicious.

RTG.928.062 RINGS AND BROOCH FROM A SAXON ELVISH HOARD.

HOMINIDS

Nymphs

LATIN NAME
*Homo fata
nympha*

HABITAT
Varied

LIFESPAN
c.10,000 years

SIZE
Human

**INFORMATION
SOURCE**
*Own Field
Report*

DISTRIBUTION
*Europe, Middle
East and India*

HE TERM 'NYMPH' IS A generic one for an exclusively female class of faery that has adapted to almost every environment on Earth, including the sea. Most nymphs are almost indistinguishable from humans, although their bewitching beauty and erotic power sets them apart from the common horde.

In general, cryptozoologists follow the ancient Greeks and classify nymphs by habitat, using names derived from the Greek. Thus, river nymphs are called potamids, meadow nymphs are called leimoniads, nymphs of ponds and pools are known as limnads, and so on. This classification reflects the nymphs' close association with nature, which is one of their defining characteristics.

SHORE THING

Water nymphs are the most widespread members of the species. Riverine nymphs are found throughout Europe and also in India, while marine nymphs, such as the oceanids, who live on the open sea, have spread around the globe and are known as far afield as Hawaii (where they are called *hina*).

Most nymphs lead a solitary existence and live in clearly defined territories of their own, although some aquatic nymphs tend to congregate in small groups. The nymph protects and maintains her territory, and her own health is closely linked to

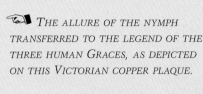

THE ALLURE OF THE NYMPH TRANSFERRED TO THE LEGEND OF THE THREE HUMAN GRACES, AS DEPICTED ON THIS VICTORIAN COPPER PLAQUE.

that of her habitat. The hamadryad of Greece and Italy, for example, takes up residence in a single tree with which she establishes a close symbiosis.

If her arboreal home dies or is felled, she perishes too. In general, however, nymphs have a very high life expectancy, said by the Greek scholar Plutarch (*c.*46–*c.*120 AD) to be around 9720 years. Today, however, few nymphs live out their full term, because pollution and development by humans have damaged the delicate balance of their environment to their detriment.

FOOD, SEX AND DEATH

Details of these secretive and shy hominids remain elusive. They are said to be gifted musicians and prophetesses. The reproductive cycle of this all-female species has confounded students for centuries, although the legends of nymphs seducing humans could provide a clue. Diet, too is a mystery. According to one report, dryads – nymphs of the woodlands – enjoy honey, olive oil and milk. Aquatic nymphs, such as the German *nix* and the

HYLAS AND THE NYMPHS (1896), BY JOHN WATERHOUSE, SHOWS THE POWERFUL SEXUAL ATTRACTION NYMPHS CAN EXERT ON HUMANS.

French *drac*, are well known for dragging or luring humans into the water and then drowning them, possibly in order to eat.

Like other faery creatures, they project a 'glamour field', which may account for both their incredible beauty and the alleged consequences of viewing it. A human who merely glimpses a nymph is said to go blind, whilst seeing one naked is reputed to be fatal. This could be due to an unusually strong glamour field that is even more dangerous when the field is unshielded by clothes.

NYMPH-MANIA

Nymphs are practically ubiquitous in Greek myth, where they are hotly pursued by libidinous Gods and men alike – the latter oblivious to the problems of exposure to the dazzling glamour field of the nymph and then somehow surviving the experience. A few of the more notable nymphs include: Thetis, mother of Achilles; Eurydice, beloved of Orpheus; Echo, unrequited lover of Narcissus; and Carmentia, a water nymph said to have taught the Romans how to read and write and to have created the Roman alphabet.

The apparently fertile offspring of unions between humans and nymphs have led many scholars to argue that they must be a sub-species of *Homo sapiens*. However, they clearly share some faerie features with other species of *H. fata*, and it seems unlikely that they could have evolved these independently. They might well represent an evolutionary link between the two species.

A FANCIFUL DEPICTION OF BRETON NYMPHS DANCING AROUND A MEGALITHIC MONUMENT. IN FACT THERE ARE NO RECORDS OF FLYING NYMPHS.

SOME SCHOLARS BELIEVE THAT THIS WELL-KNOWN FRESCO OF DANCERS FROM KNOSSOS, IN CRETE, IS ACTUALLY A TRIO OF NYMPHS. THERE ARE SUGGESTIONS THAT THE MINOAN KINGS KEPT A HAREM OF NYMPH HANDMAIDENS IN THE ROYAL PALACE.

The very word 'nymph' is loaded with connotations of bewitching beauty, sexual allure and mystery. Although they are dangerously attractive to humans, nymphs are in fact a species of nature-loving faery that are uniquely adapted to a range of natural niches, from meadows and mountains to grottoes and trees.

LES BELLES DAMES
SANS MERCI

Fairies

LATIN NAME
*Homo fata
vulgaris*

HABITAT
*Various; mainly
underground*

LIFESPAN
Varies

SIZE
*Mainly 2-4 ft
(0.6-1.2 m)
high*

**INFORMATION
SOURCE**
*Own Field
Report*

DISTRIBUTION
Worldwide

Puck: thanks to shakespeare, one
of the world's best-known fairies.

Archive note:
When funds permit, the CSL commissions a panel of
independent experts to conduct a special report into a major
cryptozoological problem or area of interest. A recent
legacy from the estate of the pioneering cryptozoologist
Dame Barbara Quinnell prompted the fellows to launch a
multidisciplinary investigation of her favourite subject –
the elusive fairy. Here are some excerpts from this work in
progress, which is being conducted by Finn O'Brien of
Skibbereen University in the West of Ireland.

TYPES OF FAIRY

THE WORD FAIRY ITSELF
STEMS FROM THE OLD
FRENCH FAE OR FAY
(FAIRY), WHICH IS
DERIVED FROM THE
CLASSICAL FATAE, OR
THE FATES. NOT THAT
THIS TRIO OF GODDESSES
BEGAT THE ENTIRE
GENUS OF FAIRIES; THE
CONNECTION IS
MERELY LINGUISTIC.

There is a great deal of confusion between the different races
of fairy, and dividing them into species and sub-species is
sometimes an arbitrary exercise. It is difficult even to com-
pile a full list of the thousands of names given to
individuals, groups and types of fairies, even in just the
dialects and languages of the British Isles. Many fairies, of
course, keep their names a closely-guarded secret, for fear of
it being used against them (as it was against the bogle
Rumpelstiltskin). In general it is advisable to avoid
offending the fairies by making only oblique references to
them - e.g., as 'the Good Folk'.

The fairy races are generally held to have diverged from
the human line of descent quite recently and current genetic
research places their area of origin in the Mediterranean.
They successfully spread to most parts of the world, except
for a few key areas where local species presented stiff resis-
tance. Nymphs excluded fairies from Greece, elves expelled
them from Scandinavia and Germany, and pixies created several
fairy-free zones in the west of England.

The most numerous and widespread of the fairy races is the
common fairy, *Homo fata vulgaris* under the CSL classification. Even within this species there is a bewildering variety
of shapes and sizes, from the noble Irish sidhe to the lowly
sprites of England. This diversity stems from a combination of
rapid adaptation to different ecological niches, together with
the ability to cast a glamour over (enchant) the viewer and
change shape at will. Nonetheless there is a clear distinction
between solitary fairies who spend most of their time alone or
in small groups and what many writers call 'trooping fairies'
- those who live in communities, often with their own highly-
developed social hierarchies.

SOLITARY FAIRIES

Solitary fairies are very diverse in appearance, ranging from
tiny flower fairies to ogre-sized monsters. They are often
ugly, dirty, unkempt and naked, or dressed in an eccentric and
individualistic fashion. They have similar habits and
lifestyle to their relatives, like brownies, hobgoblins,
bogles and goblins. Together with the profusion of local and
dialect names for fairies in the many countries where they are
found, this can lead to confusion. Common types include will
o'the wisps, flower and toadstool fairies, and pucks - as
immortalised in Shakespeare's A Midsummer Night's Dream.

TROOPING FAIRIES

Trooping fairies tend to be fairly homogenous in form, standing between 3 and 4 ft (0.9-1.2 m) high. They usually look like beautiful humans, wearing green or red clothes, riding horses and bearing old-fashioned weapons such as swords and spears. They are often accompanied by many tiny fairies called sprites, and are usually led by larger individuals of 6 ft (1.8 m) or taller, sometimes called heroic fairies.

Many well-known types of fairy fall under this category, including the daoine sidhe (pron. 'theena shee') - the major group in Ireland. The sidhe, who are relics of an ancient and mighty race of fairies, the Tuatha de Danaan (pron. 'tootha day dannan'), live mainly in fairy hills - hence their other name: 'people of the mounds'.

A 17th-century English woodcut of a moonlit dance in a traditional fairy ring.

MINOR TROOPING FAIRIES

HABITAT	NAMES
WALES	FAIR FAMILY
	TYLWYTH TEG
	BENDITH Y MAMAU
	(MOTHER'S BLESSING)
	ELLYLLON
	GWYLLION
SCOTLAND	SEELIE
ISLE OF MAN	SLEIGH BEGGEY
	FERRISHYN
SOUTH AFRICA	ABATWA
WEST AFRICA	AZIZA
SWITZERLAND	FANTINE
IRAN	PERI
USA	NAGUMWASUCK
	NAN A PUSH
ITALY	FATA

A 16th-century Flemish depiction of fairies living in a hill, just like the Irish Tuatha de Danaan.

An important aspect of trooping fairy life is its feudal, hierarchical social structure. The Scottish Seelie (like the sidhe and the tylwyth teg) are aristocrats, ruled by a monarch and living in a society closely resembling the courts of medieval Europe. Some of these monarchs' names are familiar to us through legend and literature. In Shakespeare's A Midsummer Night's Dream, Oberon and Titania - held by some to be the High King and Queen of all British fairies - rule a coalition of English trooping fairies. Other famous rulers include Fin Bheara and Midhir, legendary kings of the Tuatha, Ethal Anbual of the sidhe and Queens Mab and Micol from England.

Seelie can be mischievous and even dangerous, but they are rarely malicious. They are opposed by the Unseelie court, evil fairies who include the Sluagh, or Host, often held to be the spirits of the evil dead. This counterbalance also exists in Wales, where the evil fairies are called the gwyllion, and Ireland, where they are called the adh sidhe; elves have a similar division.

HOMINIDS

Fairies

FAIRY HISTORY

C.3000 BCE

Successive waves of
invasion leave Ireland
under the control of the
Fomorians and Firbolgs -
races of ogres, goblins
and trolls. Britain and
northern France success-
fully colonised.

C.1500 BCE

The Tuatha de Danaan, fairy
people who worshipped the
Goddess Dana, arrive from
the East. After a short and
troubled period of co-exis-
tence, the Tuatha make war
on the goblin races. The
Fomorians are destroyed and
the Firbolgs driven into the
remote western islands of
Ireland.

C.1000 BCE

The human Milesians arrive
(possibly from Spain) and
defeat the Tuatha. Most of
the latter flee west to
the Blessed Isles - Tir
Nan Og - which become a
fairy paradise. Those who
remain grow smaller and
less powerful.

C.900 BCE

The Tuatha take refuge
in the hills and waters
of Ireland as the daoine
sidhe -the 'little peo-
ple' or 'people of the
mounds'. Scattered indi-
viduals spread through-
out the land as solitary
fairies. Fairy peoples
in the rest of the
British Isles suffer a
similar fate.

C.600 BCE

The daoine
sidhe are
defeated by
Eochaid, High
King of
Munster. Their
power diminishes
and they fade
from human
affairs.

FAIRYLAND

NAMES FOR THE
ARCHIPELAGO WHERE
FAIRIES LIVE:
TIR NAN OG
AVALON
HY BRASIL
THE ISLES OF THE
BLEST
PLANT RHYS DWFEN.

FAIRY HABITATS

After the defeat of the Tuatha by the Milesians, there
was a great schism between those fairies who went
overseas and those who stayed in the British Isles.
Those that chose to leave now occupy a number of
islands in the Atlantic whose location is a
geographical mystery. They do not appear on any human
maps, are rarely seen by modern shipping or aircraft
and are invisible to satellite imagery.

Those who still live in Britain live underground in
mounds or barrows, some of which can raise up to
reveal great halls within, others of which have
passages leading to vast, twilit caverns. Fairy hills
are marked with fairy rings or by a hawthorn tree.

Solitary fairies either live in trees (hence the
famous old saying: 'fairy folk are in old oaks'); in
weedy ponds or under toadstools; in ruins; in caves;
under bridges or occasionally in houses.

430-460 AD

St Patrick converts the Irish to Christianity. The old beliefs are suppressed and fairy power is diminished still further.

c.1500 AD

The Nagumwasuck, a fairy tribe attached to the Passamaquoddy Indians, leaves North America in a stone canoe. They are never heard from again.

1520-1610

Queen Mab reigns as monarch of the British fairies.

1560-1700

Under the influence of Puritanism, fairies are seen as minor demons. Witch hunts in New England are a major assault on people who have befriended fairies.

1600-1750

Some European solitary fairies travel to New World (America and Australia) with European colonists.

1830-1855

Fairies with grey skin and blue clothes sighted in the Isle of Man.

1800-1880

European artists such as Henry Fuseli, Richard Dadd and Richard Doyle create rich, romantic images of fairyland.

DADD'S FAIRY FELLER'S MASTERSTROKE.

1922

Public interest in fairies is renewed by British author Sir Arthur Conan Doyle, who publishes convincing photographs of the 'Cottingley fairies' taken by cousins Elsie Wright and Frances Griffiths.

1931

Female fairies, about 1.5 ft (0.46 m) tall, seen in a garden in Warwickshire, in the English Midlands.

1983

Frances Griffiths admits Cottingley fairies were fakes.

Fairies

FAIRY MAGIC

As part of the Quinnell program, the Sternberg Forensic Laboratory at Penn State University is conducting a series of controlled experiments to test the numerous folklore fairy recipes and remedies. Some of their tests follow.

A recipe to invoke fairies

A team of postgraduate forensic scientists set out to test the famous invocation from the 17th-century manuscript in the Bodleian Library (MS. Ashmole 1406), which the author used to summon a fairy by the name of Margarett Barrance. The theory was that by summoning a fairy one can trap it using a glass and force it do one's bidding.

LAB REPORT
We were sceptical about 'binding' a fairy to a piece of glass, a proposition that defies the laws of physics. We also failed to see how the hen's blood could have any effect if the glass were fumigated. However, we proceeded with the experiment, using a 3 in x 3 in (7.5 cm x 7.5 cm) piece of lead crystal.

A local fairy called Fremsley was selected for invocation.

METHOD
Crystal steeped in hen's blood for three weeks; washed with Lourdes water and thoroughly aired; three one-year-old hazel wands stripped and inscribed with name 'Fremsley' while chanting name; wands buried under Miller's Mound on Weds; Fremsley invoked on Fri.

RESULT
Not proved. Fremsley did not manifest himself, therefore efficacy of crystal-binding could not be evaluated.

D. Crosby, Research Assistant

An excellent way to zett a ƒayrie, but ƒor my selƒe I call marzarett ðarrance but this will obtaine any one that is not allready bound.
ƒirst zett a broad square christall or Venus zlasse in length and breadth 3 inches, then lay that zlasse or christall in the bloud oƒ a white henne 3 wednesdayes or 3 ƒridayes. Then take it out and wash it with holy aqua and ƒumizate it. Then take 3 hazle stickes or wands oƒ an yeaRe zroth, pill them ƒayre and white, and make soe longe ar you wRite the spiRitts name, or ƒayRies name, which you call 3 times, on every sticke being made ƒlatt one side, then bury them under some hill whereas you suppose ƒayRies haunt, the wednesday beƒore you call her, and the ƒriday ƒollowinze take them uppe and call hir at 8 or 3 or 10 oƒ the clocke which be zood plannetts and howres ƒor that turne. ðut when you call, be in cleane ꞇiƒe and turne thy ƒace towards the east, and when you have her bind her to that stone or ꝣlasse.

Ways to See Fairies

The team set out to test some time-honoured formulae to help catch sight of fairies:

a) catch sight of one between two blinks of eye.

METHOD
A randomised sample of 100 students (Group T) were thoroughly briefed on fairy identification and asked to try blinking rapidly for four periods of five minutes a day, twice in the morning, twice in the afternoon. A control group (Group C) of 100 further students received the same briefing, but were only instructed to keep a sharp lookout for fairies for the same amount of time. The experiment lasted for four weeks, making a total of 22,400 observation sessions.

RESULT
Insufficient evidence for proof. Although more fairies were seen were seen by Group T, the total was too low for the differential to be statistically significant. Attention should be given to the possible use of alcohol and hallucinogenic drugs in the sample groups.

b) on a full moon, on Midsummer's Eve, look through a self-bored stone (one with a natural hole in the middle) from some fresh water.

METHOD
Researchers stood in various lakes and rivers and made the required observations.

RESULT
A success. All three saw fairies at some point in their evenings.

c) hold four grains of wheat on a four-leafed clover.

METHOD
Vacuum-packed wheat and clover were posted to 1,000 people worldwide, together with detailed instructions.

RESULT
Inconclusive. Although 12 sightings were reported, all came from Ireland, Wales and Scotland. Further research needed to find out why.

d) use a traditional ointment made for seeing fairies.

METHOD
Researchers followed this recipe, based on an 18th-century book of fairy lore.

RESULT
Unsuccessful. Enough ointment was made for 25 applications, but no fairy sightings were reported.

1. Mash a handful of four-leafed clovers in a pestle and mortar.
2. Mix with petroleum jelly.
3. Infuse for 15 minutes.
4. Strain the mixture and decant into sterilised dark jars. Leave to cool.
5. Spread the ointment on your eyelids for up to an hour of uninterrupted fairy viewing.

seen squinting through stone – Friday.

After two weeks of blinking: RESULT!! Sunday.

Blinkety blink – hey presto! – Tuesday.

PAGE FROM AN OBSERVER'S SKETCHBOOK.

Fairies

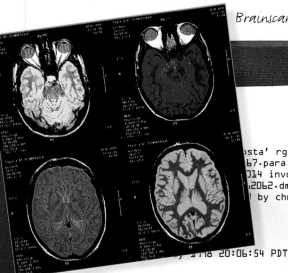

sta' rgc@sp.para.br
67.para.br ([204.62.740.250])with SMTP id YBB39682 for
014 invoked by uid 2); 29 May 1998 03:06:55 -0000
2062.dmail@sp.para.br>
by christina.com with ESMTP id UHG738409
18 20:06:54 PDT

A COLLEAGUE FROM THE SAO PAOLO INSTITUTE FOR PARANORMAL STUDIES IN BRAZIL SENT ME THIS EXCELLENT ANALYSIS OF THE FAIRY POWER OF ILLUSION AND ENCHANTMENT KNOWN AS GLAMOUR.

Finn,

Thanks for all your encouragement and support in my negotiations with the Quinnell Trust and the CSL. You have been so helpful, and I feel I know you as a personal friend. Strange, no?

The grant will enable me to conduct a series of close observations of European fairies, and will help my ongoing investigation of one of the greatest challenges in paranormal science: to explain the amazing disturbances of natural laws which surround fairies. In short, to solve the mystery of glamor.

Fairies use glamor to become invisible and to disguise objects, people and places. They are able to change their size, shape and appearance, so that they look like animals, or to become so beautiful that humans lose their senses and are bewitched. They can addle human senses so that they become lost and directionless. This is a favorite trick of the Welsh fairies, the gwyllion. Fairies can also remove the essential goodness (or foyson) of food, leaving only the flavorless appearance,

There are many theories about the nature of fairy glamors, but the main explanations are as follows:

1. Fairies have the power to manipulate electromagnetic fields, altering sound and light as they pass through space.
2. Fairies are skilled hypnotists who can induce hallucinations or implant powerful false memories.
3. Fairies are able to administer powerful mind-altering drugs or potions to people without them finding out.
4. Fairies can temporarily alter the molecular structure of matter to create a force-field or zone in which the laws of physics cease to apply.
5. Fairies can also affect the gravitational fields around them, since there are many reports of them being able to fly. Wings on fairies are generally held to be decorative rather than functional.

A recent area of scientific interest is the phenomenon of fairy time. Visitors to fairy lands find that time passes far more slowly there, and a year spent in fairyland can be the equivalent of a century in the human world. The old Irish tale of Oisin illustrates this well. According to legend, Oisin spent a few years in Tir Nan Og but was eventually allowed to return - with the strict injunction that he should never touch the ground. He finds that hundreds of years have passed and Ireland is much changed. At one point, he stooped from his horse to help some men lift a stone trough, and brushed the ground. At once, his body caught up with time, and he fell down, an ancient, wizened man. Oisin seems to have escaped lightly - many humans who have been to fairyland crumble to dust when they touch mortal soil.

The current thinking is that fairies have found a way to exploit Einstein's theory of relativity, which states that time passes more slowly as objects approach the speed of light. However, the mechanism by which they do this remains a mystery. It may be worth noting here that missing time is a common element of alien abduction scenarios.

Fairies are credited with the gift of prophecy, but they are reputed to be unreliable prophets, partly because they do not like to look upon evil. They therefore report only what pleases them. Given that the normal fabric of space-time appears to be distorted by the fairies, it is not hard to imagine that they have some method of seeing the future.

Finn, I am now making arrangements for my travels. I expect to be in Ireland later this year, and will send you details of the experiments I plan to carry out there. You know, we Brazilians do not often get the chance to go abroad. Meanwhile I am so looking forward to meeting you at last. I read your Ph.D. thesis on Fairy Dancing and found it really very stimulating. Maybe when we meet, you will teach me Irish dance and I will teach you the samba in return. A fair exchange, no? And, Finn, I saw the photo of you in the CSL Review - you look so handsome and strong! I can just imagine your arms around me and your cheek close to mine as we move across the floor. And afterwards

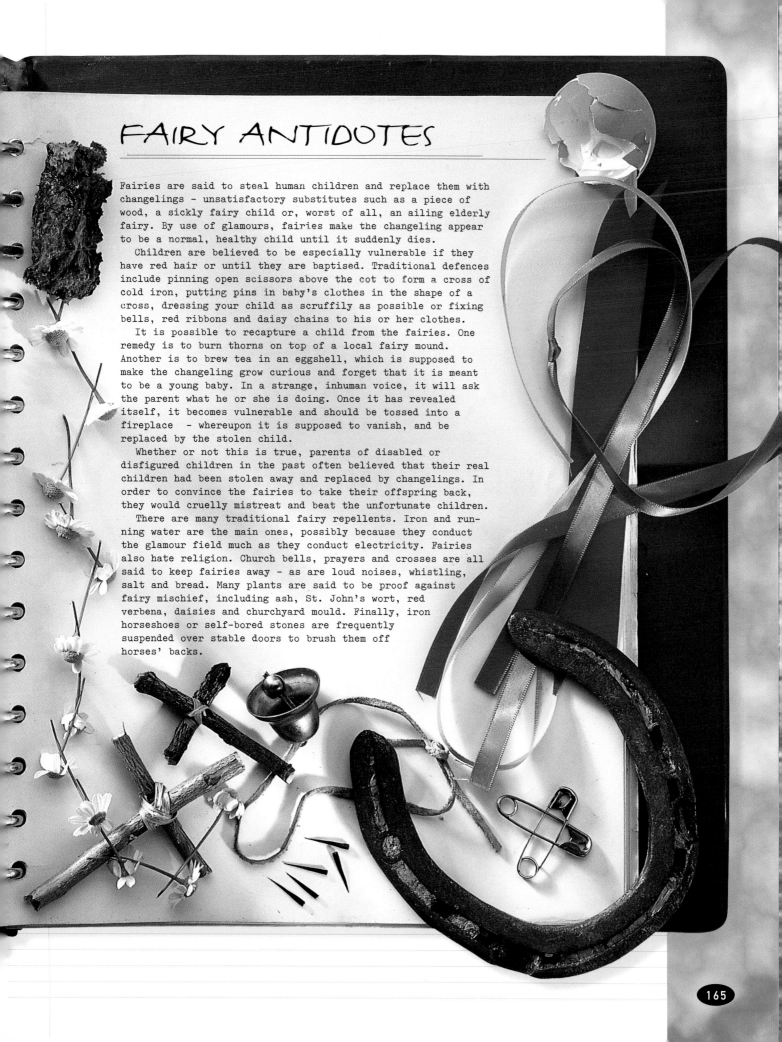

FAIRY ANTIDOTES

Fairies are said to steal human children and replace them with changelings - unsatisfactory substitutes such as a piece of wood, a sickly fairy child or, worst of all, an ailing elderly fairy. By use of glamours, fairies make the changeling appear to be a normal, healthy child until it suddenly dies.

Children are believed to be especially vulnerable if they have red hair or until they are baptised. Traditional defences include pinning open scissors above the cot to form a cross of cold iron, putting pins in baby's clothes in the shape of a cross, dressing your child as scruffily as possible or fixing bells, red ribbons and daisy chains to his or her clothes.

It is possible to recapture a child from the fairies. One remedy is to burn thorns on top of a local fairy mound. Another is to brew tea in an eggshell, which is supposed to make the changeling grow curious and forget that it is meant to be a young baby. In a strange, inhuman voice, it will ask the parent what he or she is doing. Once it has revealed itself, it becomes vulnerable and should be tossed into a fireplace - whereupon it is supposed to vanish, and be replaced by the stolen child.

Whether or not this is true, parents of disabled or disfigured children in the past often believed that their real children had been stolen away and replaced by changelings. In order to convince the fairies to take their offspring back, they would cruelly mistreat and beat the unfortunate children.

There are many traditional fairy repellents. Iron and running water are the main ones, possibly because they conduct the glamour field much as they conduct electricity. Fairies also hate religion. Church bells, prayers and crosses are all said to keep fairies away - as are loud noises, whistling, salt and bread. Many plants are said to be proof against fairy mischief, including ash, St. John's wort, red verbena, daisies and churchyard mould. Finally, iron horseshoes or self-bored stones are frequently suspended over stable doors to brush them off horses' backs.

Dwarves & Gnomes

LATIN NAME
*Homo
diminuensis*

HABITAT
*Mines and
caverns*

LIFESPAN
200+ years

SIZE
*3 ft (1 m) high,
or less*

**INFORMATION
SOURCE**
CSL Review

DISTRIBUTION
*Northern and
Central Europe*

DWARVES AND GNOMES ARE VERY similar. They share the same way of life, and are both closely associated with the earth, mining, metalworking and the hoarding of treasure. They are, however, easy to tell apart. Dwarves are generally around 3 ft (1 m) high, with a stocky, badly-proportioned body shape known to medicine as achondroplastic dwarfism. This means that their limbs are unusually short, while their heads and torsos are well developed, and thus appear over-sized. Gnomes, on the other hand, are usually smaller than dwarves and perfectly proportioned, resembling miniature human beings. Males of both races have long beards, and both species tend to dress the same way, wearing rough brown garments and caps. According to some authorities, dwarf women are also bearded. They are certainly few in number, and only have a few children. The low birthrate, combined with a long gestation periods of 18 months, keep the dwarf population low. The gnome population suffers the same constraints and is of a similar size.

TRIPLE TROUBLE

The homeland of the dwarf is in Scandinavia, where there are three types. Black dwarves are morose and solitary. Brown dwarves are more gregarious, and thus more likely to interact with humans, but they are mischievous. They have been

THE LITTLE PEOPLE

The halfling races are down-to-earth, practical creatures with a sense of mischief. They seem more like humans than their faery cousins, but in fact they are genetically closer to the latter, with whom they share many characteristics.

THE MAIN DIFFERENCE BETWEEN DWARVES AND GNOMES IS THEIR PHYSICAL PROPORTION. THE DWARF (LEFT) HAS A STOCKY BUILD AND A DISPROPORTIONATELY LARGE HEAD AND BODY. THE GNOME (RIGHT) HAS THE SAME PROPORTIONS AS A HUMAN BEING AND TENDS TO BE SLIGHTER OF BUILD AND SHORTER THAN THE DWARF.

Dwarves are renowned for their fabulous wealth and the wonderful products of their smithing. In Norse myth the *dvergar*, as they are known, created Thor's hammer, Mjolnir, Odin's ring of perpetual wealth, Draupnir, and the goddess Freya's Brisingamen necklace. In the Teutonic legend of the Nibelung, dwarves create Siegfried's cloak of invisibility and magical sword Balmung. The fateful hoard of treasure that changes hands in the tale is the property of Alberich, the dwarf-king.

FRIENDS IN HIGH PLACES

Usually dwarves and gnomes greedily hoard their precious stones, metals and marvellous artefacts, but should a mortal win favour he or she will be well rewarded. On rare occasions, humans are granted a visit to their wonderful mountain halls, to join in the feasting and revelry and usually return to the surface laden with wealth.

Although mountain dwarves are usually friendlier than mine-dwelling ones, few dwarves actively associate with humans. An exception are the Swiss *barbegazi*, whose name is probably derived from *barbe-glacée*, French for 'frozen beard'. *Barbegazi* are white-furred dwarves with huge feet that can be used as skis, who sometimes help shepherds round up lost sheep. *Barbegazi* prefer high altitudes and low temperatures, and are rarely seen.

Dwarves have spread around much of the world – they are known to the Inuit, for instance – but are only a significant presence in Northern and Central Europe. Regional names for dwarves include: *ludki*, in Slavic; *lutki*, in Hungarian; *duergar*, in Northern England; and the Norse *dvergar* and Swiss *barbegazi* described above.

accused of kidnapping human children to work in their mines. White dwarves, the type that has settled most widely in Northern Europe, are usually better disposed towards humans, although they remain proud and jealous of their privacy. They are comfortable above ground, emerging on spring nights to feast and carouse – but always being certain to return underground at sunrise. Any dwarves unlucky enough to be caught on the surface during the day are trapped there, and must wait until night falls before they can get home.

Dwarves and gnomes alike are keen metal-workers, and are experts in every stage of the process from mining the ore to smelting, smithing, and fine craftsmanship such as filigree work. With a life expectancy of two centuries or more, dwarves are able to build up a tremendous amount of expertise and skill, which is passed on from generation to generation through lengthy apprenticeships.

MINER KEY

Powers similar to their faery cousins have long been attributed to dwarves. Their caps, for instance, are said to confer invisibility, and stealing one puts its owner under your power. Experts, however, argue that this impression stems from confusion between fairies, hobgoblins and brownies, and that dwarves do not have the same powers as *Homo fata*.

One area in which gnomes and dwarves undoubtedly are gifted is that of 'geological perception'. They sense much that would be hidden to even the most experienced human miner, and are able to sniff out ores and gem stones and detect the inclines and faults in which these precious resources are formed. The 16th-century alchemist Paracelsus said that gnomes moved through the earth like fish through water.

THE ABILITY OF DWARVES AND GNOMES TO DETECT DEPOSITS OF GEMS COULD BE DUE TO AN ACUTE SENSE OF SMELL AND A SIXTH 'SONAR' SENSE, OR IT MAY SIMPLY BE ANCIENT WISDOM.

HOMINIDS

Pixy

LATIN NAME
Homo fata pixa

HABITAT
Moors and rural areas

LIFESPAN
Unknown

SIZE
Usually less than 3 ft (1 m) high

INFORMATION SOURCE
Field Report

DISTRIBUTION
Cornwall, Devon, W. Somerset and W. Dorset

BACKGROUND

England's West Country is one of the few areas of Europe largely free of fairies. Instead, this region is the preserve of the pixies, also known as the pigsies, pisgies and, in Cornwall, the piskies. According to local legend, the pixies defeated the fairies in a pitched battle and drove them east of the River Parret, which flows roughly north-south through western Dorset and Somerset).

VIXEN TOR, ON DARTMOOR, NEAR PIXY HILL — A KNOWN HAUNT OF PIXIES.

3 June. Widecombe in the Moor, Devon

I have come to the heart of Dartmoor in the hope of catching sight of a pixy. Widecombe in the Moor is a major centre for tourism and outdoor activities, and I am staying at a bed and breakfast in the hope of hearing some traveller's tales. People here are very chatty, and I soon picked up some interesting leads.

A middle-aged couple from St. Austell, in Cornwall, told me that their Cornish piskies are slightly different from the local variety. In Cornwall they tend to appear as wizened old men, or in the form of hedgehogs, which they called urchins. A young woman from Somerset explained that in her area the pixies are known for their mischievous ways, and will steal horses and ponies in the night to run

them round circles known as gallitraps, which are like the fairy rings of the rest of the country. She said that they even come into houses and throw pots and pans, but can be placated by leaving out a bowl of clean water for washing their babies, and by sweeping the hearth so that they can dance upon it at night.

A snub-nosed young man with a mop of red hair and a jaunty green cap said that there was a gallitrap up on Pixy Mound, some miles to the west. He appeared to be squinting at something, so I turned to see what it might be, but when I turned back he had finished his glass of milk and disappeared.

4th June, Widecombe in the Moor

I set off bright and early and made good time over the first few miles. Cresting a rise I came to a low stone wall and hopped over a stile into a wide field. Making my way towards the gate on the other side, I experienced a

A SOUVENIR FRIDGE MAGNET FROM CORNWALL. SEEING A PISKY IS CONSIDERED TO BE A GOOD OMEN IN THE WEST COUNTRY, ALTHOUGH A CLOSE ENCOUNTER IS NOT WITHOUT RISK.

GOOD LUCK from THE CORNISH PISKY

moment of disorientation, and found myself back at the stile. I put it down to the hot sun and set off again, keeping my eyes fixed on the gate.

After some 10 minutes of walking I realised that it was taking an inordinately long time to cross the field, and turned round to see how far I had come. There - behind me! - was the gate, some hundred yards distant. A strange feeling came over me, and I realised that I was being pixy-led, under the influence of a confusing faery glamour. It was exciting to know that I was drawing close to my quarry, but disturbing to realise

SUBMITTED BY
Dr. John Eliot FCSL
DATE   LOCATION
3-5/6 1992   Devon, England
CATALOGUE No
CXPc 6 # 209

LOCAL CHILD WITH COAT TURNED INSIDE OUT
AND HAT ON BACKWARDS TO WARD OFF PIXIES.

I remembered what the Somerset lass had told me the day before: if you put one foot inside a gallitrap, you can see the pixies, but if you put both feet in you will become their prisoner. Should a criminal put even just a toe inside the ring, he would be hanged for certain.

I tentatively put my right foot into the ring. There was a sudden laugh from nearby. Looking up, I saw the red-headed youth from the day before, perched on a rock. He greeted me warmly, and sauntered into the gallitrap. 'Hob's foot!' he exclaimed, 'Come and look at this'. He indicated something in the grass, and I was just about to join him – but something held me back.

that I might wander for hours over the same field. Fortunately I was forearmed with information. I turned my jacket inside out, put my hat on backwards and began singing loudly – all known remedies to deter pixies and cast off their glamour. Sure enough, I was able to cross to the gate without any more trouble.

On reaching Pixy Mound, I soon found the gallitrap – a ring of darker grass with mushrooms punctuating the perimeter.

In a flash it came to me. One of his ears peeked from beneath his green cap, and I could clearly see that it was pointed! The youth was a pixy, trying to trick me into the gallitrap. Realising that he'd been spotted, he gave an impish laugh, doffed his hat with a bow and disappeared! I returned to my billet with a traveller's tale of my own.

This is the pixy who cheekily tried to lure me into the gallitrap.

RAMBLERS ARE ADVISED TO TAKE CARE TO AVOID WALKING INTO GALLITRAPS LIKE THIS.

169

A fragment from a map found in Erceldoune, and believed to be part of Thomas the Rhymer's own map of Fairyland.

THOMAS THE RHYMER

Humans who have dealings with the fairies usually lose (in various combinations) their wits, their loved ones and their lives. The 13th century Scot, Thomas of Erceldoune, seems to have been one of the rare exceptions. A poet whose work has survived for six centuries, he was popularly known as Thomas the Rhymer or True Thomas. According to legend, the Queen of Fairyland carried him off for a seven-year stint as a gastarbeiter in her realm. The prices she exacted for his return to his own world were an inability to lie and the curse of prophesying in rhyming couplets. On the whole, Thomas probably got off lightly. In old age he vanished, led into the forest one night by two deer. A case, no doubt, of the call of the wild.

AN EXTRAORDINARY FIND

Historical documents and deeds signed by Thomas and his son attest that he lived from *c.*1220 to *c.*1297, and was known as Thomas Learmont or Thomas Rymour de Erceldoune. Traditional ballads and folk tales describe his adventures in Fairyland and the terms of his return. His fame was assured when he correctly predicted the death of the Scottish king Alexander III in 1286, and the Battle of Bannockburn in 1314.

Given his familiarity with Fairyland, it is hardly surprising that Thomas has already been studied by CSL members. A susurrus of excitement therefore ran through 100 Piccadilly recently when reports came in of an extraordinary find in an Ayrshire antique shop. A diary had come to light, the quondam property of one 'Sleekit' Snoddie, DD, antiquary and 'meenister' of Erceldoune 1725–1753.

CSL-sponsored excavations based on Snoddie's diary have recently unearthed the parchment map shown on the preceding pages and three fragments of a document. Although radiocarbon testing and other procedures are still underway, Society experts are already hailing the artefacts as authentically 13th-century. They could be among the most exciting archaeological finds of the decade because the map shows signs of being nothing less than Thomas the Rhymer's own map of Fairyland. The three text fragments are reproduced opposite. The first is shown as an original with a typewritten translation. The fragility of the second and third fragments rendered photography undesirable: they are therefore given as typewritten transcripts only.

an moſt Richlie
caparisoneð was she,
with ſine ſilks all girt aboſe,
an bells all oſ silver, lest
ſiſty in numbre,
ðið hange pon her ſaire
mounce's mane.
her voice was like oſ angells,
an she ðið summone me to
ſet beſiðe her.
An nowe Thomas, ye mun
Riðe wi' me,
to lanð moſt sweet an ſey,
an ye maun ſerve thro
weel or wae,
as may chaunce tae be.
An so we raðe, thro lighces
moſt strange,
ðeset on alle ſiðes by moanes,
ſor neer ſorty nighces,
thro a ſea oſ blooðe anð
ðowne lanes moſt pleasant,
an presencly we ðið come to
a right gooðe place,
a ſaerie lanðe oſ pleasant aspect.

TRANSLATION
The silks she was clad in, rich they were indeed,
Silvern bells, nigh on sixty, on the neck of her steed,
'Come sit down beside me, dear Thomas,' quoth she,
'To the Land of the Fairies you'll ride now with me.'
'Be it ill luck or good luck you will serve me well.'
Then we rode out together through lights that gleamed fell,
Through pathways and moaning and blood we did ride
For full forty nights, and I at her side,
'Till we came to the vale that's called Heartsease always—
The Land of the Fairies, where I passed many days.

Fragment 2:
.....-ing my third day in this new land I was further dazzled and amazed. Drawing near to a great hill I beheld that it rose up on pillars, and within was a great feast with ....pale-faced children of mortal aspect, who looked imploringly at me, and mimed that I should not eat of the feast. Whereupon the Queen, seeing the direction of my gaze, said to me:

'Sweet Thomas, you need not fear the eating of our fairy food. We have brought you here on account of your wisdom, to act as a counsellor for our royal person. We would not see you harmed.

Eat and drink, and pay no heed to these little mortals, who are but fodder for the Teind.'

And so we went up to the High Table ....tastes of the world, yet more intense and savoury .. in their revelry..dark-eyed nymphs and lusty sprites...women with the wings of insects, beasts with the breasts of maidens, and they swept in closer and pressed...touch...tiny hands......-

Thomas the Rhymer

Eugene Tristejambon's frontispiece to the 1865 illustrated edition of The Ballad of True Thomas.

Fragment 3:
then....Hob's lane and....Fiddler's....many leagues....to our faery steeds....but yards. And presently we came to high cliffs and looked out over Plant Rhys Dwfen and the Floating Isles, and beyond, to the far-off coast of Wales. "Your Majesty, why....I saw....sadness and despondency.

....home, my love?" she said to me. I looked away, to the far North ....you must return, this very eve."

I was greatly afraid, on hearing this. Why must I return? Would not the years of mortal passing fall upon my head in one fatal rush ere I touched the earthly ground?

....I have spun....glamour....seven in number are the mortal years of your absence. Go home Thomas, and with you take my gifts, so....
"Wherefore....the time of the Teind, and I would not have you taken....more.

'....' signifies indecipherable passage.

EDITOR'S NOTE:
'TEIND': A REGULAR LEVY OF SOULS PAYABLE BY THE QUEEN OF FAIRYLAND TO THE DEVIL.

Leprechaun

LATIN NAME
Homo fata sutor

HABITAT
*Inside hills;
wine cellars*

LIFESPAN
200 + years

SIZE
*0.5–2 ft
(0.15–0.6 m)
high*

**INFORMATION
SOURCE**
Postcards

DISTRIBUTION
Ireland

NOTE:
THE NAME CLURICAUN IS THOUGHT TO BE A DERIVATION OF
LEPRECHAUN. THE WORD IS DERIVED FROM THE GAELIC
LUACHARMÁN ('PYGMY'), OR LEITH BHROGAN ('ONE-
SHOEMAKER' — LEPRECHAUNS
ARE, IT SEEMS, SKILLED
COBBLERS). OTHER VARIATIONS
INCLUDE LEPRACAUN,
LEPRECHAN, LURIGADAUNE,
LOGHERY MAN AND LURICAUNE.

The Lepracaun or Fairy Shoemaker

April 6th, 1935

POST **CARD**

CORRESPONDENCE

THE VULCAN SERIES

FOR ADDRESS ONLY

Bunty old chap —

View halloo and all that! Strangest thing
happened last night. I'm staying at Kenmarnly
Manor — frightful old pile — with old 'Bugger'
Hopkins (you remember, the fellow who used to
fag for Atkins Minor). Well last night I went
down to the wine cellar for some port, and saw
the rummest thing — a tiny little fella, got up
in a leather apron, red coat, blue stockings and
silver-buckled shoes! 'Well,' I said to him, and
who the devil may you be?'. 'To be sure,' says
he, 'oi'm just after moindin' the woine, loike.'
Put me in mind of a leprechaun, he did.
You know, the little fellas who make shoes all
day, and hide pots of gold about the place.
Apparently, if you can catch one and keep your
eye on him, he'll lead you to a fortune. Sounds

Published by G. Mew, Post Office, Wootton Bridge.

BRITISH MANUFACTURE

Bunty Wingfield-Stratford
The Grange
Little Binkley
Sussex
ENGLAND

like bally nonsense to me.
'I say.... are you a leprechaun, by any chance?" says I.
'No,' says he, 'oi'm a cluricaun ya daft eejit!' And do
you know, he bally well vanished!
Of course, I was hogwhimpering drunk
at the time!
Tally ho!

Bigglesworth x

April 9th, 1935

POST

THE VULCAN SERIES

FOR ADDRESS

CORRESPONDENCE

Bunty old bean,

Here's a doodle of the wee cluricaun fellow I spotted in the cellar the other night. I may
have been steamed but I can't shake
the memory of the little blighter!
Not bad eh? I've had the
old sketch pad out
quite a bit
recently. Not
much else to do
round here, to
be honest ...

Pip pip!

Bigglesworth x

Published by G. Mew, Post Office, Wootton Bridge.

BRITISH MANUFACTURE

Bunty Wingfield-Stratford
The Grange
Little Binkley
Sussex
ENGLAND

HOME
HELP

This sub-species of fairy has established a curious symbiotic relationship with humans. In return for a roof over its head, a warm hearth and the odd morsel, a brownie can be a valuable help around the home, farm or workplace.

PAUL HEY

BROWNIES LOOK LIKE short, scruffy men and women dressed in ragged brown clothing. Many of them have no noses (only nostrils) and fingers that are all joined together, like mittens.

They are helpful creatures, doing chores left undone by servants and farm tasks such as reaping, threshing, mowing, herding and guarding livestock. This makes them popular with owners of houses, farms or mills, but human help is usually more hostile, as brownies may punish lazy servants or expose their misdeeds. In return for their hard work, brownies should be given the best milk and cream, and the choicest cakes and bread.

GREED IS *NOT* GOOD

Normally brownies are invisible, but they will sometimes show themselves to a favourite family member. Just like fairies, they can also use special powers to steal the essence of food (the *foyson*), leaving only the appearance.

Those who wish to live in harmony with a brownie must follow strict rules of etiquette. Firstly, brownies should never be directly rewarded for their labours.

Food should be left where they may find it, as if by accident. On the other hand, the lucky recipient of a brownie's favours should never take them for granted, or become greedy. There is a famous tale about the brownie Maggy Moloch, who was so useful about the farm that the farmer dismissed all of his human helpers. Maggy was so annoyed that she transformed herself into a malicious household goblin (boggart) – a typical brownie act of revenge.

A BROWNIE BY ANY OTHER NAME

Brownies are known as *bodachs* or *broonies* in Scotland, and a stupid brownie is called a *dobie*. The extinct *killmouli* (with an enormous nose but no mouth) used to work in the textile mills of Northern England. Similar creatures occur in much of the rest of Europe. The Welsh *pwca* or *bwca*, the *hobs* of England and the *nisse* (derived from the Norse) are all local names for this peculiar, but on the whole benign, hominid.

Unobserved by the family – but keenly watched by the cat – a brownie warms himself at a hearth in the north of England. He will make sure that the fire stays lit.

LATIN NAME
Homo fata domesticus

HABITAT
Homes, farms and mills

LIFESPAN
Unknown

SIZE
about 3 ft (1 m) high

INFORMATION SOURCE
CSL Review

DISTRIBUTION
Scotland, NE and Central England

HOMINIDS

Banshees

LATIN NAME
*Homo fata
maerora*

HABITAT
Variable

LIFESPAN
Variable

SIZE
Human

**INFORMATION
SOURCE**
Letter

DISTRIBUTION
Ireland,
Scotland

THE CRYPTOZOOLOGICAL

*Wherein this year of our Lord, Eighteen Hundred and
Ninety-Nine, I, Michael Shaughnessy McGillivray
O'Flaugherty, 4th Lord of Armeath, 19th Marquis of
Roachford, do hereby aver that this shall be a true and honest
record of matters pertaining to the O'Flaugherty family, to be
given to my eldest son, Shaughnessy Michael Almont
O'Flaugherty, to dispose of as he sees fit and proper.*

My dearest Shaun,
*By the time you come into receipt of this document I shall be laid in my
grave, and you may already know more of this matter than you would wish.
When my own father died (God rest his soul!) a similar letter was placed in
my hands, and I repeat to you now the tale which he bequeathed to me.*
*Our family, Shaun, is among the oldest in Ireland. The true Celtic
blood flows in our veins, and no other, and thus has it always been. With this
Celtic heritage has come a strange and fateful burden, for our family is haunted
by a bean sidhe, a fairy woman, rendered by the English invader as 'banshee'.
You will already have heard her mournful cry, as I heard her keen on the
day that my father died. Aye, but it is a terrible sound, Shaun, an unearthly
one. I remember that your mother's hair stood on end and that your aunt
went terribly pale.*
*This bean sidhe is known to Celtic peoples throughout these Isles — in
Scotland she is called the bean-nighe, or The Washer at the Ford; in
Manx she is the lhiannan shee, doubtless she is related to the hags of England,
and the nocnitsa of Eastern Europe. Whenever she is heard (for she is rarely
seen) it foretells a death in the family to which she is attached.*
*Cousin Connor, who lives in Scotland, says that before a death the bean-
nighe will be seen washing the funerary vestments in a stream. Correctly
approached she can be made to answer questions and grant wishes.*
Our own family spirit dates back to 1609, when the 1st Marquis of

Roachford, by all accounts an evil man, got a local girl with child. Attempting to hide his shame he murdered the girl and buried her body beneath the great oak in the walled garden. Two weeks later the girl was seen again, a beautiful woman wearing a grey cloak over a green dress, who set up a terrible wailing. The Marquis died that very night — from terror according to some.

Since that time, the passing of any O'Flaugherty has been marked by the cry of the bean sidhe. Now that my time is near we will soon hear her keen once more. I pray, dear Shaun, that she will not call for you for many a long year.

Your loving father.

Signed this Thirteenth day of May, 1899

Michael O'Flaugherty

Michael Shaughnessy McGillivray O'Flaugherty, Lord of Armeath, Marquis of Roachford

And Witnessed by

John Galveston   *Carruthers*   *Wm Aldecott*

The Right Hon.   The Very Reverend   William Aldecott, Esq.
John Galveston, QC   Derek P. Carruthers

Goblins & Orcs

LATIN NAME
Goblins: Homo kobalis
Orcs: H. kobalis orcus

HABITAT
Caves and caverns; human habitations

LIFESPAN
Goblins: 30 years; orcs: 40 years

SIZE
Goblins: c. 3 ft (1 m); Orcs: c. 5 ft (1.5 m) high

INFORMATION SOURCE
CSL Review

DISTRIBUTION
Eurasia and North America

G OBLINS AND ORCS, CLOSELY RELATED races of the species *Homo kobalis,* are renowned for their vicious tempers, low cunning, lack of morals and depraved appetites. These qualities rank them among the nastiest hominids known to man. Not only do they share several common characteristics – from a tribal social structure to a dislike of sunlight – but they also share a common status in human folklore, where they have a reputation as mischievous household spirits and nursery bogeys. This is a serious underestimation of their true nature, for they are, in fact, dangerous and violent creatures capable of inflicting real harm on humans.

DIRTINESS IS NEXT TO UNGODLINESS

It is generally agreed that both goblins and orcs are sub-species of *H. kobalis.* Some cryptotaxonomists have argued that goblins and orcs should be classified as members of a single subspecies, citing a range of anatomical similarities. However, the differences between the two races – especially the variation in size – are now considered decisive evidence in favour of their separation.

Like most other kobaloids, goblins and orcs are ugly and dirty, with mottled skin, patches of hair and a rancid odour. Goblins are small and wizened, with leathery brown skin and twisted, almost bestial faces. They have small pig-like eyes, broad flat noses, thin sneering lips and an array of sharp but filthy teeth. Goblins' hands have long fingers and sharp nails, which accumulate filth so that any scratch quickly becomes infected. Typically, a goblin will wear ragged clothes with an unkempt and dirty appearance; some goblin gangs go about equipped with crude weapons and leather armour.

GLOOM ROOM

Orcs look even less human than goblins, with brownish-green leathery skin and pig-like snouts with protruding, tusk-like lower incisors. Orc bands are likely to be equipped for battle, with chain mail, shields, spears and scimitars, marked with the symbols and motifs of their tribe.

The need to avoid sunlight forces goblins and orcs alike to make their homes in dark and gloomy caves, caverns and underground passages. In a large tribe, these may extend to vast, warren-like mazes. Goblin hideaways are far removed from areas of human habitation, and can be found only in remote wilderness or mountain areas.

Sometimes, however, goblins invade human homes and take up residence in the same manner as some other faery creatures. Many faery species can be useful in the home, but goblins can be relied on to make trouble, and householders are advised to evict them swiftly and ruthlessly.

MAD, BAD AND DANGEROUS TO KNOW

Goblins and orcs spend most of their lives in darkness and isolation, quarrelling with other hominids and ambushing passers-by. They are, however, becoming very rare.

The goblins' place in the evolutionary framework has been the subject of intense cryptozoological study. It seems likely that there have been several branchings off the line of hominid descent within the last 2 million years, one of which has evolved into modern humans, the others evolving into other hominid species. Goblins and orcs are most closely related to the other kobaloids – the kobolds, troglodytes and boggarts – and then to their much larger cousins, the ogre and the troll. Evolutionary biologists place them as close to us as to their most distant faery relatives, the elves and fairies.

RELATIVELY SPEAKING

One avenue of scholarly enquiry has concentrated on the original inhabitants of Ireland, the Firbolgs (meaning 'bog dwellers'), and their supercession by the *Tuatha de Danann* and other races. It is argued that these represent evidence for the early presence of non-human hominid races, with the Firbolgs frequently identified with an ancestral goblin race. If evolutionary precursors of goblins were widespread in remote parts of Europe before *Homo sapiens* arrived, their timeline appears to correspond with that of *H. neanderthalis* and branch off the human line of descent within the last 500,000 years. Palaeocryptoanthropologists have suggested, with some justification, a crucial bifurcation in the hominid family tree, making goblins, giants, ogres and trolls the descendants of Neanderthal man, while tracing a separate evolutionary path for humans, fairies, elves and halflings.

LIVE FAST, DIE YOUNG

Goblins and orcs follow a much-accelerated version of the human reproductive cycle. Neither their personal repulsiveness, the violence of their courtship or the viciousness of their mating prevent them from breeding rapidly. Their fast population growth is inevitable given that they reach sexual maturity as early as 6 years old, have a gestation period of just 6 months and an average 'litter' of four or five offspring. Goblin creatures tend to be highly-sexed, and are capable of interbreeding with humans and other hominids, although the resultant offspring are, thankfully, sterile. This is thought to be the origin of many changeling children.

Fortunately, the population of orcs and goblins is kept in check by the endemic violence of goblin and orcish society. The natural lifespan of these creatures is considerably less than that of humans, and very few individuals live long enough to die of natural causes.

Both these sub-species of *Homo kobalis* have a tribal social organisation. Members of the tribe live together in a community nominally headed by a chief – usually the strongest and most cunning of the lot. In practice, however, goblins are

SEE INTRODUCTION TO HOMINID SECTION FOR MORE DETAILS (P. 150). SEE ALSO FAIRIES, GOBLINS, ELVES, PIXIES ETC. (PP.154–177 PASSIM).

Goblins & Orcs

individualistic, and they largely ignore their tribal chieftain unless threatened with violence.

The exception to this rule is the Goblin King, a formidable figure who wields authority over all goblins, irrespective of tribe or race. In theory, the crown is handed down from father to son, but as with all other walks of goblin life, brute force and low cunning are as important as lineage.

RUDE HOUSEGUESTS

When goblins take up residence in a human household, the result can be disastrous. Generally, however, they avoid cities, preferring to plague isolated rural households or very old buildings. Their behaviour is at best annoying and at worst, vicious. They are much given to hiding and breaking things, teasing pets, scaring children, and working small mischiefs like souring milk, cracking eggs, knotting threads, tangling string and making fruit fall off trees before it is ripe. Goblins also have the power to induce nightmares by the simple method of inserting them into the slumbering victim's ear. People who are unfortunate enough to become host to goblins can take steps to placate them with offerings of food and milk before scaring them off with fierce dogs and crosses.

Helpful or friendly goblins are the exception to the rule, and reports of any such creatures should be treated with considerable suspicion. The creatures are probably not goblins at all, and are likely to be brownies, elves or other faery folk.

Luckily, infestations are remarkably rare. As a rule, goblins, like orcs, avoid living in settled areas, preferring to haunt remote moors, desolate hills and mountain peaks, old ruins and abandoned mines. They skulk in these lonely places, squabbling among themselves as they wait to ambush the unwary traveller, and greedily hoarding the meagre treasures they have obtained from rare passers-by.

THE ILLUSTRATOR ARTHUR RACKHAM DREW THIS IMAGE OF THE DOMESTIC ENGLISH GOBLIN BILLY BLIND AND THE UNFORTUNATE OBJECT OF HIS ATTENTION. THE RED CLOTHES SUGGEST THAT HE IS A BLOODTHIRSTY HOMINID LIKE THE SCOTTISH REDCAP.

They pose great dangers to humans, but they reserve particular hatred for elves, dwarves and gnomes, attacking them on sight and horribly torturing any taken prisoner. This hatred is reciprocated by the faery races, who fight back using every weapon in their armouries. Humans are advised above all not to get caught between the two sides, as the crossfire can be deadly.

Goblins and orcs are renowned for their voracious and omnivorous appetites, favouring meat (carrion or fresh) and even eating human flesh. Most horribly, they frequently indulge in cannibalism, and orcs in particular habitually make a meal of their lesser hominid cousins.

The goblin is not gifted with extensive magical powers, and there are aspects of its nature which a quick-witted human can use to his advantage. For example, apart from being inhumanly ugly, goblins and orcs can always be spotted by the presence of a physical defect or deformity that betrays their nature. The form of this defect varies widely, from outsized feet or noses, to extra fingers or the presence of a tail.

CHEAP TRICK

Travellers captured by goblins or orcs can usually make their escapes by setting the creatures against one another. This is easily done by raising the question of division of loot. One tactic is to accuse one goblin of pocketing spoils for himself; another is to claim that you paid one off earlier and ask him whether he shared the money with the others. As they attack one another, it is easy to make your getaway.

In modern times the goblin has been relegated to the realm of fairy tales and children's stories, but in the past they were an ever-present danger, waylaying travellers, damaging homes and even stealing children. Human concern about their activities has declined in direct proportion to their falling numbers and shrinking habitat. Goblins and

181

☞ *As goblins declined in Europe, medieval stonemasons decided to capture their image in the form of church gargoyles (ornamental stone carvings designed to act as rainspouts), using them also to frighten off real goblins. They remain vital sources for goblin historians.*

orcs were common in the ancient world, but by the Middle Ages human encroachment on the great forests and wilderness areas of Europe had reduced their numbers considerably. Pockets of goblin infestation continued, and they gained notoriety as consorts of witches and devil-worshippers.

RED IN TOOTH AND CLAW ... AND HAT

There were particularly virulent infestations in the Border country between Scotland and England, where evil goblins known as redcaps (from their habit of dyeing their hats in their victims' blood) took up residence in old abandoned castles. The danger posed by their vicious predation of travellers prompted the local authorities to mount a concerted campaign to eradicate the redcap, but Border folk maintain that some survive to this day, still haunting lonely ruins, and still wearing their gruesome headgear.

As the presence of goblin races in Europe was contracting, the spread of European colonists to the New World provided pastures new. Scottish immigrants unwittingly provided transport for the evil cannibalistic goblins called *hobyah*, who terrorised lonely colonial homesteads until their vulnerability to fierce dogs was discovered – after which they were quickly eradicated.

Since then goblins have steadily retreated from the human world, and are now restricted to sparsely populated and wilderness areas. They live

☞ *An early 20th-century engraving of an orc-like creature. As so often in such drawings, the artist is clearly confused by the fauna of the cryptozoological world, and has incorporated elements of imps, demons, orcs and goblins to create a single, misleading image.*

on in print, however, and are a common feature in fairy tales and fantasy literature, from Christina Rossetti's poem *Goblin Market*, to JRR Tolkien's world-renowned *Lord of the Rings* trilogy.

SWIM FOR IT

Other strains of goblin in Europe include the French *croquemitaine* and the *Fuath* of the Scottish highlands. In Germany, the Goblin King is closely identified with a fearsome legendary figure, the Erlking (featured in Goethe's *Der Erlkönig*) who lures children to their deaths in the forest. In fact, the Erlking is probably a dark elf.

Further afield are the *koalinth*, a mutated form of marine goblin – *Homo kobalis aquascrofa* – with webbed feet and gills, and creatures whose exact taxonomy remains uncertain, being so remote from the other kobaloid races: the *bhuta* of India, and the *tilyakai* of New Guinea, whose tiny arrows are said to cause malaria.

Kobolds & Knockers

LATIN NAME
Homo kobalis cuniculi

HABITAT
Mines

LIFESPAN
Unknown

SIZE
About 1.5 ft (0.45 m) high

INFORMATION SOURCE
Field Report

DISTRIBUTION
Germany and Britain

 **REPORT**

ONE OF CORNWALL'S MANY ABANDONED TIN MINES.

FIELD NOTES

9 June. Trewithick, Cornwall
The tin mines that pepper the landscape here have been derelict for most of this century. According to folklore, they were a favourite haunt of the knockers, and the older villagers remember many stories from the old days. The noise of knockers at work underground was often a sign of a rich vein of tin ore ready to be mined, and although they were easily offended (by whistling, swearing or the sign of a cross), few people were frightened of knockers: their worst revenge was a harmless shower of small pebbles.

BACKGROUND NOTES
Following my expedition to Dartmoor in search of the pixy, I seized the chance to stay in the West of England and investigate the knockers - mine-dwelling goblins of Cornwall, more widely known by their German name, kobolds. This term is not to be confused with 'kobaloids' - the generic term for goblin creatures.

10 June. Old How's Mine, Trewithick
Lenny Barker, from the village post office, agreed to take me down this mine, which was the last to be closed and still has functioning lift gear. We descended into the gloom with our head lamps, and Barker led me through several hundred feet of tunnel to the rock face.

The knockers looked angry and surprised at our intrusion into their tiny workshop. They hurriedly threw pebbles at us before making their escape.

CObALT - NAMED AFTER KOBOLDS.

A VUG FROM GERMANY, COMPLETE WITH MINING TOOLS ABANDONED BY KOBOLDS.

Lenny was highly amused to see that I had brought a pick, but I set to work at the seam with a will. It was hard going, but after 15 minutes of noisy banging he suddenly bade me be silent. Sure enough there was the distinct sound of activity from the other side of the rock face. 'They make plenty o'noise,' observed Barker, 'but they b'aint be doing no work.' Knockers and mine goblins in other parts of the world are famous for giving the appearance of industry without ever actually producing anything.

I resumed my digging, and a few more blows loosed a large rock from the face, revealing a 'vug' - a crystal-lined cavity in the rock. Nestled inside were three tiny figures (about 1.5 ft or 0.45 m high) wearing old-fahioned miners' gear. One of them had a tiny anvil, and was busily repairing a the tools of the others. It seemed to be some kind of miniature workshop or foundry.

I made a sudden exclamation and Barker whistled in surprise. All three of the knockers turned towards us shouted angrily ans started throwing pebbles. Suddenly our lamps went out: when they came back on, the knockers were gone. Lenny and I beat a hasty retreat, but on his insistence we left a placatory offering, in the form of some tasty morsels from the Cornish pasties we'd brought with us for lunch.

SUPPLEMENTARY NOTES AND RESEARCH
H. k. cuniculi is found in several mining areas, including Wales, where it is known as the coblynau. Generally the coblynau are friendlier than the Cornish knockers, and may lead miners to rich seams. They have also been spotted above ground, wearing spotted handkerchiefs on their heads and performing Morris dances.

The kobolds of Germany are much less friendly. They cause mine disasters, and do not always stay underground, choosing occasionally to plague homes or whole communities. One famous kobold, Hoedeken, denounced unfaithful wives; another, Goldemar, exposed the wrongdoings of corrupt clergy. The wichtlein of Southern Germany are especially ominous: they announce the imminent death of a miner by tapping three times.

A KNOTTED, SPOTTED HANDKERCHIEF, AS WORN BY A COBLYNAU — THE DANCING KOBOLD OF THE WELSH VALLEYS.

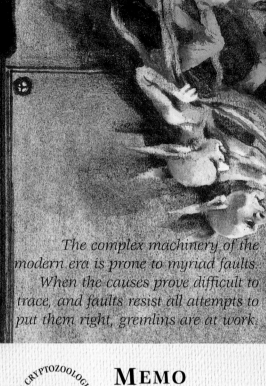

The complex machinery of the modern era is prone to myriad faults. When the causes prove difficult to trace, and faults resist all attempts to put them right, gremlins are at work.

HOMINIDS

Gremlins

LATIN NAME
Homo kobalis vexus

HABITAT
Machinery

LIFESPAN
5–10 years

SIZE
*6–21 inches
(15–50 cm)*

**INFORMATION
SOURCE**
CSL Review

DISTRIBUTION
Worldwide

THE CRYPTOZOOLOGICAL SOCIETY OF LONDON

MEMO

From: John Clifford
(Production Manager)
To: Jane Kreak (Editor, CSL Review)

Sorry, we aren't going to be able to run the *Gremlins* piece this month. As you know, this article has been beset by technical problems.

First, the author was unable to file the article by email – his computer kept crashing. He then posted it on a floppy disk, but the package got left in the rain somewhere and the disk was corrupted. Eventually he had to dictate it over the phone – which took several attempts as his home phone was out of order and we had to rely on his dodgy mobile phone. We then somehow managed to lose the article in the system and had to type it all back in again.

Things could only get better, you might have thought – but we then had terrible problems trying to illustrate the piece. Our photographer came down with pneumonia and our artist broke a finger. For some reason picture libraries couldn't help us either – seems a lot of pictures have been misfiled or gone missing.

We struggled on and got something together on the computer – then some idiot deleted it! Honestly, this article is jinxed if you ask me.

Anyway, here's what we've managed to do so far. We've now missed the print deadline, but perhaps we can sort it all out by next issue.

John.

SPANNERS
WORKS
IN THE

A COMPUTER VIRUS AND
A SERIES OF HARDWARE
FAULTS WERE LATER
IDENTIFIED AS THE
CAUSE OF THE PROBLEM.

184

REMLINS WERE UNHEARD OF A CENTURY ago, yet now they are practically ubiquitous. What is more, they seem to thrive in modern, high-tech environments. The emergence of this new sub-species of goblin has been followed with interest by the CSL, from the initial reports to subsequent attempts at field investigations, all of which were unfortunately aborted due to technical difficulties.

NATURAL HISTORY

Gremlins are almost certainly derived from boggarts, whom they closely resemble, in miniature form. It seems likely that they evolved towards the end of the 19th century, from an isolated population of boggarts at the Fremlin brewery in Kent, SE England. Their miniature form and mechanical expertise represent an important adaptation of the somewhat archaic boggart to the rapid technological innovation of the last 150 years. According to some authorities their name derives from a conflation of the words 'goblin' and 'Fremlin', but it seems more likely that the derivation is from the Old English root *gremian*, 'to vex'.

Gremlins seem to have a particular affinity for aircraft, and the massive increases in aircraft production brought about by World Wars I and II led to consequent explosions in the gremlin population. Today they are busily colonising the technology of the computer age, and have adapted their usual repertoire of mechanical and electrical tricks - loosening screws, nudging connections, etc. - to include crashing networks and getting floppy disks stuck

```
84hjrh88h483hehhhd
///DISK ERROR 00937728TRG
//SYSTEM ERROR\ 7463 at drive E:\CSL\
review\50\gremlins\743
line error 1.32
script failure type G
+++++++++++++++Y/N    Y
"Please wait ........."
```

RECOVERED TEXT STARTS HERE

< &;> The brewers and engineers of the Fremlin brewery were amongst the first to notice the Gremlin Effect, as it later came to be called.

Despite the theoretically foolproof nature of their methods and equipment, various mechanical processes would go awry, usually due to simple, inexplicable mishaps.

< &;> Pilots and mechanics of the Royal Flying Corps, created in 1912, noticed similar minor but irritating glitches. They rarely caused crashes, but frequently kept aeroplanes grounded. The problem had worsened by World War II, and Pilot Officer Kelvin McSprune of the RAF was the first to formally identify the existence of the Gremlin Effect.

< &;> A notable feature of the Effect was that the fault was inevitably caused by the most trivial of problems, such as a loose washer, but was only ever discovered after the mechanics had laboriously dismantled the entire engine. On rare occasions gremlins could be useful - they might help a crippled bomber back to base against all the odds - but usually only to save their own skins. Gremlins won a lasting place in the public imagination when one starred in a Warner Bros. cartoon with Bugs Bunny.

< &;>The electronic age has proved to be a bonanza for gremlins. Not only are there trailing wires to fray, connections to loosen and microchips to burn out, but complex software offers almost unlimited opportunities for mischief. "Debugging" software is a major task in any high-tech company, and many large

A BRITISH AIRMAN STRUGGLES TO PUT RIGHT DAMAGE DONE BY GREMLINS. SOME MILITARY HISTORIANS SAY THAT GREMLIN SABOTAGE HELPED TO HASTEN GERMANY'S DEFEAT IN WORLD WAR II.

corporations now employ several computer engineers simply to deal with < &;>
< &;> < &;> < &;>

```
738 383 system error code -21 stack full
611 291 system error code -03
092 977 system error code -09 bus failure
system failure OK
system failure OK
14:24:08++++++++++"Please disconnect"
14:24:28++++++++++firewall 35 invoked by
G FR 01+++++++
14:24:48++++++++++autoquit protocols
commenced with code 57.132.03
14:25:03++++++++++"Shutting down ..."
14:25:17++++++++++SYSTEM SHUT DOWN
```

Trolls

LATIN NAME
Homo kobalis hyperborealis

HABITAT
Caverns

LIFESPAN
Up to 300 years

SIZE
*4–11 ft
(1.2–3.3 m) high*

INFORMATION SOURCE
Own Field Report

DISTRIBUTION
Scandinavia, Shetlands, Orkneys

BACKGROUND NOTES

Trolls (or trow, as they are known in Shetland and the Orkneys) can vary widely in size. In the sheltered valleys, deep caves and more temperate parts of Scandinavia they can grow tall and powerful, using their strength to catch and eat humans. In more exposed areas, and throughout Shetland and the Orkneys, trolls are stunted and wizened. Though still dangerous, smaller trolls may occasionally render people small services, although they prefer to avoid humans altogether.

FIELD REPORT

15 August, Jötunheim National Park.
Yesterday we came up the Sognafjorden by steamer from Bergen. A long drive up the steep-walled valley from Leikanger has brought us to the edge of the National Park, traditional home of ancient Norse giants and trolls. It was here that Peer Gynt escaped the Troll-King's Hall, and here that I hope to find traces of their existence.

16 August, Jötunheim National Park.
Here, icy blue lakes nestle between jagged peaks, a breathtakingly beautiful vista that makes it easy to imagine these mountains as the home of ancient powers. High up on the mountain, my guide pointed out two misshapen lumps of stone, carved by the wind and ice into strange poses. Local legend has it that they are the remains of two trolls, caught above ground by the dawn and turned to stone.

17 August, Jötunheim National Park.
Today we crossed a glacier to pick up an old trail that led to a bleak valley pocked with small caves. Closer investigation of one revealed a litter-strewn tunnel disappearing into the dark. A foul smell lingered about the mouth of the cave. My guide was unwilling to go any further.

On the way back to the hostel, he explained that the trolls were renowned for the vileness of their homes, and

Awe-inspiring, troll-friendly Jötunheim National Park.

The frightening creature I disturbed in the cave.

CHB.583.190
PIPE RECOVERED FROM
TROLL CAVE NEAR
SUNDSVALL, SWEDEN.

were known to blind their captives, supposedly as a favour to spare them the unpleasant sight.

18 August, Jötunheim National Park.
I returned to the caves we visited yesterday, determined to explore the cave properly this time. Wearing a gas-mask, and carrying a powerful torch, I started off down the tunnel. I soon heard an evil muttering ahead, so I turned off the torch and inched

A TROLL BOOK FROM FINLAND. NOTE THE EXTRAORDINARY SCRIPT, BASED ON THE ANCIENT RUNIC ALPHABET.

A TROLL DRINKING HORN. SUCH WORKMANSHIP IS CHARACTERISTIC OF THE SMALLER, MORE ARTISTIC TROLLS.

forwards. The mossy wall of the tunnel gave off a faint phosphorescence, and in the ghostly light I saw a squat, greyish creature hunched over a jar. It grunted like a pig, then stood up and moved off. It had leathery skin covered with filthy rags and sported a necklace of what looked like small skulls.

When it had gone I looked in the jar, which was full of an evil-looking liquid. Lifting my mask for a sniff, I was overpowered by a rancid stench that made me gag with nausea. Guttural shouts from further down the tunnel signalled that it was time to beat a hasty retreat, and I hurried back to the safety of daylight. My guide later explained that I had probably found some of the foul brew that the trolls drink in place of beer. He warns that it will be dangerous for me to return, and suggests we restrict our walks to the usual hiking trails.

SUPPLEMENTARY NOTES AND RESEARCH
The trows of Orkney and Shetland are more civilised than their Scandinavian cousins, and they enjoy good music. The islanders can spot a trow by its grey coloration and its habit of walking backwards whenever it knows it is being watched.

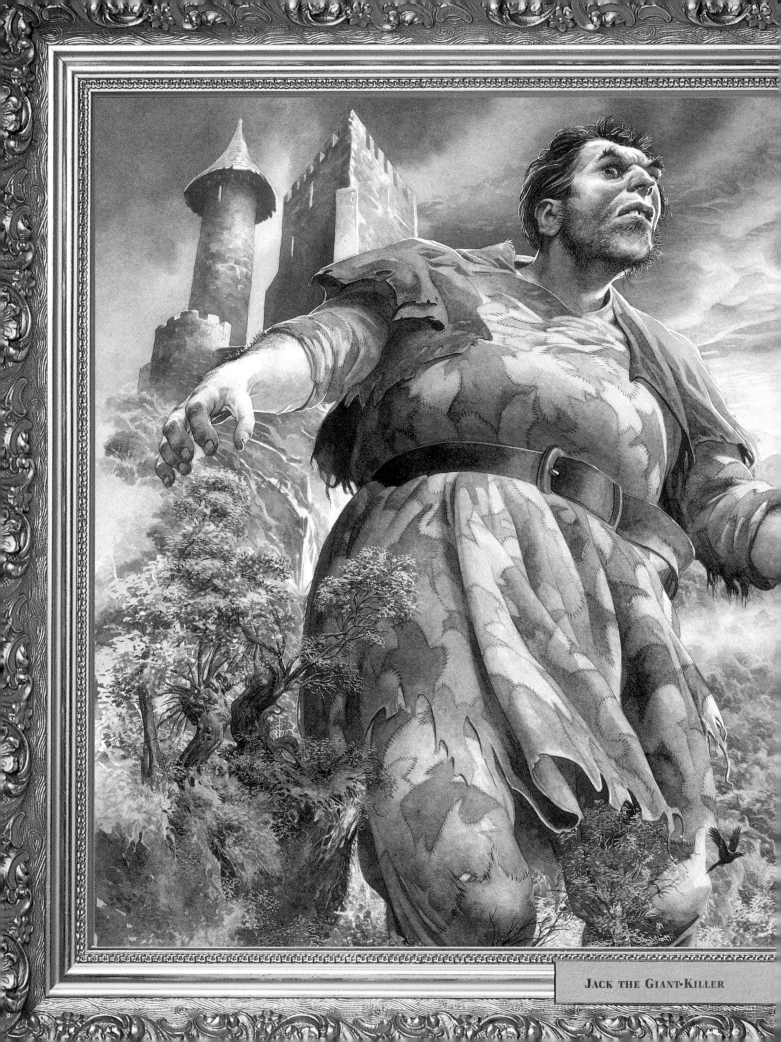

JACK THE GIANT-KILLER

by Nicholas Harris, MCSL

JACK THE GIANT-KILLER'S GUIDE TO THE

Two remarkable documents, a Middle English text and the map shown here, were recovered in 1949 during work on a bomb-damaged site next to London's Guildhall. The two documents seem to be the early equivalent of a Michelin guide, but they do not concern food. The subject matter is giants – where to find them, what their strengths and weaknesses were and the extent of their wealth. A number of the giants featured in the map are those that were encountered by the Cornish farmer known as Jack the Giant-Killer, following his change of career from dragonslayer to giant-killer. While we cannot be sure of its authenticity, the map and accompanying text appear to be a direct account of Jack the Giant-Killer's own encounters. They were purchased for the Society by the Dowager Duchess of Rothmarch, in memory of her husband, a former President of the CSL killed at Dunkirk. The CSL commissioned the painting on the previous pages as part of its Great Encounters series.

GIGANTOMACHIA BAEDEKERIS

Giants of quality are becoming increasingly hard to find. Connoisseurs cherish fond memories of the fine Norman giants of yesteryear, while only the faery folk can recall the once great specimens of Scotland and Ireland – the mighty beings who created Giant's Causeway and Fingal's Cave. Alas! – gone are the heady days of yore when Gog and Magog battled Brutus' enormous companion Corineus 'pon Albion's chalky ramparts. Nonetheless there remain some cheeky little numbers scattered about these sceptred shores, and if you are prepared to spend a little time you can still find a giant worthy of the name.

1 ST MICHAEL'S MOUNT, CORNWALL

Going by the name of Cormoran, this unfriendly fellow is a real traditionalist. He enjoys eating people, locking up maidens, amassing treasure and is as ugly and stupid as they come. My tip for success is simple decapitation – bring him down to your level by getting him to stand in a deep pit.
Verdict Highly recommended for those who like their giants old-fashioned.
Size ★★★ **Wealth** ★★★ **Stupidity** ★★★★

2 NORTHAMPTON

Dull Midlands town notable only for the presence of local villain, Blunderbore. Blunderbore is renowned for his lack of hospitality, and has a fondness for locking visitors in a tall tower. Fortunately he is as inveterately stupid as his fellows. He is much given to loitering by the tower and in this lies his weakness. With skilful use of a noose lowered from the window of the tower the giant may be easily ensnared. He is then at your mercy.
Verdict Requires a little more finesse than average, but hardly a classic.
Size ★★★★ **Wealth** ★★★ **Stupidity** ★★★

3 CERNE ABBAS, DORSET

This is one giant who really grabs the attention! He's already made his mark with the locals who, impressed with his assets, have immortalised him as a hill carving. But don't be distracted by his most obvious features – he's got more than one club, and enjoys nothing more than bashing people's heads in. I favour 'tackling' him where it hurts the most.
Verdict This fellow's standing proud at the moment, but could get cut off in his prime.
Size ★★★★★ **Wealth** ★
Stupidity ★★★

4 CAERNAVON, WALES

Wales is probably the outstanding region for quality giants in Britain today, and Caernavon is leading from the front. The Giant of Caernavon is a real peach of a giant, scoring highly in the classic virtues of ugliness, stupidity and gullibility, and offering some fresh twists. For instance, he likes to toy with his prey by being hospitable – so use the old bag of porridge under the shirt ploy. You know, pretending to be making room for more food by slicing open your 'stomach' when in fact you're slitting open the bag secreted under your shirt. The giant will attempt to follow your lead, ensuring a fatal stomach-ache.
Verdict A wake-up call for jaded palates, the Caernavon giant heralds a fresh challenge for giant-killers everywhere.
Size ★★★ **Wealth** ★★★★ **Stupidity** ★★★★

GIANTS OF ENGLAND AND WALES

To really annoy him, when you appear the next morning, unscathed, tell him that you felt a few pesky gnat bites during the night. The giant will be scared witless and will gibberingly offer you a hearty breakfast. Finish him off by showing your super-human strength – pretend a cheese is a stone and squeeze some water out of it. Watch him scarper like a frightened rabbit.

Verdict Mature palates seeking a rich, multi-layered experience should look no further.

Size ★★ Wealth ★★★★ Stupidity ★★

6 TYWYN AND BORTH, WALES
This pair offer a rare *pas de deux*. In the traditional stone-throwing mould, these giants normally pay little attention to one another. Taken on their individual merits there is, frankly speaking, little to choose between them in terms of bone-deep ignorance, hulking physicality and overall superfluity to the needs of the world in general. Some entertainment can probably be found if you can manage to convince each that the other has started a fight. Usually a period of days follows in which they work out what they think has been happening. Then, the penny drops, and you can sit back and watch the fireworks (and boulders) fly.

Verdict A tasty treat for beginners and connoisseurs alike, providing the ideal opportunity for typical giant-killer trickery.

Size ★★★★ Wealth ★★ Stupidity ★★★★★

5 CONWAY, WALES
For those seeking slightly more recherché thrills, I heartily recommend this slightly avant-garde example. More of a challenge than the normal numbskulls, the Giant of Conway requires a bit of lateral thinking to outwit. Like all bullies, however, his real weakness is that he's a great big coward. Use brain to give the impression of brawn and you've got him. Make sure you don't use the bed he provides – substitute a log for your sleeping body and sit back while the giant thrashes hell out of it.

Giants

LATIN NAME
Homo gigantus

HABITAT
*Mostly moun-
tainous regions*

LIFESPAN
80–200 years

SIZE
*14–200 ft
(4.27–61 m) tall*

**INFORMATION
SOURCE**
CSL Review

DISTRIBUTION
Worldwide

THE MILE HIGH CLUB

*Many human beings are high
and mighty, big and tall or
heroically proportioned, but
true giants are in a class –
and species – of their own.*

MANY CULTURES AROUND THE GLOBE record in myth or legend that before their ancestors arrived the land was already inhabited by giants (see below). Yet today most scholars believe this race to be extinct. For present-day cryptozoologists this is a tragedy, because giants represent one of the most impressive branches of hominid descent, as well as a fascinating biological conundrum.

The upper limit of human height is around 9 ft (2.7 m), and Robert Wadlow (1918–40) is the tallest man on record at 8 ft 11 inches (2.72 m). Human 'giants' have been known throughout history, often becoming warriors or rulers of renown. Goliath and Briareus are two well-known examples from Biblical and Classsical myth respectively. Yet such outlandish size occurs only as the result of a pathological condition known as gigantism, where a tumour of the pituitary gland causes the bones to keep growing. This condition usually shortens the sufferer's life – Wadlow died at the age of 22, his head so far from his feet that he was unable to feel the injury to his feet that caused a fatal infection. He was still growing, but the human body is simply not engineered to function well at that size.

BEETLE-BROWED BIG BOYS

True giants, on the other hand, are a species of hominid that never reaches a height of less than 14 ft (4.27 m). Most male giants are enormously strong, but stupid and clumsy. They tend to be thick set, with huge limbs, ominously low brows and heavy features. Female giants are rare, and tend to be smaller, more intelligent, and friendlier than the males.

Although some giants build great castles, and a few even achieve a modicum of relative sophistication, most of them have a level of civilisation that harks back to the Stone Age. They use clubs, rocks and simple stone tools and live in caves or rough-hewn dwellings. As many a folk tale testifies, these backward individuals are generally ill-disposed towards humans.

Giants are not social animals. They are either solitary, or live in mated pairs. Only rarely do giants gather, and these occasions usually end in trouble. A famous example is the Giant's Causeway in Antrim, N. Ireland. Commonly mistaken for a natural rock formation, the causeway is actually the result of an attempt by the giants of Ireland and Scotland to build a land link between Antrim and the West coast of Scotland. The assembled giants quickly fell to squabbling and the causeway was never completed, although remains can still be seen at Fingal's Cave on the island of Staffa, off the Scottish coast.

☞ *THE GIANT'S CAUSEWAY IS ONE OF
SEVERAL CIVIL ENGINEERING PROJECTS
LEFT UNFINISHED BY GIANTS. OTHERS
INCLUDE MONUMENT VALLEY, AYERS
ROCK AND PARTS OF ICELAND.*

HEAVYWEIGHTS

The largest living animal, the blue whale (*Balaenoptera musculus*), is able to achieve its great size (up to 150 tons [152 tonnes]) because it lives in the sea, supported and cooled by the water. The largest living land animal is the elephant, considerably smaller at a maximum of around 5 tons (5.08 tonnes). What interests cryptozoologists most about giants is that, biologically speaking, they are simply too big to exist. Giants can weigh up to 40 or 50 tons (40.64 or 50.8 tonnes), which puts an enormous strain on their bodily systems. There are three major restrictions that affect the size of land-based creatures, especially mammals:

First, animals are supported by skeletons that must be strong enough to bear their weight. The

GIANT. MACHNOW AT BREAKFAST.

Human oddities rather than true giants, people like Chang (left) and The Great Machnow (above) helped to raise the public profile of giants. Their public appearances and regularly-published photo sets attracted a devoted following.

problem here is that as overall size increases, the size of the bones must increase exponentially. A creature twice as large as an elephant will, therefore, need bones four or eight times bigger. This extra bulk means that muscles, joints and organs such as heart and lungs have to grow in parallel. Many of the body's softer organs would collapse under their own weight. Members of the *Homo gigantus* species do indeed have massive skeletons, but the bones are hollow, and composed of material both stronger and lighter than ours. A number of companies are trying to mimic this remarkable material, hoping to exploit its properties for commercial gain.

HEART OF THE MATTER

Second, all large creatures have difficulty circulating blood evenly to all parts of the body, for gravity causes it to pool in the feet. Again, the heart must increase in size exponentially to meet the demands placed on the circulation. Giants do have huge hearts, but they also have a number of secondary pumping 'stations' throughout their bodies and a system of one-way valves to prevent the blood flowing in the wrong direction.

Finally, as animals get bigger, the ratio between their surface area and their mass gets smaller, making it harder for them to keep cool by radiating heat. A giant risks overheating simply by virtue

HOMINIDS

Giants

of its size. *Homo gigantus* sleeps a lot to keep his metabolic rate low, and can tolerate much higher internal temperatures than other mammals. Giants also prefer cool climates.

Further consequences of enormous size include slow transmission of impulses around the body because of the distances involved, which makes giants slow and clumsy; a small brain, which generates less heat and is lighter than a large one, but means that giants can be very stupid and prone to neurological disorders such as epilepsy; and internal organs which are simplified to keep down body mass.

GIANT STEPS

Like some of the other hominid races, it appears that *Homo gigantus* spread around the globe before early Man, colonising most corners of the Earth. Many cultures have legends which tell how their fore-fathers fought with resident giants for possession of the land. In the Book of Numbers, the Israelite spies Joshua and Caleb reported that the Promised Land was peopled by a race of giants called the Anakim; Brutus and his Trojans, the legendary first Britons, had to fight the giant Gogmagog and the others of his race; and when the Spanish *conquistadores* reached Mexico, the Indians told them that the original inhabitants of the land had been giants, and even showed them some enormous ancient bones. One Spaniard, Bernal Diaz del Castillo, reported seeing a thigh bone as tall as a man. The Portuguese navigator Ferdinand Magellan (*c.*1480–1521 AD) was the first of a number of visitors to Patagonia who recorded the presence of giants.

As some of the Earth's oldest hominids, giants play a central role in mythology. According to Greek legend and Norse sagas, the Earth was created from the body of a giant, and other giants were the first Gods, later having their rule usurped by the Aesir and Olympians respectively. The word 'giant' itself comes from the Greek *gigantes* – the sons of the Earth, who sprang from the blood of Uranus and waged war on Olympus. This war was known as the Gigantomachy (war of the giants), and was a favourite subject for ancient Greek artists, appearing on the Treasury at Delphi, for instance. Greece had other giants, too. The man-eating *laestrygones* sank most of Odysseus' fleet, and Odysseus also had a battle with the one-eyed

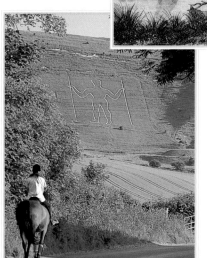

THE BERRY REGION OF FRANCE IS A LOW LYING MARSHY AREA BETWEEN THE CHER AND INDRE RIVERS. IN THE 19TH CENTURY IT WAS HOME TO A NOTORIOUS GIANT, ATTRACTED BY THE FAT LIVESTOCK OF THIS FERTILE FARMLAND.

THE 'LONG MAN OF WILMINGTON' IN EAST SUSSEX, SOUTHERN ENGLAND, WATCHES PASSING TRAFFIC. HE MAY WELL BE A FULL-LENGTH SELF-PORTRAIT.

giant cyclops. The Norse giants, known as the Jötnar, were also the enemies of the Gods. From their base in Jötunheim, in the Norwegian mountains, they threatened both Valhalla and Earth. They coveted the wealth and beauty of the Gods, and Thor was constantly kept busy fighting them.

GONE TO GROUND

Giants have used their enormous strength to kill humans (whom they often eat) and gather treasure. Naturally this has made giants favourite targets for heroes looking to prove themselves, and as a result they are now extremely rare. By the Middle Ages most of the remaining giants had withdrawn to remote castles in mountainous areas, or, like the Chenoo (the Stone Giants of the Iroquois) learned to blend in with the landscape to escape notice.

Not all giants were unfriendly to man. In Britain local traditions record those like the giant of Grabbist, who enjoyed the typically stupid giant's pastime of throwing rocks but had a good heart. The giant of Carn Galva, in Cornwall, who protected the people of the fishing villages of Morvah and Zennor from the evil giants of the nearby Lelant Hills, was another benevolent giant.

Fierce or friendly, *Homo gigantus* is virtually consigned to the history books. The shrinking modern world, it seems, no longer has enough space for the larger-than-life.

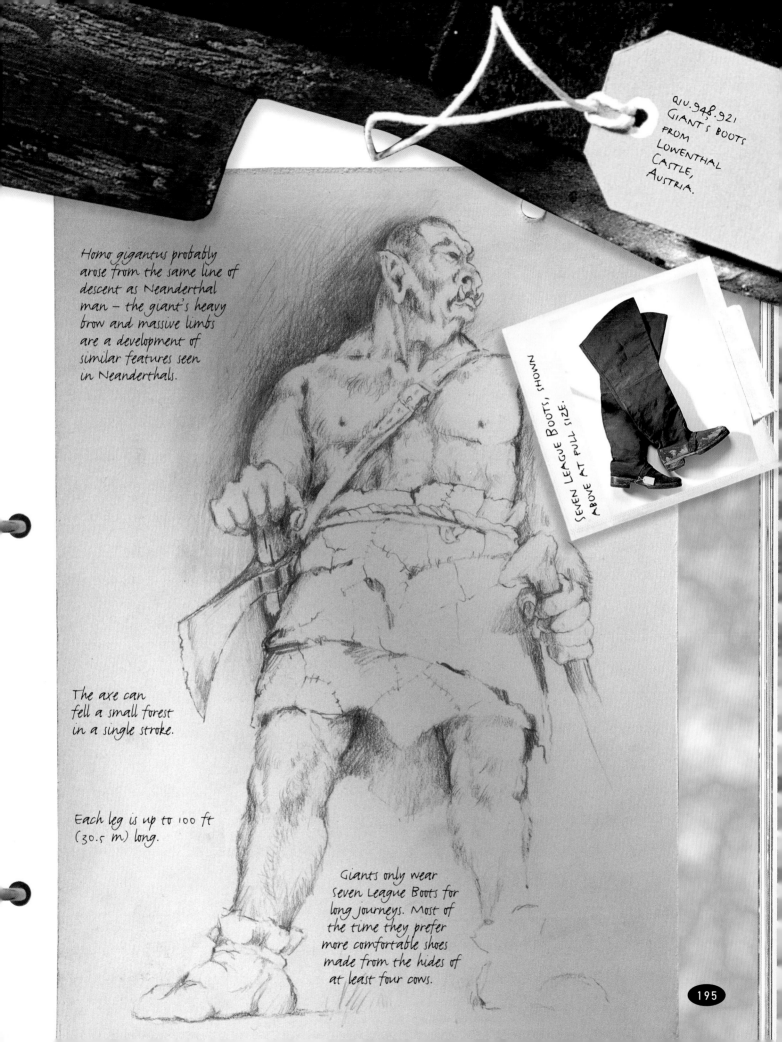

Homo gigantus probably arose from the same line of descent as Neanderthal man – the giant's heavy brow and massive limbs are a development of similar features seen in Neanderthals.

SEVEN LEAGUE BOOTS, SHOWN ABOVE AT FULL SIZE.

The axe can fell a small forest in a single stroke.

Each leg is up to 100 ft (30.5 m) long.

Giants only wear Seven League Boots for long journeys. Most of the time they prefer more comfortable shoes made from the hides of at least four cows.

195

MOMOTARO

by Nicholas Harris, MCSL

MOMOTARO

The origins of the Japanese folk hero Momotaro ('Peach Boy') were quite unusual (see below). With the help of his adoptive family, however, he grew up and embarked on a highly successful career in what we would term oni *downsizing – or Japanese ogre containment. These exploits earned him the capital to diversify into netsuke manufacture and he died known as 'The Peachboy King'.*

LAST OF THE *ONI*

The Japanese legend of Momotaro relates how a poor, childless couple found a giant peach stone in a river. They brought it home and opened it to find an infant boy within. The couple named him Momotaro after the circumstances of his birth and adopted him. Once grown, he left home to conquer Onigashima, the island of the ogres (or *oni*). He accomplished this with the help of a dog, a monkey and a pheasant whom he met on his journey. Momotaro, dutiful son that he was, then used some of the riches he had gained to ensure a tranquil old age for his adoptive parents.

Reproduced on the preceding pages is Inikko Harichi's depiction of Momotaro's overthrow of the *oni*, simply entitled *Onigashima* (1953). Harichi, one of the greatest exponents of the post-war Japanese 'Western Method', rejected traditional techniques for more Western ones. In the painting Momotaro and his three companions have already dispatched one *oni* and are squaring up to a second. Momotaro's *oni* knockout method was to let the dog bite the *oni*, the pheasant fly in its face and the monkey jump on its back. The rest was easy.

Harichi has not simply illustrated a charming folk-tale, however. His painting depicts a crucial moment in Japanese history: the final battle between ogres and humans for control of the islands. *Onigashima* therefore occupies pride of place in the Oriental Room at 100 Piccadilly. *Oni* predated the human population but in time were forced to retreat in consternation from the mainland.

The initial influx of humans into Japan probably pushed the *oni* close to extinction. By about 400 AD they recovered their numbers sufficiently to encroach again on the main islands. At this time, however, the first powerful city states arose and began to organise punitive sorties and pre-emptive strikes against the *oni*. But the ogres were based in offshore strongholds which were difficult and even suicidal to attack. A terrible fate awaited humans who were captured by the creatures – they could expect to be imprisoned, tortured and finally eaten.

According to leading Orientalist and CSL Fellow, Dr David Ghoul, the legend of Momotaro almost certainly dates from around this time and records the successful anti-*oni* campaigning of a particularly strong warlord. As with Western figures like Arthur or Hercules, the exploits of a real human figure have been built up over the centuries to become part of folklore and legend. The peach connection is unclear – possibly this 5th century warlord used a peach emblem as his personal symbol.

Dr Ghoul even goes so far as to suggest a possible location for the island of Onigashima. He argues that early records identify it as the stronghold of Akandoji, a name reflected in the presence of modern place-names like Ako in Hyogo Prefecture near Osaka. There are many islands off the coast in this area and it is there that Dr Ghoul places the real-life focus of the Momotaro legend.

THE CRYPTOZOOLOGICAL SOCIETY OF LONDON

LEGEND HAS ASSOCIATED AKANDOJI'S NAME WITH THIS FEARSOME MASK.

AN *oni* CAST OUT.

HOMINIDS

Ogres

LATIN NAME
*Homo anthro-
pophagus*

HABITAT
Various

LIFESPAN
40–60 years

SIZE
*7–15 ft
(2–4.5 m) high*

**INFORMATION
SOURCE**
Correspondence

DISTRIBUTION
Worldwide

Department of Comparative Anthropophagy
University of Cancello
Alto Adige
Italy

23 March 1986

Dear Professor Tilson

I read with interest your recent contribution to the Society's Journal. My own researches have brought me to the view that ogres are close relatives of the giants, but nearer to humans in size. As a result they tend to interact more with human communities. This is rarely a good thing, because ogres are distinguished by their fondness for human flesh (hence their Latin name: anthropophagus means 'man-eating').

Ogres are generally massively built, with powerful muscles, heavy shoulders and thick necks. They often have pointed ears, piggy eyes and boar-like snouts and tusks, thus prompting comparisons with orcs (see page XX). In Japan, where ogres are known as oni, they have a particularly distinctive appearance, with horns, three digits on each hand and foot and sometimes a third eye.

In the wild, ogres generally live in caves or thick woods. They may take up residence in towns or castles where, after looting, raping and eating the local populace, they are inevitably dispatched by a human hero. Children and young maidens are their favourite diet, but they can subsist on livestock, or even survive extended periods of fasting, though this tends to worsen their already choleric dispositions. Ogres can be found in most countries but their appetites make them unpopular, and they tend not to live to a ripe old age. Their numbers are also kept down by a propensity for eating their own children.

In many parts of the world ogres build houses out of edible sweetmeats in order to attract human children. Like giants they rely on their keen sense of smell to sniff out humans. Ogres also enjoy the occasional advantages of magical aids, such as Seven-League Boots that enable them to cover huge distances very quickly. The best way to avoid becoming an ogre's (or ogress') dinner is to employ a mixture of guile and flattery, because ogres are only slightly more intelligent than giants.

I look forward to further exchanges between us and to the greater understanding of the ogre by the world at large.

Auguri,

Ubaldo Quasiveramente

Ubaldo Quasiveramente

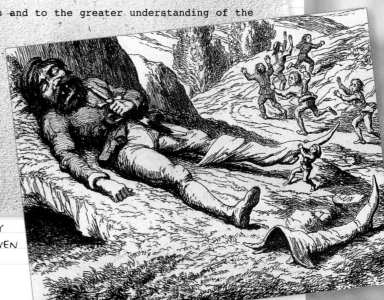

YPSILANTI, AN INFAMOUS 17TH CENTURY BOHEMIAN OGRE, IS DEPRIVED OF HIS SEVEN LEAGUE BOOTS IN A MOMENT OF VULNERABILITY.

HOMINIDS

Apemen

LATIN NAME
Various

HABITAT
Usually mountainous/ forested regions

LIFESPAN
Unknown

HEIGHT
3–9 ft (1–3 m)

INFORMATION SOURCE
CSL Review

DISTRIBUTION
Worldwide

THE EXISTENCE OF APEMEN, SUCH AS the Bigfoot and the yeti, is now widely accepted even in in conventional zoological and scientific circles. As a result, they are probably the best-known animals of the entire cryptozoological menagerie. Like the orang-utan and the gorilla, apemen shun human company, preferring to live in the remotest areas. Recently, cryptozoologists have started to appreciate the wide range of regional and local variants of the species, with different types of apeman reported from Sumatra, China, Russia and many other places. Europe once had a population of apemen, variously known as woses, woodwoses or wild men, although these had died out by the end of the Middle Ages.

The traditional image of the apeman is a towering monster covered in thick fur, resembling a cross between a man and an ape. It is important to note, however, that not all apemen are the same. The Sumatran *orang pendek* is short and slender, while the Mongolian *almas* is said closely to resemble Neanderthal man. It seems likely that there are at least three different types of apeman, but they are all probably living fossils – obscure survivors of the prehistoric age.

PREHISTORIC MIGRANTS

Most reports of the yeti and Bigfoot agree that they conform to the traditional big ape picture, as do some descriptions of China's *yeren* and Pakistan's *barmanu*. The most plausible explanation of these beasts is that they are descended from the prehistoric ape *Gigantopithecus*, which supposedly died out 300,000 years ago, and lived in Central Asia. Perhaps *Gigantopithecus* migrated across the Bering land bridge, and survives in wilderness areas in both Asia and North America.

Apemen such as the Bigfoot and the yeti are perhaps the best known crypto-zoological creatures of the present day, and are among the most widely accepted in conventional scientific circles.

GONE APE?

200

The *almas* creature reported in Mongolia and parts of Russia seems to be a quite different creature. Many of the descriptions sound more like a primitive and hairy 'wild man' than an ape-like creature, but with Neanderthal features such as high cheekbones and heavy brows. Europe's extinct woodwoses also fit this description. The most likely candidates here must be Neanderthals – *Homo neanderthalensis* – who have somehow survived the extinction of their race 30,000 years ago.

AN ERECT SURVIVOR

A third type of apeman is the diminutive *orang pendek* and other pygmy-sized creatures like the Nepalese *teh-lma* or the *batatut*

from Borneo. Suggestions for its identity vary from a new form of orang-utan to a surviving variant of *Homo erectus* – the first hominid to migrate out of Africa and start to colonise the rest of the world.

The table displayed by the Chinese apeman below demonstrates the very wide distribution and variety of apemen generally.

THIS PARADE OF APEMEN SHOWS JUST A FEW OF THE MANY VARIATIONS ON THE THEME OF A GIANT, HAIRY HUMANOID WITH APE-LIKE HAIR. LEFT TO RIGHT: THE AUSTRALIAN YOWIE, A WILD MAN SEEN IN THE USSR IN 1941, A 17TH-CENTURY ENGRAVING OF A JAVANESE WILD MAN, A 20TH-CENTURY CHINESE APEMAN AND A HAIRY EUROPEAN GREEN MAN.

APEMEN AROUND THE WORLD

Africa	Nandi bear, chemosit
Australia	Yowie, poolagarl, kalkadonis, narragun
Borneo	Batatut
China	Yeren ('wildman'), xueren, hsileh-jen
Europe (until the Middle Ages)	Wose, woodwose, Green Men, Wild Men of the Woods
Fiji	Vélé
Guadalcanal, Solomon Islands	Mumulon
Hawaii	Menehune, nawao
Himalayas	Yeti (from Sherpa dialect, 'yeh-teh'), mi-go, metoh-kangmi, teh-lma, dzu-teh, rimi, tok, nyalmo, temu, mirka, sogpu, shukpa
Iran	Nasnas, dev
Japan	Hibagon
Malaysia	Kaki besar
Mongolia	Almas
New Zealand	Maero, macro
North America	Bigfoot, sasquatch, wendigo, bushman (in early reports), mo-mo, skunk ape, Lake Worth Monster, wauk wauk, Ice Giant, Jersey Devil
Pakistan	Barmanu ('big hairy one')
Russia	Alma, almast, almasty, kaptar
Siberia	Chuchunaa
South America	Maricoxi
Sumatra	Orang pendek ('little man'), orang letjo ('gibbering man'), sedapa
Venezuela	Vasitri

HOMINIDS

Yeti

LATIN NAME
Probably
Gigantopithecus

HABITAT
Unsettled high
valleys in
remote areas

LIFESPAN
Unknown

SIZE
7–10 ft
(2.1–3 m) tall

INFORMATION
SOURCE
Field Report

DISTRIBUTION
Mountains of
Central Asia

CSL
SUBMITTED BY
Marjorie Evans-Hartson
DATE 29/3-20/7 1962
LOCATION Sikkim: India/ Nepal Border
CATALOGUE № C2 YE 18 #3
LONDON
THE CRYPTOZOOLOGICAL SOCIETY OF LONDON

REPORT

One of the earliest Western reports of the yeti is that of the 13th-century monk and philosopher Roger Bacon. He recorded that in the 'high rocks' of Tibet and China there lived hairy wild-men, whom the natives would capture by leaving out bowls of liquor and getting them drunk. Such reports were rare, and until the 19th century, when European travellers began making regular excursions to the Himalayas, Central Asia remained a relatively unexplored country – a terra incognita for Westerners.

During the 19th century, however, such expeditions became increasingly common, and strange stories began to filter back from adventurers, mountaineers and cartographers. In 1832, B. H. Hodgson, the British Resident at the court of Nepal, reported that his porters had run in terror from a shaggy creature that stood on two legs. They insisted that it was a demon, but Hodgson thought that it might have been some sort of ape.

One of the first mentions of the term yeti comes from 1882, when Major L. A. Waddell saw footprints in the snow on an expedition in Sikkim, in Northeast India. The sherpas told him that they had been

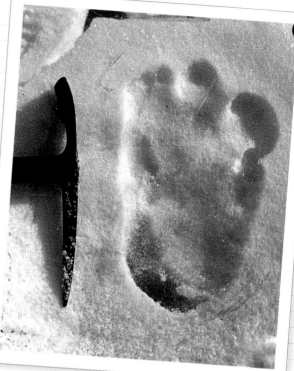

ERIC SHIPTON'S FAMOUS PHOTOGRAPH OF A 13-INCH LONG, 8-INCH WIDE (33 x 20 CM) YETI FOOTPRINT, TAKEN IN 1951. THIS PRINT WAS ONE OF A CLEAR TRAIL ACROSS THE MENLUNG GLACIER, NEAR MOUNT EVEREST, AT AN ALTITUDE OF 18,000 FT (5500 M).

A TYPICALLY SENSATIONALIST VIEW OF THE YETI, FROM A FRENCH MAGAZINE PRINTED AT THE HEIGHT OF THE YETI CRAZE OF THE 1950s.

made by the hairy man of the snows, the yeh-teh, which loosely translates as 'that-there thing'.

However, the yeti really hit the headlines in 1921, when Lieutenant-Colonel C. K. Howard-Bury was on an expedition in the Everest region. His sherpas pointed out three strange creatures moving across the flat expanse of a snow field at about 23,000 ft (7000 m). On reaching the snow field, Howard-Bury found a number of huge footprints which his porters apparently attributed to a creature called the metoh-kangmi, later translated by journalist Henry Newman as 'Abominable Snowman'. This name helped to spark off a period of immense public interest in the yeti.

Interest reached fever pitch when Eric Shipton's returned from his 1951 expedition with photographs of a yeti's footprint, taken high on the south-west slope of Menlung-tse. The picture showed a five-toed print about 13 inches (33 cm) long, with anatomical features that clearly marked it as non-human. This remains the most conclusive proof of the yeti's existence.

However, popular belief in the yeti was dealt a blow in 1960, when Sir Edmund Hillary - one of the mountaineers who had conquered Everest - returned from an expedition bearing a skullcap said to be made of yeti skin, borrowed from a Tibetan Buddhist monastery. Public interest in the yeti declined sharply after the cap was tested and shown to be made of ordinary goatskin from a local herd.

It was against this background that Dame Marjorie Evans-Hartson, the eminent mountaineer and long-time associate of the CSL, undertook to lead the Society's third expedition in search of the yeti.

FIELD REPORT
May 20, Kanchenjunga Base Camp, 4000 m
Meant to be wrong time of year for blizzards, but you try telling that to the local weather gods. Bloody blizzard won't let up. Porters still taking stuff up to the Second Camp, poor blighters. You've got to admire their spunk!

This is what the damn creature loked like close up. It lumbered off pretty quick after it caught sight of me.

Funny-looking feet the thing has - a bit like hands somehow.

yak 20
Filter
MADE FROM FINEST VIRGINIA TOBACCO
JANAKPUR CIGARETTE FACTORY

MADE IN NEPAL

GDP.872.889 BLUE SHEEP WOOL FROM THE NEPAL HIMALAYA.

NOT.787.182
YETI FINGERTIP,
UNKNOWN ORIGIN.

May 22, Kanchenjunga 2nd Camp, 5100 m
Germans have left a terrible mess here. Apparently none of them made it back from the summit. Shame. This is where that Greek fellow, Tombazi, spotted some sort of creature, back in '25. He reckoned it was just some old hermit. As we shovelled dahl batt into our mouths this evening we got to talking about it, and Sherpa Ngozah said it was probably a meh-teh. He says they come this high when they're crossing from one valley to the next. Well, having climbed 3000 feet in a couple of days, this made me pretty angry. I asked him why the hell we aren't just looking for them in the valleys, but he says the only way you can spot the beasts is against the white background of the snow fields.

Yeti

May 24, Dhal Monastery, 3600 m
The head lama here seems a decent enough
cove. He rummaged around in his cell and
showed us some interesting relics,
including a yeti scalp which he admitted
was only an imitation, made out of the
skin of a serow, a local type of goat. He
then brought out a pretty manky looking
old finger, which he insisted was the real
thing. Blenkinsop, the monkey expert, got
pretty bloody excited. Told me it looked
like a gorilla's finger. 'Don't be bloody
stupid,' I told him, 'there aren't any
gorillas in the Himalayas.' 'Exactly,' he
said, doing that eyebrow thing that
irritates me so much.

May 27, Kanchenjunga 2nd Camp
Up and down like a bloody yo-yo, here we
are again. Woke up this morning to the
sound of excited sherpas. Apparently
someone got into the beer last night.
Made off with some of the food too. Well,
I didn't see what the fuss was - until
they pointed out a footprint in the snow
by the storage tent. It was really odd.
The second toe was as big as the first,
and the whole thing was a good 15 inches
long. Blenkinsop, hopping around like a
maniac, got out his clobber and made a
cast of the print.

May 28, Kanchenjunga, 6300 m
Tally ho! This morning I was scanning up
ahead with the glasses when I saw a dark
figure making its way across the snow.
Sure enough, when we got here we found a
set of prints just like yesterday's. Rum
thing, though. They stopped at this sheer
rock face. No way of climbing it that I
could see. Ngozah started to fiddle
nervously with his gloves.

First, distant, glimpse of a yeti. He eventually disappeared
behind a crag in the rock face. Visibility good, but weather
starting to deteriorate.

MEH 28/5/62

FOOTPRINTS PHOTOGRAPHED BY DAME MARJORIE
ON THE LOWER SLOPES OF KANCHENJUNGA.

May 29 , 6800 m

Didn't get far today. Bloody cold out. Woods started going on about frostbite. Told him not to be such a bloody nancy-boy. I lost half my right foot on Annapurna – didn't catch me moaning!

May 30 , 7200 m

Tremendous excitement all round. Climbed over a ridge about lunchtime, came face to face with the most extraordinary creature! It was about 7 ft tall – face like a monkey's arse, hairy all over, stank something rotten. Big fella too, must have weighed at least 700 lbs (317 kg).

Wouldn't you know it, I dropped my ruddy camera. The thing ran off before I could get a picture. We tried to follow it, but the ground was just too tough. Blenkinsop, eyes out on stalks, got a good look at it. Said it looked like a Gigantopithecus, but muttered about it being extinct for a good whack of time. 'Apparently not,' I observed, and tried to wiggle my eyebrows, but my face was too bloody cold. He then spotted some droppings and ran around collecting them for analysis. Lucky we spotted the creature, as tomorrow we have to start back down to base camp.

SUPPLEMENTARY NOTES

Dame Marjorie's experience shows that getting more than a brief glimpse of the yeti is difficult. It is very shy and the master of its environment, able to hide in unscaleable cliffs and high passes.

However, the yeti does leave some evidence of its passing. The spoor Maurice Blenkinsop brought back were analysed here at the CSL, and revealed similar results to those obtained from yeti excreta

brought back by Tom Slick in 1959. They contained an unknown species of parasitic nematode worm. The finger examined at the Dahl monastery is also reminiscent of the digit brought back by Tom Slick's expedition from the Pangboche monastery in Nepal, and smuggled out of India with the help of the actor James Stewart.

Future expeditions might be able to bring back more proof. For instance, there are rumours that the Tibetan monasteries of Sakya and Riwoche contain entire mummified yeti corpses.

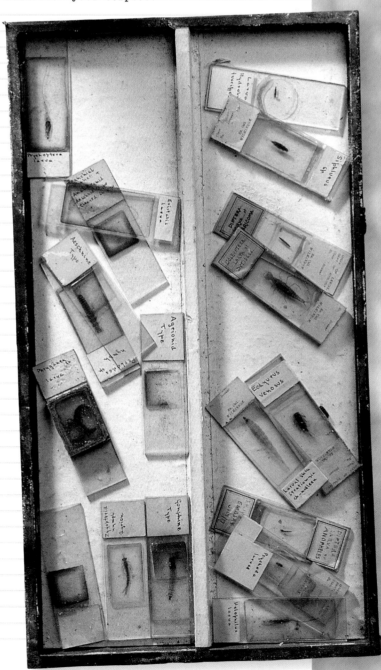

ANIMAL PARASITES FROM THE CSL'S COLLECTION, INCLUDING SOME (IN THE LEFT-HAND SECTION) RECOVERED FROM YETI DROPPINGS.

HOMINIDS

Bigfoot

LATIN NAME
Gigantopithecus

HABITAT
*Mountainous/
forested regions*

LIFESPAN
Unknown

SIZE
*7–10 ft
(2–3 m) tall*

**INFORMATION
SOURCE**
CSL Review

DISTRIBUTION
North America

Forest rangers in the national parks of Canada and the USA occasionally glimpse gigantic apes in the woods. But could so-called Bigfoot sightings actually be hoaxes carried out by pranksters in ape suits?

YOUR FEET'S TOO BIG

THE TRUE STORY OF BIGFOOT STARTS approximately 11,000 years ago, when people first crossed what is now the Bering Strait between Asia and North America. That was the period of the last Ice Age, when so much seawater froze that ocean levels fell significantly around the world. A land bridge between North America and Europe then emerged that allowed people to cross from one to the other on foot. The Native American population of the Americas is descended from these early settlers, now thought to have been nomadic hunters following their quarry on to a new continent.

It seems likely, however, that the first *Homo sapiens* in America were not the first hominids. Those migrating Ice Age hunters appear to have encountered a gigantic apeman closely related to the Himalayan yeti. This was probably a species of *Gigantopithecus* (Latin for 'giant ape'), a prehistoric creature that was thought to have died out some 300,000 years ago.

CLOSE ENCOUNTERS

The human arrivals soon made their impact felt on their environment, and are implicated in the rapid extinction of many large mammals. As the immigrants settled the land, the Gigantopithecines were driven into the mountains and forests (especially the western mountain ranges). American Indians knew the apemen by many different names, including sasquatch and wendigo, and attributed supernatural powers to them.

As white hunters, trappers and traders made inroads into the American wilderness, they inevitably encountered these creatures. In early reports they are called 'bushmen' or 'wild men'. Most of these stories are probably lost to us, dismissed as tall tales and fancies, but several survive. For instance, in 1811 David Thompson, explorer and trader, came across 14 inch (35 cm) footprints on the West coast. The local Indians told him they were made by one of the 'giants' who lived on Vancouver Island.

President Theodore Roosevelt told a story he had heard from a trapper called Bauman. In 1842 Bauman's companion was killed by an unidentified gigantic creature in Idaho.

One of the most famous tales is Albert Ostman's claim that in 1924 he was abducted by a family of *sasquatch* who lived a primitive, Stone-Age lifestyle, and only escaped by feeding the male a large quantity of potent, sneeze-inducing snuff.

Many of these tales only emerged after 1958, the year builder Jerry Crew discovered a huge, humanoid footprint on a site in Humboldt County,

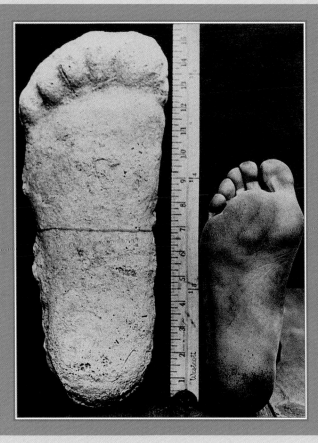

A FRAME FROM ROGER PATTERSON'S SHORT 16MM MOVIE OF 1967, CAPTURING WHAT APPEARS TO BE AN ENORMOUS DARK BROWN APE WALKING AWAY FROM THE CAMERA IN ALARM.

AT 8 FT (2.4 M) TALL, THIS SCULPTURE AT WILLOW CREEK, CALIFORNIA IS ACKNOWLEDGED TO BE A GOOD LIKENESS OF THE BIGFOOT.

Northern California. His story, and photographs of the cast he made, were a media sensation. The name Bigfoot came into general usage, and the countryside was filled with hunters and monster watchers. Hundreds of sightings followed; according to some estimates, well over 1000 people in the US have seen a Bigfoot.

MONKEY SEE, MONKEY DO

The reports show that male Bigfeet are at least 7 ft (2.1 m) tall, with a heavily muscled physique and huge shoulders. Females are slightly smaller, with sagging breasts. Coloration is variable, from short black hair with silver tips to shaggy red fur. There has even been one report of an albino *sasquatch*, from Washington state. The Bigfoot's eyes are often described as glowing and red, which may indicate an adaptation for night vision, suggesting a nocturnal lifestyle. Another common feature of reports is a terrible smell that accompanies the creature. In some cases this smell is released in response to danger, and may thus be a defence mechanism akin to the skunk's. In Florida Bigfoot is known as the Skunk Ape.

What vexes zoologists and cryptozoologists alike is the continuing paucity of hard evidence for Bigfoot's existence. Droppings and hair attributed to

the *sasquatch* usually turn out to be something else – on one occasion, manmade fibres. In June 1982, forest patrolman Paul Freeman discovered fingerprints left by an 8 ft-tall Bigfoot in Tiger Creek, Oregon, but these do not constitute definitive proof.

The single best piece of evidence remains the so-called Patterson film. This was shot by Bigfoot hunter Roger Patterson in October 1967, at Bluff Creek, near Eureka, California, a traditional Bigfoot haunt. It clearly shows a 7 ft-tall female *sasquatch*, with black, shiny hair and drooping breasts, who turns away and ambles across a clearing in an ape-like fashion.

SUITS YOU, SIR

The creature in the Patterson footage is either an ape-like creature unknown to science, or a hoax. Most people assume the latter, a conclusion which has been encouraged by persistent rumours that a well-known Hollywood special effects man has admitted to making the 'monkey suit'. In fact the individual in question strenuously denies this, and the Patterson film has still never been proved to be a hoax. According to some experts, the springy gait of the creature Patterson filmed could not have been consciously created – even by the most athletic human wearing a suit.

A HUMAN FOOT IS DWARFED BY THE CAST OF A BIGFOOT PRINT FOUND AT BLUFF CREEK SHORTLY AFTER ROGER PATTERSON MADE HIS FILM.

HOMINIDS

Vampire

LATIN NAME
*Homo
sapiens
chiroptera/
immortuus*

HABITAT
*Graveyards,
castles*

LIFESPAN
Indefinite

SIZE
Human

**INFORMATION
SOURCE**
Field Report

DISTRIBUTION
Worldwide

FIELD  REPORT

In 1924 a Transylvanian woman was buried with horseshoes nailed to her hands and feet, a wooden stake through her chest and heavy stones on top of her coffin. The people who buried her believed with absolute certainty that she was a vampire – one of the living dead, a ghoul risen from the grave to spread corruption and pestilence, capable of surviving only by drinking the blood of the living.

The Vampire or Spectre of Guiana.

The Venezuelan Great Vampire Bat (*Desmodus rotundus*) goes to work on the teat of a sow.

Of course today this seems incredible. Living in the 1990s, it is difficult for us to imagine the kind of superstition or the depth of fear that would drive 20th-century Europeans to mutilate a dead body so grotesquely. However, over 150 years of vampirical research by the CSL attests that such fears are far from groundless. Almost from the inception of the Society, our investigators have delved into this murky mystery.

Reproduced here are the surviving parts of the Society's very first Field Report, submitted in 1848 by Douglas George Pendleton. One of the Society's founders, Pendleton was a noted antiquarian scholar who vanished in Brazil's Mato Grosso under mysterious circumstances in 1877.

The vampire was already a staple of Gothic fiction by 1897, when Bram Stoker wrote the seminal vampire novel <u>Dracula</u>. The first great literary success in the genre was John Polidori's <u>The Vampyre</u> (1819), with its Byronic antihero Lord Ruthven. In the 1840s, the serial <u>Varney the Vampire</u> gripped the public imagination. It was against this background that Douglas Pendleton made the long journey to the remote principality of Wallachia, recently freed from Ottoman bondage but still extremely backward.

LEFT AND BELOW: TWO ITEMS FROM THE SOCIETY'S EXTENSIVE COLLECTION OF VAMPIRE DOCUMENTS AND EPHEMERA.

No. 1.]   Nos. 2, 3 and 4 are Presented, Gratis, with this No.   [Price 1d.

VARNEY THE VAMPIRE OR THE FEAST OF BLOOD

A ROMANCE OF EXCITING INTEREST.

BY THE AUTHOR OF
" GRACE RIVERS; OR, THE MERCHANT'S DAUGHTER."

LONDON: E. LLOYD, SALISBURY-SQUARE, AND ALL BOOKSELLERS.

astonishing contrast between the splendours of Buda and Pest and the rural poverty that surrounds us here. The peasants are little better than the serfs of old, their homes mere dilapidated hovels and the general condition of the populace is woeful. As the carriage passes, they stare in mute incomprehension, as if we were visitors from the Moon.

1st December. Strehaia, Wallachia.
This morning we saw the strangest thing. The carriage slowed as we approached a crossroads, and I beheld a party of grim-faced men grouped around an open coffin. Signalling the driver to stop, I observed with mounting puzzlement as they first garlanded the corpse (which was laid face down) with wild roses and garlic, then scattered fine seeds about her. My incomprehension turned to horror as they proceeded to hammer nails into her hands and feet, and drove a stake of sharpened wood through her body. I leapt to the door to protest this outrage, but was held back by my travelling companion, an impressively bearded priest. This stern patriarch explained in broken German that the corpse was that of a young woman who had taken her own life, and must therefore be interred in this fashion. To my mind it was an ungodly business, and the experience has helped to inspire in me a sense of profound gloom and melancholy.

The unnerving scene at the crossroads.

VTR.046.849
SHARPENED STAKE WITH TRACES OF BLOOD, PLUS LOCAL MALLET. PROVENANCE: CALMANESTI, WALLACHIA.

The corpse, staked out like a mock crucifixion, is ready for the coup de grace — a stake through the heart.

3rd December. Filiasi

Arriving at dusk, we passed the graveyard on the edge of this small town. I espied a strange figure, dressed in sheets, hunched upon the ground as if searching for something. Muttering prayers, my fellow passengers crossed themselves, and the driver urged the horses on. As we came up the main street the church bells began to toll, and the entire populace seemed to glance about themselves nervously before hurrying indoors. The houses here are all decorated in the most peculiar fashion, with strings of garlic hung about the doors and wild roses growing around the windows, and beds planted with wolfsbane, dog rose, hemlock and wormwood. As we alighted, I noticed that the road was scattered with rose thorns.

The other passengers dispersed rapidly, and I made my way to the inn. As I passed through the low, garlic-scented doorway, I was greeted by the ferocious snarls of a huge black dog with the most bizarre markings painted on its head — a second set of eyes, rendered in garish colours. The innkeeper took the dog in hand, and stared at me suspiciously. He quickly divined that I was a foreigner, and spoke rough but serviceable English.

Over a mug of blood-red wine and a thick but tasteless stew, I inquired as to the legion of oddities which his village presented to the visitor's eye. When

I explained the purpose of my visit he found his tongue, and, pausing only to stoke the mightily roaring fire, poured forth a torrent of information. The garlic, wild roses and other plants all had but one function: to deter the approach of that thing which I had come to seek — the wampyr. These bloodthirsty ghouls could also be scared off by fierce hounds, particularly when augmented with extra eyes as I had observed. The rose thorns, and the seeds I had seen scattered on the poor suicide the day before, were employed to distract the revenant, for it would feel compelled to count every one, and thus be kept busy until the dawn, when it must return to its grave. Seeds were scattered in the graveyard for the same purpose.

At this point I mentioned the strange, shrouded figure I had seen in the graveyard at dusk, and the innkeeper grew pale. "Tomorrow," he declared, "you will see how we deal with the undead. But tonight, we will speak no more." In spite of all my questions, I could get no more from him, and he curtly bade me good night.

The vicious guard dog at the inn, complete with a painted pair of eyes to scare the wampyr.

4th December. Filiasi

At noon the villagers gathered in the town square. With stern and solemn purpose, they made their way to the graveyard. There were many fresh graves there, and a young girl on horseback was led around the graveyard, stepping over each plot in turn. Before one such grave the horse suddenly shied and reared up. This was the sign the villagers had been looking for, and they fell to, digging with picks and shovels until we heard the sound of tools on wood.

Looking into the grave, I saw a coffin with a loosely-fixed lid. From one corner trailed a soiled winding sheet. The box was lifted from the grave, and the priest came forward to tear off the lid. Within the rough-hewn coffin lay a rosy-cheeked, pink-lipped figure that more closely resembled a sleeping youth than a two-week old corpse. Its hair and fingernails were long and ragged, there was a smear of blood about its mouth, and the tips of two long canine teeth could be seen.

The coffin lid was removed to reveal a body more sleeping than dead

The priest sprinkled holy water on a shovel, a mallet and a sharpened stake of hawthorn wood. Crossing himself, one man positioned the stake above the chest of the corpse while another swung the mallet. As the wood drove through its heart, the corpse started and opened its eyes! To our horror it reached up and grasped the stake, emitting a ghastly scream as blood spurted from the wound! The sexton stepped forward with the shovel and cut the creature's head off with a single blow.

The hideous undead corpse, with all its raiment, was burned on a hawthorn pyre. As smoke climbed into the frosty December sky, the townsfolk and the priest joined in chanting a strange, atonal liturgy. Back in the village, I drank a full bottle of wine, and was not alone in this employment. Tomorrow I shall return to England, where the dead remain buried and garlic is restricted to fancy foreign cooking, which is as it should be.

COMMENTS ON THE PENDLETON DOCUMENT BY DR ALAN KULA OF THE CSL HISTORY WORKING GROUP.

Pendleton's account, a classic of early cryptozoological investigation, is as remarkable for its omissions as it is for the light it sheds on life in 'vampire country'. Pendleton makes no mention of mysterious Counts, hypnotic stares, transformations into bats or many of the other attributes associated with vampirism today. Bram Stoker's novel <u>Dracula</u> - and its subsequent film adaptations - have muddied the waters by drawing on a variety of European folklore traditions, as well as the real historical figures of Vlad Dracul and his son Vlad Tepes, the Impaler, the cruel and bloodthirsty rulers of 15th-century Wallachia.

A CONTEMPORARY LIKENESS OF VLAD TEPES, THE ORIGINAL DRACULA AND (RIGHT) A WOODCUT RECORDING ONE OF HIS MANY IMPALINGS.

Another prototype of today's fictional vampire may have been Elizabeth Bathori, the Countess of Hungary. In 1610, she was found guilty of murdering over 600 young girls and bathing in their blood in order to preserve her own youth. She was convicted of sorcery, and imprisoned for the rest of her life.

Putting both fiction and history to one side, bloodthirsty undead revenants have existed in various parts of the world for some time. The Ancient Assyrians went in fear of eery <u>ekimmu</u>, and the Romans were preyed upon by the <u>striges</u>, which took the form of birds. Vampires disappeared from Britain in c.1300, but they were common in continental Europe for much longer: Bulgaria had an epidemic in 1863.

In 19th-century New England it was thought that people who died of tuberculosis would return as vampires. The diaries of author Henry Thoreau record how several bodies were exhumed and burnt, and their ashes were fed to relatives as a prophylactic measure. Though diminished in number, isolated cases continue to appear in the present day. An exhibition of 'mummified vampires' held in Jakarta in 1997, for example, drew huge crowds.

<u>Variants and related creatures</u>
There are dozens of national and regional vampire variants. Many of these are said to be ghosts or spirits, but all share characteristics such as blood-sucking or shape-changing. They include: the Portuguese <u>bruxa</u>; the Indian <u>vetala</u>; the North American <u>anchanchu</u>; the South American <u>azeman</u>; the Trinidadian <u>sukuyan</u>, and the Malaysian <u>bajang</u>.

BRAM STOKER, THE IRISH AUTHOR, PICTURED ON HIS VISIT TO THE CSL IN 1899 — UNFORTUNATELY, TWO YEARS TOO LATE FOR HIM TO MAKE THE DETAILS IN HIS VAMPIRE CLASSIC DRACULA CORRECT.

FOR MORE BLOODSUCKING, SEE CHUPACABRAS — P. 76.

FIELD REPORT

This is a partial list and brief explanation of some of cryptozoology's most interesting and unusual creatures.

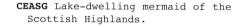

ABATWA South African race of fairies. They live in anthills and only show themselves to sorcerers, pregnant women and children under four.

ADARO Melanesian mermen who travel of rainbows.

AHNIZOTL Aztec water creature. A hybrid of dog and monkey, with a head on the end of its tail.

ALFAR Nordic elf.

AMEMAIT Hybrid of lion, crocodile and hippo.

ARIMASPIANS Race of one-eyed people, famous for battling with griffons for their gold.

BAGIM Australian harpy.

BARBEGAZI Swiss-French race of Alpine gnomes. They estivate (sleep through the summer) and emerge only when it is very cold. They have large feet that they use as skis.

BARGUEST Shaggy black dog with big eyes, found near churchyards.

BEN-VARREY Mermaid found around the Isle of Man.

BI-BI Chinese winged fox. Its call resembles that of the wild goose.

BODACH Chimney-dwelling bogey.

BONNACON Buffalo-like creature that defends itself by rearward discharge of volatile chemicals.

BRUSCAS Portuguese female vampire that drinks the blood of its own children.

BUCCA Cornish hobgoblin or kobold.

BUCENTAUR Hybrid creature with bull's body and human torso and head.

CATOBLEPAS Foul-smelling creature with a buffalo's body, hippo's legs, warthog's head and long neck.

CEASG Lake-dwelling mermaid of the Scottish Highlands.

CLURICAUN Irish wine-cellar dwelling leprechaun.

CORRIGAN Breton fairy renowned for substituting fairy changelings for human babies.

DHAMPIR In Transylvania, the son of a vampire — the only person capable of seeing and killing invisible vampires.

DRAC French nymph that dwells in watery caverns.

EACH UISGE (pronounced ech ooshkya) Celtic waterhorse.

ERLKING Germanic goblin.

FIRBOLG Primitive Irish race: 'people of the bogs'.

GLAISTIG Half-human, half-goat hybrid of the Scottish Highlands.

HAYK Armenian giant.

HEKATONCHEIRE Greek giant with 100 arms and serpent's legs. These creatures aided the Titans in their battle against the Gods.

HEMICYNE Hybrid of human and dog, native to the shores of the Black Sea.

HIPPOCAMPUS Sea-steed with the head and forelimbs of a horse, webbed hooves and a fish's tail.

HIPPOGRIFF Offspring of a horse and a griffon, once tamed and used as aerial mount.

HOBYAH Cannibalistic goblin that lives in the woods of Scotland and New England.

HOO Another name for phoenix.

ICHTHYOCENTAUR Hybrid sea-creature with the head and torso of a human, the tail of a fish and the forelegs of a horse.

ITZPAPALOTL Aztec hybrid of woman and butterfly.

JALPARI Punjabi water nymph.

JÖTNAR Norse giant.

KALAMAKARA Hybrid of lion and crocodile.

KALERIPOEG Estonian giant.

KAPPA Japanese water demon, a hybrid of frog, tortoise and monkey.

KARKADANN Hybrid of unicorn and rhinoceros.

KI-LIN Chinese hybrid of deer, horse, lion and unicorn.

KILYAKAI Evil goblins from New Zealand. Their tiny arrows cause malaria.

KNOCKERS Cornish fairies who live in tin mines.

KOALINTH Marine hobgoblin with gills and webbed feet.

KRIOCAMP Mesopotamian hybrid of ram and fish.

KU Giant dog native to Hawaii.

KUJATA Monster native to the Islamic world: a vast bull with 4000 eyes, ears, mouths, nostrils and feet.

LAMASSU Colossal winged bull with human head.

LEPRECHAUN Irish member of the fairy family.

LUDKI Slavic dwarves. Can be driven away by the sound of church bells.

MAKARA Indian sea-monster, a hybrid of fish and mammal.

MANTA Giant cuttlefish from Chile.

MARA Danish female vampire.

MOKELE MBEMBE African cave- or lake-dwelling elephant-sized beast, with a long neck and a reptilian appearance. Possibly a type of brontosaurus.

MUSCA MACEDDA Sicilian demon that takes the form of a fly.

NAGA Indian hybrid of snake and human that lives underground guarding hoards of treasure.

NAGUMWASUCK Fairy race of the North American Passemequaddy. Shy and ugly, they travel in stone canoes.

NAIN ROUGE Dwarf species accused of starting the great Detroit Fire of 1805.

NANDI Giant flesh-eating bear of East Africa.

NASNAS Yemenite hominid resembling a human being sliced vertically in half.

ONI Japanese ogre.

ONOCENTAUR Member of the centaur family with the body of an ass.

OPINICUS Griffin-like monster with lion's body and legs, eagle's head, neck and wings and camel's tail.

PERYTON Hybrid combining a deer's head and legs with a bird's feathered head and body. Native to the Mediterranean, it casts a man's shadow and flies in large flocks.

PISKY Alternative word for pixy.

PIXY English West-Country members of the fairy family renowned for tricks and generally ludic behaviour.

PUK Type of household dragon of the Baltic states.

RAMARA Fish that fastens on ships' keels to keep them steady in rough seas.

ROANE Scottish seal-maiden.

ROC Vast, legendary birds now found only on Madagascar.

RUKH See ROC.

SASABONSAM West African forest monster with hairy body, large bloodshot eyes and long legs.

SELKIE Seal-maiden of the Shetland and Orkney islands.

SIMURGH Persian half-dog, half-bird with the powers of speech and healing.

SISIUTL Canadian snake with three heads: a man's in the centre and two snake's heads at either side.

SKRIMSL Icelandic sea serpent.

SQUONK Hominid of the Pennsylvania woods. It cries constantly in despair at its wrinkled, warty skin, and if captured it dissolves in a flood of its own tears.

TENGU Japanese hybrid of human and bird.

TO Burmese hybrid of lion and deer.

TRITON Merman.

TYLWYTH TEG Welsh fairy that communicates using sign language.

VAMPIRE Bloodsucking undead human.

WYVERN Two-legged, true-winged European member of the dragon family.

YALE Antelope-like animal with a boar's tusks and jaws, an elephant's tail and a goat's beard.

YAMA-UBA Mountain spirit of Japan, with snakes for hair, similar to the Classical Medusa.

ZOTZ Mayan dog-headed, winged demon.

Index

S-Y

STOKER, BRAM - YOWIE

CSL REVIEW ARTICLES

FIELD REPORTS

The Cryptozoological Society of London and Carroll & Brown would like to thank the following:

Dr David M Burn, PhD, FCSL; Captain Paul Stoker-Bryan, RN (retd.); Dr Pinkus, MD; Tonianmo Wilson; Sameer; Centrevine Ltd; Conservator Systems, Liverpool; Hilda Jennings; Abigambi-Klib; Finn Lewis; Worldly Wicked & Wise; Paddington Cemetery; Jo-Anne Stanford; Laura Price; Gerard McLaughlin; Emily Gilchrist; Gilda Pacitti; Aku Young; Katie Kohn; John Bell; Scott's of Sunningdale.

ILLUSTRATIONS BY:
Martin Knowelden, Nick Harris, Simone Boni, Coral Mula, Matthew Williams, Pavel Kostal, Simon Daley.

PICTURE CREDITS:
6   Mary Evans Picture Library
7   Hulton-Deutsch Collection Corbis UK Ltd.
8   Hulton Getty Picture Collection Ltd.
10   Mary Evans Picture Library
16   Everett Collection/Corbis UK Ltd.
17   Popperfoto
18   Popperfoto
19   Hulton Getty Picture Collection Ltd.
21   Mary Evans Picture Library
25   Images Colour Library
26   Fortean Picture Library
28   Images Colour Library
30   Fortean Picture Library
31   Taiyo Fisheries, Tokyo/Fortean Picture Library
32   National Gallery, London/AKG – London
32-3   Fortean Picture Library
33   Mary Evans Picture Library
34   AKG – London
35   (top) Mary Evans Picture Library
35   (bottom) Janet & Colin Bord/Fortean Picture Library
36   Jean-Loup Charmet
39   (top) Hulton Getty Picture Collection Ltd.
39   (bottom) Mary Evans Picture Library
43   AKG – London
44   Robert Le Serrec/Fortean Picture Library
44-5   Mary Evans Picture Library
45   (top) AKG – London
45   (bottom) Mary Evans Picture Library
46   (top) Rene Dahinden/Fortean Picture Library
46   (bottom) Fortean Picture Library
47   (top) Fortean Picture Library
47   (bottom) Popperfoto
48   Barnard/Fox/Hulton Getty Picture Collection Ltd.
48-9   Hurriyet/Associated Press
50   Loren Coleman/Fortean Picture Library
52   Debbie Lee/Fortean Picture Library
54   Fortean Picture Library
56-7   AKG – London
57   Mary Evans Picture Library
59   Roger Kohn
61   (left) Roger Kohn
61   (right) Roger Kohn
63   Bridgeman Art Library
68   Sipa/Rex Features
70   Roger Kohn
71   Roger Kohn
75   (left) Mary Evans Picture Library
75   (centre) Fortean Picture Library
75   (right) Roger Kohn
78-9   AKG – London
79   AKG – London
80   Hulton Getty Picture Collection Ltd.
81   (left) Hulton Getty Picture Collection Ltd.
81   (right) Fortean Picture Library
82   AKG – London
84   Images Colour Library
85   Fortean Picture Library
86   (top) Lars Thomas/Fortean Picture Library
86   (bottom) Roger Kohn
87   Mary Evans Picture Library
88   Roger Kohn
89   Werner Forman Archive
90   (top) Roger Kohn
90   (bottom) Roger Kohn
91   Michael Fogden/Oxford Scientific Films
92   Leszcynski/Animals Animals/Oxford Scientific Films
94   Images Colour Library
95   (top) Lars Thomas/Fortean Picture Library
95   (bottom) Mary Evans Picture Library
96   Mary Evans Picture Library
98   Hulton Getty Picture Collection Ltd.
99   Hulton Getty Picture Collection Ltd.
100   AKG – London
101   Lauros-Giraudon/Bridgeman Art Library
102   Roger Kohn
104   Bridgeman Art Library
106   Werner Forman Archive
110   Mary Evans Picture Library
111   J.C. Francolon/Frank Spooner Pictures

Acknowledgements

112 (top left) Images Colour Library
112 (top right) Images Colour Library
112 (bottom) Crown Copyright/Health & Safety Lab./Science Photo Library
113 Mary Evans Picture Library
115 (top left) Erich Lessing/AKG – London
115 (top right) Mary Evans Picture Library
115 (bottom) Hulton Getty Picture Collection Ltd.
119 AKG – London
120 Mary Evans Picture Library
121 (top) National Museums of Scotland
121 (bottom) Hulton Getty Picture Collection Ltd.
122 Hulton Getty Picture Collection Ltd.
126 (top) Erich Lessing/AKG – London
126 (bottom) Hulton Getty Picture Collection Ltd.
127 (top) AKG – London
127 (bottom) AKG – London
130 (top) Jean-Loup Charmet
130 (bottom) Fortean Picture Library
134 AKG – London
134-35 Images Colour Library
135 AKG – London
136 (top) Roger Kohn
136 (bottom) Roger Kohn
137 Zooid Pictures
138 AKG – London
139 AKG – London
140 Jean-Loup Charmet
141 (left) AKG – London
141 (right) Images Colour Library
142 (top) Rex Features
142 (bottom) Chris Catton/Survival Anglia/Oxford Scientific Films
145 Hulton Getty Picture Collection Ltd.
147 Fortean Picture Library
150 (left) Mary Evans Picture Library
150 (right) Richard Galpin
151 (left) Wellcome Centre for Medical Science
151 (right) Fortean Picture Library
156 Bridgeman Art Library
157 (left) Mary Evans Picture Library
157 (right) Roger Kohn
158 Mary Evans Picture Library
159 (top) Mary Evans Picture Library
159 (bottom) Fortean Picture Library
161 (top left) Mary Evans Picture Library
161 (top right) Tate Gallery/ET Archive
161 (bottom) Fortean Picture Library
164 (bottom) Lawrence Dutton/Tony Stone Images
166 Images Colour Library

168 Images Colour Library
169 (top) Roger Kohn
169 (bottom) Robin Redfern/Oxford Scientific Films
173 Images Colour Library
174 Mary Evans Picture Library
175 (top) AKG – London
175 (bottom) Mary Evans Picture Library
180 Mary Evans Picture Library
181 (top) Images Colour Library
181 (bottom) Fortean Picture Library
182 Lawrence Dutton/Tony Stone Images
185 Hulton Getty Picture Collection Ltd.
186 Roger Kohn
187 Roger Kohn
192 Tom Till/Tony Stone Images
192-93 Hulton Getty Picture Collection Ltd.
193 Hulton Getty Picture Collection Ltd.
194 (top) Mary Evans Picture Library
194 (bottom) David C. Tomlinson/Tony Stone Images
199 (top) Fortean Picture Library
199 (bottom) Hulton Getty Picture Collection Ltd.
200 (left) Fortean Picture Library
200 (right) Fortean Picture Library
201 (left) Fortean Picture Library
201 (centre) Fortean Picture Library
201 (right) Images Colour Library
202 (top) Hulton Getty Picture Collection Ltd.
202 (bottom) Mary Evans Picture Library
204 David Murray
206 Cliff Crook/Fortean Picture Library
207 (left) Rene Dahinden/Fortean Picture Library
207 (centre) Patterson/Gimlin ©1968 Dahinden/Fortean Picture Library
207 (right) Rene Dahinden/Fortean Picture Library
208 (top left) Hulton Getty Picture Collection Ltd.
208 (bottom left) Stephen Dalton/Oxford Scientific Films
208 (right) Stephen Dalton/Fortean Picture Library
213 (top left) Images Colour Library
213 (top right) Mary Evans Picture Library
213 (bottom) Hulton Getty Picture Collection Ltd.